Linguistic Fundamentals for Natural Language Processing II: 100 Essentials from Semantics and Pragmatics

Synthesis Lectures on Human Language Technologies

Editor
Graeme Hirst, *University of Toronto*

Synthesis Lectures on Human Language Technologies is edited by Graeme Hirst of the University of Toronto. The series consists of 50- to 150-page monographs on topics relating to natural language processing, computational linguistics, information retrieval, and spoken language understanding. Emphasis is on important new techniques, on new applications, and on topics that combine two or more HLT subfields.

Neural Network Methods for Natural Language Processing
Yoav Goldberg
2017

Syntax-based Statistical Machine Translation
Philip Williams, Rico Sennrich, Matt Post, and Philipp Koehn
2016

Domain-Sensitive Temporal Tagging
Jannik Strötgen and Michael Gertz
2016

Linked Lexical Knowledge Bases: Foundations and Applications
Iryna Gurevych, Judith Eckle-Kohler, and Michael Matuschek
2016

Bayesian Analysis in Natural Language Processing
Shay Cohen
2016

Metaphor: A Computational Perspective
Tony Veale, Ekaterina Shutova, and Beata Beigman Klebanov
2016

Grammatical Inference for Computational Linguistics
Jeffrey Heinz, Colin de la Higuera, and Menno van Zaanen
2015

Automatic Detection of Verbal Deception
Eileen Fitzpatrick, Joan Bachenko, and Tommaso Fornaciari
2015

Natural Language Processing for Social Media
Atefeh Farzindar and Diana Inkpen
2015

Semantic Similarity from Natural Language and Ontology Analysis
Sébastien Harispe, Sylvie Ranwez, Stefan Janaqi, and Jacky Montmain
2015

Learning to Rank for Information Retrieval and Natural Language Processing, Second Edition
Hang Li
2014

Ontology-Based Interpretation of Natural Language
Philipp Cimiano, Christina Unger, and John McCrae
2014

© Springer Nature Switzerland AG 2022
Reprint of original edition © Morgan & Claypool 2020

Linguistic Fundamentals for Natural Language Processing II:
100 Essentials from Semantics and Pragmatics

Emily M. Bender and Alex Lascarides

ISBN: 978-3-031-01044-6 paperback
ISBN: 978-3-031-02172-5 ebook
ISBN: 978-1-68173-622-8 epub
ISBN: 978-3-031-00183-3 hardcover

DOI 10.1007/978-3-031-02172-5

A Publication in the Springer series
SYNTHESIS LECTURES ON ADVANCES IN AUTOMOTIVE TECHNOLOGY

Lecture #43
Series Editor: Graeme Hirst, *University of Toronto*
Series ISSN
Print 1947-4040   Electronic 1947-4059

Linguistic Fundamentals for Natural Language Processing II: 100 Essentials from Semantics and Pragmatics

Emily M. Bender
University of Washington

Alex Lascarides
University of Edinburgh

SYNTHESIS LECTURES ON HUMAN LANGUAGE TECHNOLOGIES #43

ABSTRACT

Meaning is a fundamental concept in Natural Language Processing (NLP), in the tasks of both Natural Language Understanding (NLU) and Natural Language Generation (NLG). This is because the aims of these fields are to build systems that understand what people mean when they speak or write, and that can produce linguistic strings that successfully express to people the intended content. In order for NLP to scale beyond partial, task-specific solutions, researchers in these fields must be informed by what is known about how humans use language to express and understand communicative intents. The purpose of this book is to present a selection of useful information about semantics and pragmatics, as understood in linguistics, in a way that's accessible to and useful for NLP practitioners with minimal (or even no) prior training in linguistics.

KEYWORDS

NLP, semantics, pragmatics, linguistics

For Dan Flickinger,
a good friend and mentor to us both who has inspired us
to be better linguists.

Contents

Acknowledgments

This book has benefited from thorough comments from two reviewers (one anonymous, the other Johan Bos) as well as Adam Lopez and Bec Dridan, to whom we extend our gratitude. We are also grateful for feedback and answers to queries from Francis Bond, Kristen Howell, David Inman, Elin McCready, Stephan Oepen, Woodley Packard, Miriam R. L. Petruck, and Olga Zamaraeva and wish to thank the following for their assistance with the construction and glossing of examples: Abeer AlDayel, Syed Sameer Arshad, Stergios Chatzikyriakidis, Marianne Desmets, Francesca Gola, Takao Gunji, Zev Handel, Julia Hockenmaier, Josh Hou, Alexander Koller, Nanna Inie, Valia Kordoni, Arturo Magidin, Sam Mchombo, Mythili Menon, Petya Osanova, Chongwon Park, Susanne Riehemann, Elena Santiago, Atsuko Shimada, Joanna Sio, Erica Verde, and Olga Zamaraeva. Finally, we would like to express appreciation to Graeme Hirst, series editor, and Morgan & Claypool for their encouragement to create this volume.

Emily M. Bender and Alex Lascarides
August 2019

CHAPTER 1

Introduction

#0 Understanding semantics and pragmatics is beneficial for building scalable Natural Language Processing (NLP) systems.

Anywhere there is human communication (written, spoken, or signed) captured in digital form, there is scope for an application of Natural Language Processing (NLP). This includes human-computer interactions (e.g., search engines, chatbots, spoken user interfaces, embodied communication with robots), computer-assisted human-human interactions (e.g., machine translation), as well as machine access to human-human interactions (e.g., digital discovery in legal proceedings). In the majority of cases, these applications are valuable precisely because they allow access to the meaning that speakers convey when they use language—and their value is limited by the extent to which they can do that. The relationship between the form of utterances and the content those utterances are used to convey seems transparent to us as speakers because in our everyday experience with language we exploit that relationship between utterance and meaning with great apparent ease: we do not often have to think about how to express ourselves when speaking languages we are reasonably fluent in; similarly we often don't need to deliberate for very long to infer what people meant by what they said. However, the processes of both human language production and human language understanding are in fact highly complex and furthermore guided by rich systems at many levels of linguistic structure.

We believe that an understanding of this complexity—and what has been discovered about the systems involved by researchers in linguistics—is critical to building effective NLP systems. This is especially true for the long-term goal of general-purpose NLP: that is, NLP that transfers easily across domains, tasks, and speakers. While machine learning has made impressive progress on many separate tasks (given appropriately curated data sets), the keys to generalizing beyond any specific set of end-to-end systems lie in modeling the linguistic system itself such that that model can be reused across tasks. And this can only be done based on an understanding of how language works, including how sentences come to mean what they mean (semantics) and how speakers can use sentence meaning to convey communicative intent (pragmatics).

Our goal in this book is to provide an overview of key concepts from semantics and pragmatics in a way that is accessible to students, researchers, and developers in NLP. The 100 vignettes that follow are meant to be easily digestible descriptions of key points about how meaning works in language and linguistic behavior, with further pointers into the relevant literature. The book should help readers build an appreciation for the shape of the problems of natural language understanding and natural language generation the kinds of resources that can be leveraged to approach it in a linguistically-informed manner.

We note here at the outset that this is just one perspective on natural language semantics and pragmatics: our presentation is informed by the broad literature on these topics, but where there is disagreement or open questions in the field, we will generally present a point of view without going into detail about all of the different theoretical viewpoints. In particular, we focus on formal semantics and pragmatics and what they have to say about how language works that we think would be useful for NLP students, researchers, and developers to know. There are many other approaches to semantics that are not discussed in detail here; this includes cognitive semantics [Lakoff, 1988, Langacker, 1987, Talmy, 2000] and frame semantics [Fillmore, 2006]. Furthermore, there are many interesting issues of relevance to linguistic semantics that have been discovered through NLP research but which the formal semantics literature doesn't yet address (for example, how to handle partially compositional multiword named entities [Downey et al., 2007]). These, too, will not be addressed here.

#1 Knowledge of semantics and pragmatics can inform the design of NLP systems for understanding and generation.

Some NLP tasks start with speech[1] or text, some produce speech or text, and some do both. In all cases, knowledge of semantics and pragmatics can help. Starting with the analysis direction (speech/text as input), semantically sensitive tasks include parsing to semantic representations, discourse processing, sentiment analysis, named entity resolution, and co-reference, among others. Some systems approaching these tasks are meant to be task- and domain-independent, such as a reference resolution system designed to be a component of many different larger systems. Others are quite task specific, such as a system designed to detect ad hominem attacks in a discussion forum. In either case, it is useful to know how language conveys meaning, because conventions of language, both systematic (e.g., the principle of compositionality, see #2) and highly idiosyncratic (e.g., word order, or the denotation of individual words), are pervasive.

Language imposes constraints on the messages that a sentence can be used to convey, both on the basis of the syntactic form of the sentence and on the basis of its context of use. Knowledge of these linguistic constraints can help us design NLP systems with better search strategies and higher accuracies. Conventions contribute to better search strategies because they make certain candidate messages impossible, even when non-linguistic information sources, like real-world knowledge, predict those messages to be likely [Lepore and Stone, 2015].

Let's examine an example of how linguistic convention and real-world knowledge can interact: contrast the natural interpretations of the two English discourses (1a) and (1b), from Asher and Lascarides 2003.

(1)   a. Kim switched off the light. The room became dark. Kim drew the blinds.

[1]Relatively little NLP work looks at signed languages.

    b. Kim switched off the lights (and) Kim drew the blinds. The room became dark.

The only difference in linguistic form of these discourses is textual order. But unlike discourse (1b), discourse (1a) would be highly misleading as a description of a situation where switching off the light and drawing the blinds *together* cause the room to be dark, even though real-world knowledge alone would suggest this interpretation (and indeed contributes to the natural interpretation of (1b)), thanks to the connection between drawing blinds and causing darkness. The different predictions about meaning for these two discourses stems from the order in which the sentences are uttered, and a convention that a coherent discourse should not describe events in the order "cause, effect, a further cause of that effect" without making this causal structure linguistically explicit (e.g., by saying *And a further cause of the room becoming dark…*). We'll discuss this convention (in fact, a generalization of this convention) in much more detail in #67. Since predictions about meaning are in general dependent on real-world knowledge (see #3 for further discussion), an NLP system will achieve enhanced accuracy if it distinguishes linguistic vs. non-linguistic sources of information when computing meaning, for then it can make more accurate predictions when the two sources of information provide conflicting clues about interpretation, as they do in discourse (1a).

Building NLP systems involving natural language generation (speech or text output) also benefits from an understanding of semantics. In concept-to-text generation (e.g., natural language query systems), the system must choose a message to communicate that is satisfied by its database and a corresponding natural language string that will successfully communicate that message to the user. As the database is in effect a model of the world and semantics is a theory of the relationship between natural language strings and such a model, understanding semantics is key to building successful concept-to-text generation systems.

In text-to-text generation (e.g., multi-document summarization), an understanding of linguistic semantics can similarly inform system design: For example, models of paraphrase and entailment relations can help the designer to stop a generation system from repeating itself. Similarly, understanding how the context of use constrains antecedents to pronouns and elided constructions is necessary for ensuring that they are used appropriately by the generation system. Even systems built with machine learning methods that don't have feature engineering still need this kind of knowledge for thorough evaluation.

Analysis and generation are very different tasks, but encodings of the linguistic knowledge that supports them can be shared. For example, reversible grammars [e.g., Alshawi and Crouch, 1992, Bender et al., 2002, Kay, 1975, van Noord, 1990, White and Baldridge, 2003] are so-called because they support both parsing a natural language string into a semantic representation and generating from a semantic representation a natural language string. Reversible grammars have proved useful in NLP: see Strzalkowski 2012 for a range of NLP applications, and earlier work in dialogue systems [van Noord et al., 1999] and machine translation [Müller and Kasper, 2000].

CHAPTER 2

What is Meaning?

#2 Meaning can be modeled in terms of validity and reference.

This chapter describes the basic concepts that philosophers and formal semanticists use to talk about the meaning of natural language. We will address how those concepts, when used with care, are useful for developing NLP systems.

Looking at language in terms of logic illuminates the meaning of certain key kinds of expressions, by grounding them in the validity of arguments. A valid argument is an argument where if its premises are true, then its conclusion must also be true. The meanings of certain kinds of natural language expressions play a crucial role in contributing to the validity of arguments and so one can represent their meaning by modeling that validity.

For instance, consider the following argument, which happens to be a *syllogism* [Aristotle, 1989]:[1]

$$
\frac{
\begin{array}{c}
\text{All men are mortal} \\
\text{Socrates is a man}
\end{array}
}{
\text{Socrates is mortal}
}
$$

This argument (or syllogism) is valid: if its premises are true, then so is its conclusion. Note that you can substitute *man* (and its plural version *men*) and *mortal* with anything, and the argument remains valid. So the following *argument schema* is valid:

$$
\frac{
\begin{array}{c}
\text{All P are Q} \\
\text{x is P}
\end{array}
}{
\text{x is Q}
}
$$

Or to put this another way, the argument's validity is due to the meanings of the quantifier *all* and the verb *be*. So by constructing a logic that validates the above schema, we effectively have a formally precise account of the meaning of these words. In a similar way, we can analyze the meanings of conditionals (*if*), negation (*not*), disjunction (*or*), and modals (*must*, *probably*). For instance, the following schemata are valid:

$$
\frac{
\begin{array}{c}
\text{If P then Q} \\
\text{not Q}
\end{array}
}{
\text{not P}
}
\qquad
\frac{
\begin{array}{c}
\text{P or Q} \\
\text{not P}
\end{array}
}{
\text{Q}
}
\qquad
\frac{
\text{It must be the case that P}
}{
\text{It is probably the case that P}
}
$$

[1]A syllogism is an argument consisting of two premises that contain three terms, one of which is common to both (in this case, the three terms are *Socrates*, *man* and *mortal*, and *man* is the common term), and a conclusion containing the two terms that weren't common in the premises.

In logic, the expressions in the formal language that contribute to validity are known as *logical constants*. Therefore, a theory that uses logic and its notion of validity to model natural language meaning must map natural language expressions that contribute to validity (e.g., the English words *every*, *some*, *not*, *or*, *must*) to meaning representations, which in formal semantics are also known as *logical forms*, that feature the appropriate logical constants from the logic's formal language: e.g., *every* maps to a meaning representation that will feature the quantifier $\forall$;[2] *must* will map to a meaning representation featuring the modal operator $\Box$,[3] and so on.

Natural language expressions that don't contribute to validity will correspond to non-logical constants in the formal language—e.g., predicate symbols of an appropriate arity, constants, or variables. For instance, the above syllogism can be regimented formally as shown below:

All men are mortal	$\forall x(man(x) \rightarrow mortal(x))$
Socrates is a man	$man(s)$
Socrates is mortal	$mortal(s)$

Each sentence in the syllogism is assigned its logical form, expressed in a first-order language. Notice how the words that don't correspond to logical constants (*man*, *mortal*, and *Socrates*) correspond instead to predicate symbols (*man*, *mortal*) or constants (*s*). In classical first-order logic, the formulae in the above premises validate the formula in the conclusion.

There are two alternative (and normally very closely related) ways to underpin predictions about validity in a logic: via a proof theory (which consists of a set of axioms where each axiom relates well-formed formulae in the language), or via a model theory (both of these are nicely explained and implemented in Blackburn and Bos 2005). A model theory assigns an *interpretation* to all well-formed expressions of the language in terms of a model M, which in turn is an abstract representation of the way the world is. One writes the model-theoretic interpretation of an expression ϕ as $[\![\phi]\!]^M$. For example, in classical first-order logic, each model $M = \langle D, F \rangle$ consists of a set of individuals D and a function F that maps predicate symbols and constants to their denotations: e.g., each one-place predicate symbol denotes a subset of individuals in the model M (so $F(man) \subseteq D$), and each constant denotes an individual (so $F(s) \in D$).

Model theoretic interpretations are *compositional*: that is, the interpretation of a formula is defined in terms of the interpretations of its parts and how they combine in that formula. So, for example, $[\![man(s)]\!]^M$ is defined in terms of $[\![man]\!]^M$ and $[\![s]\!]^M$. Specifically, where $M = \langle D, F \rangle$, $[\![man]\!]^M = F(man)$, $[\![s]\!]^M = F(s)$ and $[\![man(s)]\!]^M = true$ just in case $[\![s]\!]^M \in [\![man]\!]^M$ (in other words, $man(s)$ is true just in case the individual denoted by s is in the set of individuals

---

[2]This quantifier is a part of first-order logic. There's an excellent introduction to first-order logic in Gamut 1991a and Blackburn and Bos 2005. For now, it suffices to know that roughly speaking, the quantifier is defined as follows. In the syntax of a logical form, where x is a variable and ϕ is a formula, $\forall x\phi$ is a formula. In semantics, $\forall x\phi$ is true if ϕ is true, whatever individual the variable x denotes. For further details on quantifiers, see #51 and #52.

[3]Syntactically, if ϕ is a formula then $\Box\phi$ is a formula, the truth of formulae are defined with respect to possible worlds, one of which is the actual world, and $\Box\phi$ is true in the actual world if ϕ is true in every possible world.

denoted by *man*). Another example of compositionality at work is the model theoretic interpretation of conjunction, which is represented by the Boolean connective $\wedge$ and roughly means "and":[4] $[\![\phi \wedge \psi]\!]^{M} = true$ just in case $[\![\phi]\!]^{M} = true$ and $[\![\psi]\!]^{M} = true$.

These two specific examples illustrate a more general idea, attributable to Tarski [1956]. Specifically, they illustrate how a model theory specifies the conditions under which formulae are true with respect to a model M (known as *truth conditions*). Thanks to compositionality, those truth conditions in turn are based on set theory and reference: the predicate symbols and terms from which the simplest formulae in the language are built denote sets of individuals and individuals, respectively. Thus, converting a natural language sentence into its logical form defines the meaning of the sentence in terms of its truth conditions, which in turn are defined (via compositionality) in terms of reference. Further, the truth conditions assigned to formulae determine the logic's notion of validity, i.e., which conclusions follow from which premises. For instance, $[\![\neg\phi]\!]^{M} = true$ if and only if $[\![\phi]\!]^{M} = false$; so in classical logic (where a formula is always true or false), it follows from these truth conditions for negation that $\neg\neg\phi$ entails ϕ, whatever the formula ϕ.

Compositionality not only underlies the way one defines the model-theoretic interpretation of well-formed formulae in the logic; it also underlies how the logical form for a natural language expression is derived from the expression's linguistic form, however complex the natural language expression might be. In other words, as proposed in Frege's writings [see Beaney, 1997], the logical form assigned to a natural language sentence is a function of the logical forms of its parts and how they combine in syntax. Montague [1974] used Frege's principle to demonstrate how one can write a grammar that assigns the well formed phrases in a natural language both a syntactic and a corresponding semantic representation: it supports the analysis of an unbounded number of phrases via a finite number of rules. More generally, deriving meaning representations for natural language by exploiting compositionality is a major issue, which we return to in Chapter 7.

However, as we'll see in the course of this chapter and also in Chapter 3, there are often systematic and predictable relationships among the denotations of words (e.g., *chairman* is to *man* as *chairperson* is to *person*) and in formal semantics these relationships are often ignored, because the meaning of these words are expressed with non-logical constants of the formal language (i.e., predicate symbols). It's a major challenge to capture all relevant linguistic generalizations for the so-called open-class words in a formal and computationally tractable way. But validity can help here too: it can, for instance, model the fact that all (count) nouns that denote animals can also be used as mass nouns that denote their edible substance. Such relationships are expressible by what is known as *lexical rules* [Copestake and Briscoe, 1995], and these are typically expressed in the literature using a brand of logic known as *typed feature structures* [Carpenter, 1992] (see #19).

---

[4]Syntactically, where ϕ and ψ are formulae then so is $\phi \wedge \psi$.

Knowing how natural language expressions contribute to validity is very important to NLP, because natural language inference—that is, the act of drawing a valid conclusion from a natural language text or dialogue—is needed for many NLP applications. These include Recognizing Textual Entailment (RTE) [Bentivogli et al., 2009], discussed in #3 below, question answering [e.g., Kwok et al., 2001], and information extraction [Chang et al., 2006].

#3 Natural language understanding requires commonsense reasoning.

The aspects of natural language meaning that are illuminated by thinking about classical logic and its notion of validity aren't sufficient, on their own at least, for capturing the inferences that people naturally make from natural language text. People infer much more than what is made valid by classical logic. Furthermore, speakers exploit this fact when choosing what to say (see Chapters 9 and 13). To illustrate the phenomena, consider some examples from the NLP task of Recognizing Textual Entailment (RTE). RTE is the task of determining which of three entailment relationships people would typically take to hold between a *text fragment* and a natural language *hypothesis*: it's *positive* if the text fragment entails the hypothesis; it's *negative* if the text fragment entails the hypothesis is false; and it's *neutral* if their truth values are independent [Dagan et al., 2006].

RTE data sets[5] contain many examples where the entailment relationship is based on commonsense reasoning with both linguistic and non-linguistic information such as real-world knowledge, and not just logical constants such as *all* and *must* that we discussed in #2. In example (2), H1 is labeled positive, H2 negative, and H3 neutral:

(2)   Text: The purchase of Houston-based LexCorp by BMI for $2 Bn prompted widespread sell-offs by traders as they sought to minimize exposure. LexCorp had been an employee-owned concern since 2008.

H1: BMI acquired an American company.
H2: BMI bought employee-owned LexCorp for $3.4 Bn.
H3: BMI is an employee-owned concern.

Intuitively, H1 is positive because of (among other things) real-world knowledge that Houston is in America and that when you purchase something you acquire it. But these expressions correspond to non-logical constants in any classical symbolic logic—that is, *purchase* and *acquire* are represented by separate and logically unrelated predicate symbols in logical form, and *Houston* and *America* by individual constants.

Furthermore, in contrast to classical logic, the commonsense reasoning involved is inherently *defeasible*.[6] For example, it is highly natural for most people to assume that *Houston* in

---

[5]https://tac.nist.gov/data/RTE/index.html. While almost all existing RTE data sets are English, data sets for other languages are now emerging: e.g., Zeller and Padó [2013] present a German RTE data set.
[6]Defeasible inference means that when ϕ is entailed by a set of premises Γ (written $\Gamma \vdash \phi$), it does not follow that ϕ is also entailed by a superset of those premises; i.e., it's possible that $\Gamma \vdash \phi$ and $\Gamma \cup \Gamma' \nvdash \phi$.

the text fragment in (2) refers to the city in Texas, U.S. rather than the town in Renfrewshire, Scotland, even if they possess the world knowledge that both of these towns exist. The use of the term *American* in H1 reinforces this interpretation, because people tend toward interpretations of the text fragment and hypothesis that maximizes their semantic relatedness, an issue we'll return to shortly (we also discuss this aspect of natural language interpretation in more depth in #67). But unlike entailments in classical logic, adding further facts to the premises can compel one to retract this conclusion: e.g., imagine the text fragment in (2) starts with the sentence *A company from Scotland called LexCorp contributed to major upsets on the London Stock Exchange yesterday.*

Even the prediction that H2 is negative relies on commonsense reasoning that goes beyond classical logic: specifically, it relies on the commonsense assumption that BMI didn't buy LexCorp twice. Without this (defeasible) assumption, H2 is neutral, like H3.

Outside of tasks like RTE, which directly model commonsense reasoning over natural language data, commonsense reasoning is also necessary to the process of constructing a meaning representation of a linguistic utterance that precisely captures the content that the speaker intended to convey. For example, the task of identifying antecedents to pronouns has been a central issue in NLP since Winograd 1972, and Hobbs 1979 shows that commonsense reasoning is central to this task. Specifically, Hobbs uses (3a) and (3b) to show how identifying the antecedent of a pronoun is dependent on the commonsense knowledge that we use to construct a coherent meaning for the entire discourse—that is, a meaning in which the contents of the individual sentences are semantically related:

(3) a. John can open Bill's safe. He knows the combination.

  b. John can open Bill's safe. He should change the combination.

In both of the above texts, one infers that *the combination* denotes the combination of Bill's safe; this depends on real-world knowledge (e.g., that safes have combinations) plus an assumption that applies universally to discourse; namely, that the contents of these sentences in the discourse are coherently related. Coherence together with world knowledge also predicts why we interpret *he* as denoting John in (3a) and Bill in (3b). If *he* in (3a) refers to John, then the world knowledge that knowing a safe's combination enables you to open it supports an inference that the content of the second sentence explains why the first sentence is true. This is a more coherent interpretation of the discourse overall than one where *he* denotes Bill. In (3b) the world knowledge that comes into play is that changing the combination of one's safe solves a security breach whenever someone other than the owner can open it. This knowledge, together with the interpretation of *he* as denoting Bill, supports an interpretation of the coherence of the discourse in terms of *explanation*:[7] the first sentence in (3b) explains why the second is true. If *he* is instead taken to denote John in (3b) then a coherent relationship between the contents of the two sentences

---

[7]In both (3a) and (3b) the particular type of coherence relation is the same (*explanation*). One and the same coherence relation (see #7) can give rise to different interpretations because of how it interacts with world knowledge.

becomes much more tenuous, relying on highly particularized assumptions about John and Bill rather than general world knowledge about security breaches. In sum, the resolution of the referent of the pronoun in (3a,b) depends on commonsense reasoning.[8]

Commonsense reasoning also influences temporal interpretation: (4) from Asher and Lascarides 2003 is naturally interpreted as the falling preceding the helping, while in (5) the pushing precedes the falling:

(4)   Max fell. Kim helped him up.

(5)   Max fell. Kim pushed him.

These distinct temporal interpretations stem from distinct knowledge of the (default) temporal relationships among the events described: if someone falling and someone pushing them are related at all, then normally the latter causes the former, but this is not the case when the two events are falling and helping someone up. This kind of reasoning about temporal relationships is defeasible, i.e., listeners can and do update their interpretation based on further information later in the discourse. This is illustrated in (6), where the same text fragment in another context receives a different temporal interpretation from (5):[9]

(6)   a. Kim and Max were at the edge of a cliff.

      b. Max felt a sharp blow to the back of his neck.

      c. He fell.

      d. Kim pushed him.

      e. Max went over the edge of the cliff.

Yet another instance of commonsense reasoning involves what we infer from speakers' choices of how to describe entities. For example, (7) adapted from Hobbs et al. 1993 is naturally interpreted as meaning that the joggers were run over while they were jogging:

(7)   A car hit two joggers last night.

Intuitively, this inference exploits defeasible commonsense reasoning about why the speaker referred to the injured people using *joggers* as opposed to an alternative description.

Because commonsense reasoning is prevalent in understanding everyday language use, it's not only critical in NLP to the RTE task, but also to other tasks such as open domain question answering, i.e., the challenge to return an expression, extracted from some set of documents, that answers the user's question [Radev et al., 2005]. For instance, the answer to the questions in (8) (example due to Ivan Titov) should be *Trinity* and *Australia*, respectively:

---

[8] For further discussion, see Chapter 10 and especially #76.

[9] Like the discourses (1a) vs. (1b) discussed in #1, the world knowledge that contributes to the interpretation of (5) gets overridden in the richer discourse context provided in (6) by a linguistic convention against describing events in discourse in the order "cause, effect, a further cause of that effect" without making the unusual order linguistically explicit.

(8)   Lansky left Australia to study the piano at the Royal College of Music. Lansky dropped his studies at RCM, but eventually graduated from Trinity.

    1.   Where did Lansky get his diploma?

    2.   Where did he live before studying piano?

Inference is critical to finding the right answers in this case, and the inferences depend on commonsense knowledge such as the relationship between graduating and diplomas. Similarly, inference is also critical to information extraction, if that task is to go beyond representing the knowledge extracted in terms of the exact words used in the source texts [Chang et al., 2006].

Overall, then, an adequate model of natural language understanding must incorporate commonsense reasoning with linguistic and non-linguistic information. Furthermore, this reasoning must be defeasible, because the content of an utterance depends critically on contextual information that's hidden rather than observable. Thus, content is estimated under uncertainty and one can therefore change one's mind on gathering subsequent observable evidence about the context. For instance the temporal relation between falling and pushing one infers for the two sentence discourse (5) is clearly defeasible, because when this same discourse is embedded in the richer context provided by (6) one revises one's inference about that temporal relationship.

There are many symbolic logics that, unlike classical logic, make valid intuitively compelling notions of defeasible inference [e.g., Asher and Morreau, 1991, McCarthy, 1980, Reiter, 1980]. By definition, defeasible logics make it possible for a formula ϕ to be entailed by a set of premises Γ (written $\Gamma \models \phi$) and not entailed by a superset of those premises (e.g., $\Gamma \cup \Gamma' \not\models \phi$); classical logic lacks this property. Some of these defeasible logics (in particular Reiter's default logic) bear a very close relationship to the probabilistic belief model of Bayes Nets [Pearl, 1988].

#4 Meaning derived from form is different from meaning in context of use.

In #3 we saw that a full interpretation of an utterance relies on commonsense reasoning as well as the direct contribution of the words. More generally, in order to build models of linguistic meaning or natural language technology that can handle open-domain human communication, it is imperative to distinguish three different levels of meaning: (1) semantics that is derived from linguistic form, (2) the content that the speaker publicly commits to, and (3) implicatures that follow from that public commitment. Public commitment [Hamblin, 1970] is a public stance that one takes to a proposition (or a question or a request): one can be publicly committed to something without believing it; further, unlike beliefs, one must perform an action (e.g., saying something) in order to form a public commitment (for motivation in linking communicative actions directly to public commitment as opposed to belief, see #66, #90, and #93, and also Hamblin 1970 and Lascarides and Asher 2009).

The semantics that is derived from linguistic form is called *timeless, conventional, standing,* or *sentence* meaning [e.g., Grice, 1968, Quine, 1960]. It represents what is constant about the meaning of a sentence (or other linguistic object) across all possible contexts of use. Furthermore, it is supported by conventional or shared linguistic knowledge, such as might be modeled by a grammar [see Bender et al., 2015]. By contrast, in order to interpret what a speaker means to convey by using a specific linguistic form, interlocutors must apply commonsense inference, drawing on both general knowledge as well as (presumed) shared knowledge about the current linguistic and non-linguistic context. This conveyed meaning can be further subdivided into that which the speaker has publicly committed to and that which they haven't.

For example, in (9), B's utterance of *Yes* has a minimal sentence meaning: what can be derived from this form alone is very scant.

(9)   A: Is it raining?
      B: Yes.

The listener can use the (linguistic, in this case) context, however, to infer that the content of B's utterance *Yes* in this context is that it is raining. Furthermore, according to the semantics of dialogue proposed by Ginzburg [2012], Hamblin [1970], Lascarides and Asher [2009], Poesio and Traum [1998], and others, the speaker is publicly committed to that content: Note how B can't plausibly deny that what she meant by her move was *It's raining*. Specifically, the public commitments follow from *discourse coherence* [Asher and Lascarides, 2013, Lascarides and Asher, 2009]. By uttering something, speakers are assumed to be committing to making a coherent discourse contribution, and even when the coherence relation itself is left implicit, it becomes part of the content they have publicly committed to. In (9), B publicly commits to *It is raining* because B's utterance must be a coherent response to A's question, and the only coherent response it could be, given its linguistic form, is that it's an *answer*.

The word *yes* is an example of an *anaphoric expression*: it is meaningful, by which we mean that its content can be evaluated as true or false against the current state of affairs, only if one uses the context of use of the utterance containing the anaphoric expression to construct that content. Anaphora, which is the phenomenon of a phrase being meaningful only in virtue of its context of use, features in all natural languages and indeed it's ubiquitous: examples of anaphoric expressions include pronouns (e.g., *he*), VP ellipsis (e.g., *Kim did*), presuppositions (see Chapter 11 for examples), and many other linguistic constructions that will be discussed throughout the course of this book.

In dialogue (9), we see that B makes a public commitment to the content of her utterance where the content of its anaphoric expressions (in this case, *yes*) is resolved to something meaningful (i.e., evaluable against the current state of affairs). More generally, public commitments are to contents that are meaningful, and so if the speaker's anaphoric expressions are ambiguous in context, then constructing a representation of what the speaker publicly committed to is defeasible or uncertain (much like resolving linguistic ambiguity can be defeasible or uncertain).

The idea that what a speaker is publicly committed extends beyond the meaning derived from only its linguistic form is further illustrated in (10). Here the *No* uttered by B denies the *explanation* relation that connects the contents of A's individual sentences, as is made clear by the rest of B's turn:

(10)   A: John went to jail. He embezzled the company funds.
        B: No. He embezzled the funds but he went to jail because he was convicted of tax evasion.

The felicitous use of *no* to deny something is a test for whether that content has been publicly committed to. Here, what *no* refers to is not explicit in the text: rather, it is the implicit *explanation* relation between the two sentences of A's turn [Asher and Lascarides, 2003]. This *explanation* relation, which could have been marked overtly by a cue such as *because*, instead must be (defeasibly) inferred. Nonetheless, it is still available to be referred to (and denied).

The third level of meaning we distinguish is *perlocutionary consequences*: These are inferences about private cognitive attitudes, derivable from a speaker's public message or commitment, but which the speaker is not publicly committed to. Returning to (9) above, suppose that A's question was a follow up to the sentence shown in (11). In this context, it is natural to assume that B's (positive) answer to the question yields an inference that B wants A to adopt a new intention to take her umbrella (we'll discuss such inferences in more detail in #89). This is not a part of the content that B publicly commits to, however: it is not a necessary consequence of an assumption that B's move is coherent, and accordingly B can plausibly deny that this is what she meant by her utterance, as in (11).

(11)   A: I wonder whether I should take my umbrella.
            Is it raining?
        B: Yes.
        A: Oh, so you do think I should take my umbrella.
        B: I didn't say that.

The following chapters will discuss all three of these levels of meaning. Modeling all three are important to building successful natural language understanding systems and they cannot be modeled in one undifferentiated end-to-end approach. The contributions at the three levels rely on different linguistic systems: grammar and lexicon for identifying meaning derived from form, discourse coherence and commonsense reasoning (taking meaning derived from form as input) for identifying public commitments, and additional commonsense reasoning involving plans, beliefs and preferences for identifying further implicatures. In order to design scalable NLP systems, it is critical to understand the differences and connections between these layers of interpretation and the kinds of processing that support them [Bender et al., 2015].

#5 Many extant models of meaning distinguish locutionary, illocutionary and perlocutionary acts.

In #4, we distinguished three levels of meaning: compositional semantics; the content that a speaker publicly commits to when she utters something; and the effects of those public commitments on the cognitive states (e.g., beliefs and intentions) of the interlocutor and speaker.

These distinctions are similar but not equivalent to those made in the philosophy literature between locutionary, illocutionary, and perlocutionary acts [Austin, 1962, Searle, 1969]. A locutionary act is the act of saying something meaningful; for instance, the act of saying (12):

(12)   Smoking is bad for your health.

An illocutionary act is an act you perform by performing a locutionary act: for example, by saying (12), the speaker is performing the illocutionary act of *asserting* the proposition that smoking is bad for your health.

One can in fact perform several illocutionary acts with one locutionary act: under one interpretation of our example, the speaker is not only asserting the proposition that smoking is bad for your health, but by doing so she is also performing the further illocutionary act of *warning* the speaker not to smoke. This warning is known as an *indirect speech act*. An indirect speech act is an illocutionary act that speakers perform by performing a different illocutionary act. In this example, the warning is issued by asserting a proposition.

A perlocutionary act changes the cognitive states of the speaker or the addressee in virtue of the speaker performing an illocutionary act. For instance, if the addressee heeds the warning the speaker issued by uttering (12) then she forms an intention not to smoke. That the speaker causes the interlocutor to adopt a new intention is a *perlocutionary act*.

This three-way distinction between locutionary, illocutionary, and perlocutionary acts cuts across the three-way distinction between compositional semantics, public commitments, and perlocutionary consequences that we highlighted in #4. The content conveyed by a locutionary act is not equivalent to the compositional semantics of a phrase, because philosophers typically take such contents to be *meaningful*—that is, they can be evaluated against a model or the current state of affairs. This means that the content conveyed by a locutionary act is one where antecedents for expressions such as pronouns, elided constructions, or the word *yes* are resolved. For instance, in (9) (repeated here), B's locutionary act entails that it's raining, but that's distinct from the compositional semantics of *yes*, which is highly underspecified and does not entail this.

(9)   A: It's raining.
       B: Yes.

An illocutionary act is also not equivalent to a public commitment: this is because indirect illocutionary acts can be mutually understood and yet not be part of the public commitment. Recall the tests for public commitment from #4: a public commitment cannot be plausibly denied and furthermore is an available antecedent for interpreting a subsequent context-sensitive expression like *no* or VP ellipsis (which is a VP where the finite verb is omitted; e.g., *Kim did* and *Kim will too*). The content of the warning in our example (i.e., not to smoke) is not available for resolving the ellipsis in B's (anomalous[10]) utterance in (13): B's utterance cannot mean *I refuse not to smoke*, even if A and B mutually share the knowledge that A's utterance is a warning to B not to smoke.

(13) A: Smoking is bad for your health.
      B: #I refuse.

Thus, the three-way distinction between sentence meaning, speaker meaning, and perlocutionary consequences in #4 cannot be reduced to the distinction between locutionary, illocutionary, and perlocutionary acts.

#6 Philosophical concepts like indirect speech acts and common ground are useful for dialogue processing, but they have a different status from public commitments when resolving anaphora.

The philosophical literature on illocutionary acts, including indirect speech acts and the notion of *common ground* have been influential in the study of dialogue. For example, there are several proposed ways of estimating illocutionary acts from dialogue data [e.g., Stolcke et al., 2000] as well as work on understanding dialogue as a process of updating common ground, understood to be the interlocutors' shared knowledge or mutual beliefs [Lewis, 1979, Stalnaker, 1978].

This can be seen in (13) above, where, after A's turn, it is highly plausible that A and B mutually believe, or have in their common ground, that A has warned B not to smoke. But this can't be an antecedent to the elided construction in B's anomalous response, which cannot be interpreted as *I refuse not to smoke*. A further example is shown in (14). Here, thanks to the Gricean Maxim of Sincerity [Grice, 1975], after A's utterance, A and B should update their common ground to include the proposition that A believes that it's raining. However, the infelicity of B's response shows that the VP ellipsis cannot treat this belief as an antecedent.

(14) A: It's raining.
      B: #I do too.

Overall, these dialogues show that we need something separate from this notion of common ground in order to model the interpretation of anaphoric expressions. Otherwise, a natural language generation system will express content using elided constructions when it is in fact infelicitous to do so. Here, the anaphoric expressions in question are the elided complement of *refuse* and the pro-verb *do too* (see #71). Ostensibly, they should refer to *not smoking* and *believe it's raining*, respectively, both of which are in the common ground at that point in the relevant dialogue. But in reality, these interpretations of the elided constructions aren't felicitous.

---

[10]The symbol # before an utterance indicates that it is infelicitous in some way, despite being syntactically well-formed.

These considerations about anaphora show that it's useful to distinguish the semantic representation of discourse from the effects of that content on the cognitive states of the participants, including updates to their common ground. However, as Chapters 9, 10, 11, and 13 show, while this distinction is necessary, it's far from sufficient for defining the set of possible antecedents to anaphoric expressions; those constraints depend on many other factors as well.

#7 Some speech acts are relations.

Speech acts are traditionally thought of as properties of utterances. For instance, *asserting*, *questioning*, or *requesting* are, quite rightly, viewed this way. Existing dialogue corpora, such as the English Switchboard corpus [Godfrey et al., 1992] are often tagged with the DAMSL (Dialogue Act Markup in Several Layers) tagset [Core and Allen, 1997], which consists of 300 tags, and all of these are used to label individual linguistic phrases in dialogue: in other words, they are treated like properties of individual utterances.

However, looking more closely at the various types of tags in this tagset, it is apparent that while the first two can be construed to be a property of an utterance, the latter two have a meaning that's actually best expressed as a relation between utterances, rather than a property of an individual utterance. DAMSL provides the following four types of tags, and an utterance can have several tags from each type, to reflect the fact that people can perform more than one type of action with their utterance (for example, an "Answer," which is a Backward Looking Function tag, may also be a "Statement-Non-Opinion," which is an Information Level tag):

Communicative Status: Whether the utterance is intelligible and whether it was successfully completed (yes/no).

Information Level: A characterization of the semantic content of the utterance, that corresponds roughly to its illocutionary force [Austin, 1962]. For instance, the utterance *It's raining* would be tagged with "Statement-Non-Opinion," while the utterance *Is it raining?* would be tagged with "Yes-No-Question."

Forward Looking Function: How the current utterance constrains the future beliefs and actions of the participants, and affects the discourse. For instance, a "Tag-Question" (e.g., *isn't it?*), and questions generally, are forward looking in the sense that one expects a subsequent utterance to provide an answer.

Backward Looking Function: How the current utterance relates to the previous discourse. For instance, *Excuse me?* may be tagged with "Signal-non-understanding," *I don't know* with "Other answers," *yes* with "Yes-answers," and so on.

Considering the meaning of these speech act labels, the acts that are categorized as Backward Looking Functions are *relations*, because they denote a *relationship* between the content of two phrases: a prior utterance and the current one (that is being tagged with the Backward

Looking Function). Or to put this another way, marking an utterance u as Answer(u) misses important semantic information—namely, which prior question in the dialogue was u an answer to? Replacing this markup with a relation Answer(q,u)—where the annotator has to identify the prior question q that u answers—would preserve this information.

Coherence-based models of discourse [e.g., Asher and Lascarides, 2003, Hobbs, 1979, Kehler, 2002, Mann and Thompson, 1986, Webber et al., 2003] place this relational view of speech acts at center stage. In these theories, the current utterance b is attached with a *coherence relation* (e.g., *explanation, result, narration, contrast, answer*) to a salient segment a that's already a part of the discourse context.[11] Each coherence relation is a type of *relational speech act*. It is an act because elaborating some prior content, drawing a contrast with it, or explaining why some prior content is true are all things that people do with their utterances. Coherence relations also effect a change to the context, just like actions do in general: specifically, they change what is salient and available for interpreting subsequent anaphoric expressions in the discourse (see #67 for details). They are relational because successfully performing them depends not only on the content of the current utterance but also on that of the prior utterance to which the current utterance is coherently connected.[12] In fact, each coherence relation is a type of *anaphoric* relational speech act [Asher and Lascarides, 2003, Webber et al., 2003], because identifying the speaker's current act (or, equivalently, their coherent contribution) involves identifying the *antecedent* content that their current utterance relates to, and what prior content the current move relates to is rarely linguistically explicit.

Coherence relations provide a more fine-grained inventory of speech acts than assertion, question and request. Coherence relations like *elaboration, explanation,* and *contrast* are all a kind of assertion: the semantic consequences of these acts entail that speakers publicly commit to the content of their current utterance, just like an assertion so commits them. But these coherence relations (or relational speech acts) carry entailments additional to those that follow from asserting something. For example, explanation(a, b) entails not just the content of the current utterance b, but also that b is an answer to the question *why a?*, where a is the content of a prior discourse move. Coherence relations where the second argument to the relation is a question also carry entailments that are additional to those that follow from only from the speech act of questioning. For example, in (15), taken from the STAC corpus,[13] in which players of the board game *The Settlers of Catan* negotiate trades over resources [Afantenos et al., 2012b], the question *elaborates* on the partial offer that's implicated by the first indicative, so that the intended content of the question can be paraphrased as *Do you have any clay you are prepared to exchange for wood?*

(15)   A: I've got wood. Do you have any clay?

---

[11]These theories also countenance that an assertion, a question, and a request are properties of individual utterances.

[12]See #12 for examples that show coherence relations can relate the content of linguistic units to salient non-linguistic events as well.

[13]https://www.irit.fr/STAC

In the STAC corpus annotation scheme, which is based on Segmented Discourse Representation Theory [SDRT; Asher and Lascarides, 2003] this is annotated with the specific coherence relation Qelab, whose semantics supports the inference that the question is assigned the content in this context that we've just described.

Clarification requests—of which there are various kinds [Ginzburg and Cooper, 2004]—are also a particular kind of questioning, since answers to the clarification request must bear a certain semantic relation to the content of the unit that the clarification request was attending to. Exactly what type of semantic relation the answer must bear to this prior unit depends on the clarification request's type. As Ginzburg and Cooper [2004] attest, the clarification request may query a prior move at several distinct levels: what words were said in a prior utterance, or what senses a prior word (or phrase) can have, or what a prior word or phrase denotes in the current context, or even what speech act the prior speaker was attempting to perform [DeVault and Stone, 2006].

Overall, then, it's useful to include in one's representation of discourse meaning the relational speech acts (aka coherence relations) that connect one utterance to another, rather than just annotating that an utterance is an assertion, or a question, or annotating that an utterance is an answer without identifying which question it is an answer to. This is because the semantics of these coherence relations use the contents of the units they relate to support inferences about speaker meaning that go beyond those that follow from an utterance being an assertion, or a question, or an answer to some unspecified question. We'll see many examples where coherence relations prove useful for predicting speaker meaning in Chapters 9–13.

#8 Linguistic meaning includes emotional content.

Thus far, we have mostly been talking about meaning in terms of truth-conditional compositional semantics (i.e., what must be true for a proposition expressed by a utterance to be true) and inferences beyond that based on coherence relations in discourse and the like. But the meaning associated with linguistic forms that we use extends beyond what might be called propositional content and includes both emotional content and social meaning (see #9 below). Emotional content expressed by choices in linguistic form includes expression of the speaker's attitude toward the content of their utterance, expressions of the speaker's feelings about entities they are referring to, as well as indications of the speaker's emotional state carried in the speech signal.

Expressions of speaker attitude include evaluative adverbs such as *hopefully* or *fortunately* in English as in (16).

(16)   Hopefully, the line will move quickly.

(17)   Fortunately, it's not too cold outside.

In (17) the evaluative adverb *fortunately* does not change the truth conditions of the utterance. The speaker is still asserting that it is not too cold out. What *fortunately* adds is that the speaker is happy about this. The use of *hopefully* in (16) is slightly different: In addition to expressing speaker attitude (in this case, that the speaker would like the state of affairs described by the rest of the sentence to come to pass), it is also a modal adverb [Huddleston and Pullum, 2002, p. 768] and thus serves as a hedge. Where *The line will move quickly* is a baldly stated prediction about the future, the utterance in (16) doesn't commit the speaker to the belief that it will necessarily come about.

Huddleston and Pullum [2002, p. 772] note that evaluative adverbs combine only with asserted information and so don't appear in questions, commands, or attached to presupposed content, which they illustrate with the following examples, respectively:[14]

(18)   a.   *Did the soldiers fortunately get away?

   b.   *Fortunately catch the bus.

   c.   *Since Deidre fortunately recovered from her illness, she has lived in California.

Potts [2007] identifies six properties of what he calls "expressive content" (e.g., the emotive information provided by *damn* in *that damn cat*): (i) it is independent of truth conditional semantics (what Potts calls "descriptive content"); (ii) it is non-displaceable, i.e., always pertains to the current situation; (iii) it is perspective dependent, usually (but not always) pertaining to the speaker's own perspective; (iv) it is difficult or impossible to paraphrase expressive content with strictly non-expressive terms; (v) expressives are like performatives in that the mere uttering of an expressive constitutes the act that is their effect; and (vi) repeating expressives is informative rather than redundant.

Expressives in English are generally separate words (with exceptions such as expletive infixation, e.g., *un-fucking-believable*), but crosslinguistically we also find expressive meanings associated with morphology. For example, Ponsonnet [2018] provides a typology of the emotions associated with diminutive and augmentative morphology crosslinguistically. In Ponsonnet's survey, both diminuatives (deriving from forms describing a referent as small in size or quantity) and augmentatives (likewise, but big, not small) come to carry both positive and negative expressive content. This is illustrated in (19) and (20). (19), from Tacana, a language of Bolivia, illustrates the use of the diminutive *=chidi* to express compassion for the referent (in this case also the addressee), while in (20), from Tunumiisut,[15] a language of Greenland, the augmentative affix *-kaik* indicates that the speaker finds the referent to be nasty.[16]

---

[14]As Huddleston and Pullum note, *since* in (18c) is intended in its temporal sense. (18c) is fine if *since* is interpreted in its causal sense, as it has different presuppositional properties in that sense.

[15]Tersis [2009] describes Tunumiisut as a part of the Inuit dialect chain, which also includes the better described Kalaallisut [kal]. It does not appear that Tunumiisut has its own ISO 639-3 code.

[16]These examples, like all non-English examples in this text, are presented in the format of interlinear glossed text (IGT). This is a widely used format in the linguistics literature and IGT contain quite a bit of information. The first line presents the sentence or utterance in question in the target language. If the target language uses a non-Roman orthography, a second line provides a transliteration. The next line gives a morpheme-by-morpheme gloss of the sentence, indicating both lemmas and grammatical formatives. The glosses of grammatical formatives ("grams") are given in small caps. A brief explanation of each gram is given in Appendix B. Finally, there is a free translation to English. That same line contains the ISO 693-3 code for the language and a citation for the source of the example, if applicable.

(19)   Jid'iu-pe-taiti-a=wekwana   mida yawe=chidi.
       peel-COMPASS-A3-PF-PST=3PL 2SG   husband=DIM

       "[The frogs] peeled you entirely, my poor husband [Spanish *maridito*]." [tna] [Ottaviano, 1980]

(20)   tii-kaik-pa-a.
       take-AUG-INDIC-3SG.3SG

       "The nasty one takes him." [kal] [Tersis, 2008]

While there is an obvious connection to sentiment analysis here, it is important to keep in mind that the kinds of data collected in, e.g., the MPQA subjectivity lexicon [Wilson et al., 2005] or SENTIWORDNET [Baccianella et al., 2010] don't (only) pertain to expressivity in Potts' sense. In particular, MPQA includes words like *celebrate* in *supporters celebrated overnight* where the sentiment involved is displaced from the speech situation.

In addition to lexical items and morphology, emotion can also be expressed in language through prosody. Ang et al. [2002] show that prosodic cues can be used to detect frustration on the part of speakers, specifically in the context of speakers getting frustrated with HCI dialogue systems. Mairesse et al. [2012] look at spoken language reviews and find that modeling acoustic features can improve sentiment analysis accuracy in those reviews.

#9 Linguistic meaning includes social meaning.

In addition to emotional content, linguistic form can be conventionally associated with what is called "social meaning." Sometimes this is dedicated words that carry information about, for example, politeness or formality, like the word *please*, the informal vs. formal second-person pronouns in Dutch, French, German, and Italian, or the elaborate system of honorifics in Japanese, illustrated in (21) [McCready, 2019, Okushi, 1997]. (21a,c) both use the "plain" forms of the verb, constructing the situation as one in which either the speaker and addressee are close or the addressee is a subordinate of the speaker. Conversely, (21b,d) use the "polite" form of the verb and thus signal social distance. This could be used, for example, to construct the situation as one in which the speaker and addressee are not close or the speaker is a subordinate of the addressee. This set of examples illustrates another dimension of variation in the choice of the verb stem, which indicates that the recipient of the book is (21c,d) or is not (21a,b) subordinate to the giver.

(21)   a. 本　を　もらった。
          Hon wo morat-ta.
          Book ACC receive.SHON:±-PST.AHON:−

          "(I) received a book." [jpn]

       b. 本　を　もらいました。
          Hon wo morai-mashi-ta.
          Book ACC receive.SHON:±-AHON:+-PST

"(I) received a book." [jpn]

c. 本　　を　いただいた。
Hon wo itadai-ta.
Book ACC receive.SHON:−−PST.AHON:−

"(I) received a book." [jpn]

d. 本　　を　いただきました。
Hon wo itadaki-mashi-ta.
Book ACC receive.SHON:−−AHON:+-PST

"(I) received a book." [jpn]

More commonly, social meaning involves parts of the linguistic system that become imbued with associations either to groups of people or to traits associated with groups of people. These may be in directly contrasting, truth-conditionally equivalent pairs or sets (such as different pronunciations of the same word, or differing speech rates or pitch levels) or they may be related but not quite synonymous forms (e.g., near synonyms, or the Japanese honorifics listed above) [see Campbell-Kibler, 2010, Lavandera, 1978]. Forms imbued with social meaning are then available as symbolic resources that speakers can use in constructing and projecting personae as well as constructing social situations, in a process that Eckert [2003], building on Hebdige [1984], calls "bricolage."

While NLP systems that recognize and appropriately react to the fine nuances of socially meaningful linguistic variation may be far away, it is still worthwhile for NLP practitioners to be aware of this aspect of meaning, especially since it is (partly) derivable from form. Recognizing that not every contrast in form relates to truth-conditional meanings may help with error analysis. Further, a better understanding of how linguistic form reveals social information could in principle be useful in processing social media data for such purposes as tracking user opinions of brands (a kind of sentiment analysis) or detecting hate speech.

#10 There is ambiguity at many levels.

Ambiguity is a pervasive feature of natural language; at every level of linguistic structure, there are ambiguities that must be resolved in natural language understanding. For spoken language processing, this starts with the mapping between an acoustic signal and a series of words, as in the famous example of similar sounding strings *recognize speech* and *wreck a nice beach.*[17]

Another classic example of ambiguity is part of speech ambiguity, or *syntactic lexical ambiguity*, where some words have multiple possible *parts of speech* (or POS) tags. For example, *man* can be a noun or a verb:

(22)   a. A man walked in.

        b. The sailors man the decks.

[17]Tompkins [2010] attributes this example to Bell Labs researcher Homer Dudley.

This type of ambiguity is often resolved by constraints on well-formedness of sentences or phrases: for instance, the preceding determiner and succeeding verb to *man* in (22a) makes this a noun and not a verb.

There is also *semantic lexical ambiguity*, also known as *word sense ambiguity*. A word with a particular POS tag can have multiple possible senses. For instance, the noun *mogul* can refer to a mound of snow or the head of an Indian dynasty. We'll discuss this kind of lexical ambiguity in detail in Chapter 4, since word sense phenomena are quite complex, exhibiting productivity and important linguistic generalizations.

Going beyond the level of the word, we have *structural ambiguity*: there is more than one way to assign a phrase or sentence a well-formed syntactic structure. This is also known as *attachment ambiguity*. For example, the sentence (23) exhibits structural ambiguity:

(23)   I saw a kid with a telescope.

As shown in Figure 2.1., the propositional phrase (PP) *with a telescope* can attach to the noun *kid* (in which case semantically, it qualifies the individual that they saw) or it can attach to the verb phrase (VP) *saw a kid* (in which case semantically, it qualifies the event of seeing a kid). The link between sentential syntax and semantics will be discussed in detail in Chapter 7.

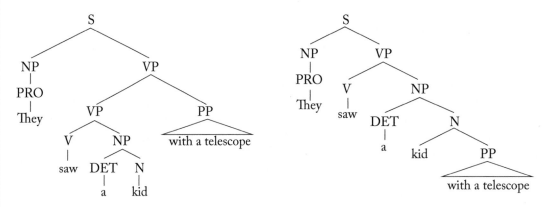

Figure 2.1: Two possible syntax trees for sentence (23).

Semantic scope ambiguity is also an ambiguity that can be exhibited at multiple levels: the level of the phrase, sentence or multi-sentence discourse. Some words, such as quantifiers (e.g., English *a*, *most*, *every*), modals (*must*, *should*), and negation (*not*) take *semantic scope*: in other words, the element they correspond to in a linguistic unit's logical form takes a formula as an argument. A phrase, sentence or discourse exhibits a semantic scope ambiguity when there are at least two alternative meaning representations for that unit, which differ in the relative semantic scope of these scopal elements. For example, the sentence (24) exhibits a semantic scope ambiguity between *a* and *must*: it can mean that there is a car that Sara must sell, or it can mean that Sara must sell some car (any car).

(24)   Sara must sell a further car to meet her targets.

The scopal order where *a* semantically outscopes *not* (i.e., there's a car that Sara must sell) is arguably a lot less salient for (24a) than the reading where *not* outscopes *a*. But the two readings have distinct truth conditions: $\exists x \Box P(x)$ entails $\Box \exists x P(x)$, but not *vice versa*. They also have distinct effects on what subsequent pronouns in the discourse can refer back to [Groenendijk and Stokhof, 1991, Kamp, 1981, Kamp and Reyle, 1993], and this in turn can help to resolve the semantic scope ambiguity: if (24) is followed by the sentence *It's that Jaguar on the car lot*, then one must interpret (24b) as *a* semantically outscoping *must*.

Presuppositions (which we'll discuss in detail in Chapter 11) can also enter into semantic scope ambiguities. For example, the possessive construction in (25) is known as a *presupposition trigger*, which introduces the presupposition that Sandy has a spouse. In (25a), this presupposition semantically outscopes *believes* (to paraphrase, (25a) means "Sandy has a spouse and Kim believes Sandy's spouse is bald"), even though syntactically the noun phrase *Sandy's spouse* is dominated by the verb *believe*. But in (25b), *believes* semantically outscopes the proposition that Sandy has a spouse (to paraphrase, (25b) means "Even though Sandy isn't married, Kim believes that Sandy is married, and (so) has a spouse, who is bald").

(25)   a. Kim believes that Sandy's spouse is bald.

       b. Even though Sandy isn't married, Kim believes that Sandy's spouse is bald.

We'll discuss the interaction between semantic scope and the interpretation of anaphoric expressions, including pronouns and presuppositions, in much more detail in #69, #80, and #81.

Finally, an utterance can be ambiguous at the level of speech acts:

(26)   A: Have you emptied the dishwasher?
       B: Is that a question or a request?

If one countenances indirect speech acts, then A's utterance can be interpreted as a question or (indirectly) as a conditional request (as B's response suggests). If one doesn't countenance indirect speech acts, then A's utterance is a question, but the communicative intention that prompted it is ambiguous: Is A's intention to simply know an answer to her question, or is it that B empty the dishwasher if it's not already emptied?

#11 What's done as a pipeline in many approaches to NLP is done in human processing via incremental interpretation/incremental building of the discourse model.

NLP systems often adopt a pipeline architecture, especially if they reason about linguistic structure: one component maps the acoustic signal to a sequence of words, which in turn may be segmented and tokenized, another then assigns those words POS tags; another then assigns the sequence of POS-tagged words a syntactic structure; yet another then identifies the type of speech act performed, and so on. The fact that human language processors can backtrack on decisions made in prior parts of the pipeline on the basis of inferences in subsequent modules shows that semantic and discourse information influences the resolution of ambiguity at the syntactic, lexical, and acoustic levels. This in turn shows that a strictly pipelined approach is not an adequate model of human language processing, and probably won't be suitable for interactive NLP tasks such as dialogue systems.

Furthermore, pipeline architectures do not afford incremental interpretation of discourse, on a word-by-word basis. In contrast, the human processor is really good at incremental interpretation. Indeed, even though the interpretation of the prefix of a phrase is necessarily incomplete, in that it does not yet correspond to a specific proposition whose truth can be evaluated against a model, human sentence processors nevertheless use these "incomplete" interpretations to resolve lower level ambiguities: for instance, structural ambiguity [Crain and Steedman, 1985] and even speech recognition [Bard et al., 2000]. There is also evidence that humans don't resolve ambiguity in contexts where the incomplete semantic representation is "good enough," given the task the comprehender needs to perform [Ferreira and Patson, 2007].

One particularly striking piece of evidence for incremental interpretation stems from so-called garden path sentences. The verb *raced* is much more likely to be a past participle than part of a passive construction, leading to the perceived ill-formedness of (27):

(27)   The horse raced past the barn fell.

In fact, this sentence is both well formed and syntactically unambiguous,[18] but as many have shown through reading time experiments [Crain and Steedman, 1985] and eye tracking experiments [Demberg and Keller, 2008, Frazier and Rayner, 1982], humans find it hard to parse. Demberg and Keller [2008] show not only that humans tend to assign *raced* its most frequent form at the point at which they read that word, but also that when their error is finally revealed to them—i.e., at the point where they read *fell*—the alternative choice is no longer easily accessible to the human interpreter to help her recover from her prior error. In other words, humans not only disambiguate POS tags before the sentence is complete, but in some cases also effectively "throw away" the alternative POS tags before one can be sure that their current choice yields a well-formed sentence.

Garden path sentences produce strong effects in reading times and eye tracking. This might suggest that the human sentence processor is working like a pipeline: subsequent evidence from sentential syntax seems unable to correct a prior error in one's decision on how to resolve a POS tag ambiguity. But that's not what's going on: further experiments, which manipulate the *discourse context* so as to create or ameliorate garden path effects, show that humans do multi-level processing all at once and incrementally, but some of those levels can't easily be changed in light of later evidence [Altmann and Steedman, 1988, Crain and Steedman, 1985]. The effect of discourse processing in (27) involves the process of finding a referent for the NP.

---

[18]It is a paraphrase of *The horse that was raced past the barn fell.*

On reading *raced*, one is faced with a choice of two possible NPs: *the horse*, where *raced* is mistakenly understood as the main verb of the sentence, or a longer NP starting with *the horse raced*, where *raced* is a passive verb in a reduced relative clause inside the NP. In contexts where the shorter NP (*the horse*) would fail to refer, readers reject that analysis and don't have a garden-path effect. This is illustrated in (28), where the context does not provide any referent for the simple NP *the horse*:

(28)   Two horses were on the farm yesterday. One was ridden past the barn; the other was kept in the stable. The horse raced past the barn fell.

One can also manipulate the discourse context to make parsing *harder* for the human processor. Altmann and Steedman [1988] show that reading times are significantly shorter when (29c) is preceded by (29a) rather than (29b), and also shorter when (29d) is preceded by (29b) rather than (29a):

(29)   a.   *NP supporting context:*
            A burglar broke into a bank carrying some dynamite. He planned to blow open a safe. Once inside he saw that there was a safe with a new lock and a safe with an old lock.

       b.   *VP supporting context:*
            A burglar broke into a bank carrying some dynamite. He planned to blow open a safe. Once inside he saw that there was a safe with a new lock and a strongbox with an old lock.

       c.   *NP-attached target:*
            The burglar blew open the safe with the new lock and made off with the loot.

       d.   *VP-attached target:*
            The burglar blew open the safe with the dynamite and made off with the loot.

Many experiments involving eye tracking also offer strong evidence that humans construct interpretations of the signal on a word by word basis and exploit those interpretations when resolving syntactic ambiguities in subsequent parts of the utterance. For example, Tanenhaus et al. [2000] show that subjects successfully fixate on the intended referent of an natural language description long before that description is complete, but after the description so far is sufficient to discriminate the intended referent from all the other salient referents in the context (on the grounds that the other visible objects in the scene don't satisfy the interpretation of the description so far).

There is a general consensus in the literature that garden path effects occur because humans interpret language incrementally. Implemented grammars and accompanying parsing algorithms that tackle interpretation incrementally do exist, e.g., Combinatory Categorial Grammar [Steedman, 1996] is designed to support incremental parsing and interpretation [see, e.g., Haddock, 1988, Stone, 1998].

#12 In face-to-face conversation, people use both verbal and non-verbal actions to convey meaning.

In embodied conversation, where the participants share the same environment (whether physical or virtual), non-linguistic objects and events can become a part of the content of the interaction. The most obvious way is through so-called *deixis*: for instance, someone can point to a mug and say *Put this in the dashwasher*. *This* is a demonstrative (also known as a deictic expression) and the pointing is a deictic gesture. Their combination serves to denote the mug that's visually salient to the dialogue participants.

Indexicals (*I*, *you*, *here*, *now* etc.) and demonstratives (*this*, *that*) are generally assigned a two-part semantics [Kaplan, 1989, Reichenbach, 1947]: one part is a rule that determines how a particular indexical or demonstrative item uses the context of utterance to select a denotation in its context of use; the other part is the denotation thereby selected. In other words, the context-dependence between linguistic meaning and the environment is encoded into the compositional semantics of an individual lexical item.

There are, however, other ways in which non-linguistic objects and events can become a part of the content of the interaction. The following is taken from the STAC Corpus [Afantenos et al., 2012b], in which human players are playing the board game Settlers of Catan. The "Server" messages describe the way in which the game state has just changed, and players track these changes on the game board that's visualized on their graphical interface; player i's utterance is what she typed into the chat interface, which (together with the game board) is also a part of the graphical interface for this game.

(30)   Server: player i rolled a 2 and a 1
       Server: player j gets 2 sheep. player i gets 1 wheat
       player i: *Woo!*

Player i's utterance *Woo!* isn't deictic, in that it doesn't point to anything in the environment. Rather, it expresses an attitude to something in the context, that must be *anaphorically* determined. Here, that something is non-linguistic: specifically the event where i gets one wheat resource card.

Finally, non-linguistic events can become a part of the content of the interaction even if the linguistic utterance contains no deictic expressions, demonstratives or any anaphoric expression. Specifically, the antecedent to a relational speech act can be non-linguistic:

(31)   *B is putting an unprotected vase in a cardboard box*
       A: Bubblewrapping fragile objects protects them in transit.

Here, A is correcting a prior non-linguistic move, not a linguistic one; furthermore, that prior non-linguistic move wasn't a communicative move! But a failure to recognize that A is correcting B's move is a failure to understand what A is doing in this interaction. More generally, understanding the interaction between linguistic units and their non-linguistic context—including visually salient events such as those in (31)—is absolutely critical to human-robot interaction if that interaction includes language. This is because people use deictic expressions, anaphora and speech acts quite naturally to appropriate salient parts of the non-linguistic context into their messages. As Hunter et al. [2015] attest, around 17% of the utterances in the STAC Corpus do this. Enabling robots to recognize such moves, and also to perform the task of *symbol grounding* (i.e., estimating which object in the visual context a linguistic description such as *the dog* refers to) calls for a much more integrated approach to visual and linguistic processing than we currently have, though recent work in this area is productive and very exciting [e.g., Dobnik et al., 2012, Forbes et al., 2015, Narayana et al., 2019, Tellex et al., 2011, Yu et al., 2016].

There are also a number of non-verbal communicative moves that speakers can perform. We already mentioned deictic hand gestures (e.g., pointing). Speakers can also use so-called *depicting* gestures: these are spontaneous and improvised hand gestures whose form resembles (either physically or metaphorically) what it refers to. For example, in (32), taken from Loehr's corpus [Loehr, 2004], the speaker depicts the mixing of mud with her gesture:

(32)   So she mixes mud…*Speaker's right hand is held loose, fingers facing downwards, and she performs a consecutive four rotation movements of this hand*

Facial expression (e.g., winking to indicate sarcasm, or raised eyebrows to indicate denial or surprise) and body posture (e.g., leaning forward to indicate engagement) can also be contentful.[19]

#13 Linguistic meaning and non-linguistic perception interact in complex ways.

In face to face conversation, speakers denote salient non-linguistic objects and events in various ways: with demonstratives (e.g., English *this*, *that*), indexicals or deictic expressions (e.g., *now*, *here*, *you*) and deictic gestures (i.e., pointing), often combined with a pronoun, demonstrative, or a definite description. For instance, while pointing at a poster of Florence, one might say *that's a beautiful city*. The deictic gesture denotes the poster, and the demonstrative *that* denotes the city of Florence that the gesture's denotation (i.e., the poster) depicts [Lascarides and Stone, 2009]. Thus, there is a specific relationship between the denotation of the demonstrative and the gesture that isn't identity, and even though it is left linguistically implicit, interlocutors can infer it.

In light of these phenomena, the context in which demonstratives, indexicals and deictic gestures receive an interpretation must include non-linguistic objects [Kaplan, 1989], such as the speaker (for interpreting *I* and *me*), the hearer (for interpreting *you*), the location of the conversation (for *here* and *there*), the time of utterance (for *now*, *tomorrow* etc), as well as salient entities (such as the poster) and their properties (such as the fact that the poster depicts Florence).

As Hunter et al. [2015] attest, however, speakers can perform linguistic moves that make a non-linguistic event a part of the content of the interaction even when the utterance doesn't

---

[19]In signed languages, facial expressions and body posture can also function as lexical items or morphological inflection, i.e., be incorporated directly in the grammar of the language [Bellugi and Fischer, 1972].

include any of the above referring expressions or deictic gestures. For example, as we showed in #12, an adequate meaning representation of (31), repeated here, must capture the fact that speaker A is correcting B's non-linguistic action: in doing so A is conveying to B that the vase she's handling is fragile and the causal connection between bubblewrapping and protection that she expresses linguistically applies to this vase.

(31)   *B is putting an unprotected vase in a cardboard box*
       A: Bubblewrapping fragile objects protects them in transit.

To put this another way, understanding how A's linguistic move is semantically related to B's non-linguistic move guides one toward a particular perception of B's action, i.e., the vase is fragile, and although B is packing it the method of packing is not sufficiently protected. Inferring these properties of B's action are effectively semantic consequences of A's linguistic move correcting B's non-linguistic one.

A speaker's linguistic move can even affect the way interlocutors perceive a non-linguistic event that is not currently visible [Hunter et al., 2018]. Suppose A says (33) and then she flicks her head toward a scratch on the wall:

(33)   My daughter Rose has been sent to her room.

A competent interlocutor infers that Rose did something to cause the scratch on the wall. But if A had said *I tried to move furniture today* instead of (33), then the conceptualization of the event that caused the scratch would be different.

Intuitively, the non-linguistic event e, of Rose causing the scratch on the wall, *explains* (33). This event e can also now influence how subsequent utterances, such as (34), get interpreted:

(34)   I was cooking dinner.

The semantic relations between e and (33) and between e and (34) are critical for accurately interpreting A's message. If we disregard the contribution of e, the sequence (33)+(34) implicates that A cooking dinner temporally overlaps sending Rose to her room. The interpretation of (33)+e+(34) has a different temporal structure: cooking dinner temporally overlaps e, which precedes the punishment. Representing the meaning of examples like (31) and (33) requires modeling the interaction between the coherence relations that speakers exploit between linguistic units and non-linguistic ones, as well as modeling how the semantics of these relations support inferences about a particular way of perceiving the non-linguistic events.

The interaction between language and perception is also of central concern in solving the symbol grounding problem within the field of human-robot interaction [e.g., Bos and Oka, 2007, Forbes et al., 2015, Tellex et al., 2011]. This work focuses on teaching a robot how to recognize objects or abstract concepts (e.g., spatial relations) via training data that consists of a set of pairs: a visual scene and a linguistic description of that scene (e.g., *This is a blue cube*, and *The red triangle is to the right of the blue cube*). Examples like (31) and (33) show that the interaction between language and perception can be complex, calling for reasoning about coherence relations that take the content of a whole clause as an argument, not just estimating the denotation of referring expressions.

#14 (Disambiguated) linguistic form produces an abstract meaning representation, while coherence and cognitive states yield more specific contents.

In the course of this book, we will distinguish the representation of meaning at (at least) three levels (see also #4):

1. *The representation of meaning that is derivable from linguistic form.*

   We'll refer to meaning that is derived purely from linguistic form as *compositional semantics*. This type of meaning representation is typically quite abstract, because we take the now well-established view that linguistic form on its own, even disambiguated linguistic form, underspecifies certain aspects of meaning (see #4). For instance, the relative semantic scope of quantifiers and other scope bearing elements such as negation (e.g., *every man did not talk*), word sense ambiguities (e.g., *I'm going to the bank*), the semantic relation between referents in a compound noun construction (e.g., whether *pottery shelf* is a shelf made of pottery or a shelf with pottery on it), and the antecedents to pronouns are all determined by the sentence's context of use, not just its syntax.[20]

2. *The public commitment that a speaker makes when she utters something.*

   We take the public commitments that speakers make when they utter something to include the semantic consequences that follows from an assumption that the speaker's utterance is *coherent*: in other words, it is coherently related to the prior discourse (or, as we saw in #12, to a salient non-linguistic event). Thus, public commitments go beyond content that is derivable just from sentential syntax. For instance, answering *No* to *Is it raining?* publicly commits the speaker to the proposition that it is not raining, something that cannot be inferred from the form of the word *no* on its own [Lascarides and Asher, 2009]. Identifying the antecedent part of the discourse context that the current utterance is coherently related to and identifying the coherence relation relies on defeasible inference (as discussed in #7 and #67), so inferring what a speaker publicly commits to is defeasible.

3. *The cognitive effects of public commitments on both the speaker and interlocutors*

   Axioms of rationality and cooperativity yield inferences about the cognitive states of the speaker and the interlocutor [Grice, 1975]. For example, Grice's Maxim of Sincerity licenses a (defeasible) inference that the speaker believes it's raining from the fact that he

---

[20]Although emotional content (#8) and social meaning (#9) are also properly part of meaning derivable from linguistic form, for the most part we will set them aside in future chapters.

uttered *It's raining*. A cooperative recipient of the request *Pass the salt* will adopt an intention to pass the salt or an intention to inform the speaker of why she can't do this.

We mentioned above that certain kinds of semantic ambiguities can persist even when all ambiguities in sentential syntax are resolved [Bos, 1995, Copestake et al., 2005]. Accordingly, Chapters 7 and 8 will use a model of grammar that underspecifies lexical sense, semantic scope, and certain semantic relations (e.g., the relation between the denotation of nouns in a compound noun construction). One could assume a model of grammar that doesn't underspecify these aspects of content; in our view, this is less important than respecting the distinction in any NLP system between the above levels of meaning.

While the grammar underspecifies lexical senses, Chapter 4 describes how word senses can be idiosyncratic, or predictable and productive, and the challenges and opportunities this represents for NLP systems. The way word meaning is systematically related to the arguments the corresponding predicate symbols select for and how those arguments can be linguistically expressed is discussed in Chapter 5. We also emphasize the need for grammars and parsers to take account of the highly particularized syntactic and semantic properties of multi-word expressions in Chapter 6.

Chapters 9–13 deal with meaning in context—in other words, the second and third levels of meaning representation we described above. Following Hobbs [1979] and many others, we will emphasize that many aspects of pragmatic meaning arise as a byproduct of reasoning about how an utterance is coherently related to a move in the discourse context. We'll discuss pronouns and other anaphoric expressions (Chapter 10), presuppositions (Chapter 11), information status, information structure (Chapter 12), and conversational implicatures (Chapter 13).

CHAPTER 3

Lexical Semantics: Overview

#15 In formal grammar, words are often represented as opaque predicate symbols, but on its own this misses a lot of important information about word meaning.

As we described in #2, natural language contains certain words whose meanings are closely related to the classical notion of validity in symbolic logic (e.g., quantifiers, modals, negation). But most natural language words do not have this elevated logical status. Formal grammars typically represent the natural language "non-logical" words in terms of predicate symbols, e.g., representing the meaning of the word *dog* with a one-place predicate; so $dog(x)$ is a well-formed formula. As discussed in #2, model theory interprets such predicates in terms of set theory: for instance, $[\![dog]\!]^M$ is a subset of the domain D of individuals in the model M, and $[\![dog(x)]\!]^M$ is true just in case $[\![x]\!]^M \in [\![dog]\!]^M$. Similarly, if the meaning of the word *love* is represented as a three-place predicate $love(e, x, y)$ between an event and two individuals [Davidson, 1980],[1] then its denotation $[\![love]\!]^M$ is a subset of the set of triples $E \times D \times D$, where E is the set of eventualities in the model M, and $[\![love(e, x, y)]\!]^M$ is true just in case $\langle [\![e]\!]^M, [\![x]\!]^M, [\![y]\!]^M \rangle \in [\![love]\!]^M$.

There is a lot that such a semantics fails to capture.[2] For example, it doesn't reflect the ways in which semantic relationships among words are dependent on commonsense knowledge (e.g., that birds have wings) and ontological information (e.g., that dogs are mammals). Researchers explore these relationships in a number of ways, but particularly via a distributional semantics, defined in terms of word embeddings—that is, one which clusters words according to whether they appear in the vicinity of the same words, or not (see #26).

Nevertheless, simply associating each natural language word with a predicate symbol does carry at least one critical piece of semantic information: the arity of the predicate symbol and the sort of arguments it takes specifies the number of entities that the natural language word qualifies and also the *sort* of entities they are (e.g., event, individual or proposition). For instance, being a

---

[1]Davidson's inclusion of the event term e has been widely adopted [e.g., Bos, 2015, Copestake et al., 2005, Kamp and Reyle, 1993, Pustejovsky, 1995]. Among other things, one motivation for this approach is that it supports the modeling of certain entailments through wedge elimination, discussed in #47.

[2]This is well illustrated by the following story, famous among linguists: At the end of a course they taught together, Barbara Partee and Terry Parsons offered to spend a session answering any questions the students had. A student asked, "What's the meaning of life?" and the instructors answered by going up to the blackboard and writing ˆ*life*' (Barbara Partee, pc, September 2017). For readers not familiar with formal semantics, simply notice that this example makes studying meaning look like an exercise in font change!

dog is a property of an individual, while *love* is a relation between an event and two individuals. However, formal semantic theories differ on how to constrain the denotation of a predicate like *dog*: some allow it to include fake dogs and someone in a dog costume [e.g., Kamp and Reyle, 1993] while others assume a fake dog is not a dog, and so the word *fake* is represented as a predicate symbol that takes a predicate as an argument to form a new predicate that in turn takes an individual as an argument—i.e., $[fake(dog)](x)$ [e.g., Montague, 1974].

Either way, like we said earlier, conceiving of the meaning of open class words in terms of predicate symbols and set theory is to miss major phenomena concerning their meaning, phenomena that we will spell out in the rest of this chapter and also Chapters 4 and 6. We will show in these chapters how the meaning of open-class words carries extremely rich information that influences processing at all levels—syntactic, semantic, and pragmatic. This rich information about meaning is sometimes systematic and predictable, in a way that (arbitrarily) associating the meaning of each word with its set of referents fails to capture. On the other hand, it is an inherent feature of word meaning that much of it is idiosyncratic, and so the challenge in any model of word meaning is to get the balance right between predictable (and productive) aspects of word meaning and idiosyncratic features of it.

#16 Lexical semantics includes word sense, semantic roles, and connotation.

Even if we approach lexical semantics via distributional models (i.e., we represent each word as a vector that is a compact representation of the context in which the word occurs; see #25 and #26 for more details), it is very useful to consider what kind of information we are attempting to capture. Semantic information associated with individual lexical items includes at least the following:

Word sense   Word senses are the different kinds of uses available for a given form (see #18). These sets of uses include distinct uses arbitrarily grouped into the same word form (*homonymy*, see #21) as well as sets of uses that follow predictable patterns (*regular polysemy*, see #19). As discussed in Chapter 4, much can be learned about how meaning works in natural language by studying productive patterns of word senses, the role of metaphor in the development of senses, and how word senses change over time. Furthermore, relations among senses can be extremely useful in NLP: for example, *hypermyny* is the relation where one sense is a supertype of another (e.g., *mammal* is in a hypermyny relation to the "person" sense of the noun *man*); *hyponymy* is the term for the relation where one sense is a subtype of another.

Semantic roles   As noted in #15 above, the opaque-predicate-symbol approach to representing word meaning in compositional semantics includes an indication of the number of arguments any such predicate takes. But there is more to predicate-argument structure than the mere arity of a predicate: different arguments relate to their predicates in different ways, known as *semantic* *roles*, discussed further in Chapter 5. Which semantic roles are at play and which argument takes which role is a matter of lexical semantics.

Connotations Finally, word choice distinctions can carry connotations beyond the direct denotation of a lexical item. For example, *child* and *kid* arguably refer to the same set of entities, but evoke different attitudes in doing so. Similarly, the word pairs *manger/bouffer* (French) and 食べる *taberu*/食う *kuu* (Japanese) involve forms that can all be translated as "eat," but where the former form in each pair is a relatively neutral description, the latter conveys informality of the eating itself and/or the description of the eating. Such distinctions in connotation are resources that can be deployed to convey emotional (#8) and social (#9) content alongside propositional content.

#17 Sometimes lexical semantics attaches to small collections of words rather than individual words.

The term *lexical* in *lexical semantics* suggests that it is a question of the meaning of individual words, and words are commonly understood to be the individual components of phrases and sentences. However, all of the phenomena relating to lexical semantics overviewed in #16 and covered in detail in Chapter 4 can also attach to collections of words. These are still a matter of lexical semantics because those collections themselves are idiosyncratic and thus must be learned as part of the language (rather than built up compositionally each time) and because they serve as the building blocks of larger phrases, just as less controversial "words" do. For example, the verb-particle pairs *pick up* and *pick out* in (35) are not contiguous within their sentences, but nonetheless jointly carry the senses "retrieve," "elevate," "choose," and "remove," respectively.

(35) a. Kim picked the kids up from daycare.

　　　b. Kim picked the litter up from the trail.

　　　c. Kim picked the color out, but Sandy approved it.

　　　d. Kim picked the seeds out from the salad.

Furthermore, these predicates have semantic roles for their arguments that are filled by other elements of the sentence (e.g., Kim is the one doing the choosing, etc.).

One could argue that the meaning of *up* and of *out* contributes to the meaning of the verb particle construction: e.g., in the "choose" sense of *pick out*, the subject chooses the color *out* of a set of alternatives, and in its "remove" sense, the subject removes the seeds *out* of the salad. But there are other verb particle constructions where this degree of compositionality breaks down: e.g., the meaning of *make out* (in all its senses) has nothing to do with the meaning of *out*.

Collections of words that have semantic or other idiosyncrasies such that they must be listed in the lexicon are called *multiword expressions* and are the subject of Chapter 6.

CHAPTER 4

Lexical Semantics: Senses

#18 A single word form can have many senses.

The same word form can appear in different contexts with different meanings. For the purpose of building dictionaries for human use and resources like the Princeton WordNet of English (WordNet) [Fellbaum, 1998, Miller, 1995], lexicographers often decide when two different uses are both an instance of the same word sense, and when those two different uses are examples of distinct senses. Some word forms will have large numbers of word senses identified, others very few. For example, WordNet 3.1[1] lists just one sense for *daffodil* ("Narcissus pseudonarcissus (any of numerous varieties of Narcissus plants having showy often yellow flowers with a trumpet-shaped central crown)"), but *make* has two senses for the noun and 49 for the verb, a selection of which is shown in (36):

(36)   a. (engage in) *"make love, not war;" "make an effort;" "do research;" "do nothing;" "make revolution"*

       b. (make or cause to be or to become) *"make a mess in one's office;" "create a furor"*

       c. (to compose or represent) *"This wall forms the background of the stage setting;" "The branches made a roof;" "This makes a fine introduction"*

       d. (cause to be enjoyable or pleasurable) *"make my day"*

Both function and content words exhibit sense ambiguities, but the meanings of function words tend to be more abstract than those of content words. For instance, the adverb *through* is assigned the following, quite abstract, five senses in WordNet:

(37)   a. (from beginning to end) *"read this book through"*

       b. (over the whole distance) *"this bus goes through to New York"*

       c. (to completion) *"think this through very carefully!"*

       d. (in diameter) *"this cylinder measures 15 inches through"*

       e. (throughout the entire extent) *"got soaked through in the rain"*

So on the whole, identifying the intended sense of a function word is less useful for discerning the topic of a text than identifying the senses of content words.

---

[1] http://wordnetweb.princeton.edu/perl/webwn, accessed April 18, 2018

While some kinds of lexical ambiguity recur across languages, in general it is not the case that the senses grouped under a single word form in one language will also be carried by a single word form in other languages. Take the Englishword *ride*, for which WordNet[2] lists two noun and fourteen verb senses. A selection of the verb senses is given in (38).

(38)   a. ride over, along, or through

        b. sit and travel on the back of animal, usually while controlling its motions

        c. be carried or travel on or in a vehicle

        d. be contingent on

        e. harass with persistent criticism or carping

        f. keep partially engaged by slightly depressing a pedal with the foot

        g. continue undisturbed and without interference

        h. move like a floating object

Open Multilingual Wordnet [Bond and Paik, 2012] relates words across languages to the same synsets (synonym sets) and associates the Japanese word 乗る *noru* with senses (38a)–(38c), but not with the others.[3] Conversely, in Japanese Wordnet [Isahara et al., 2008][4] 乗る *noru* is associated with the eight senses shown in (39), but for only the first three of those does Open Multilingual Wordnet also list *ride*. Further, the events referred to in (39d) and (39f–i) cannot plausibly be referred to with the English word *ride* (although (39d), being a mounting event, can be conceived of as a strict part of a riding event, and similarly for (39g) and (39i)).

(39)   a. ずっと乗る、あるいはを通じて乗る ("ride over, along, or through")

        b. 通常、動物の動きを制御してその背中に座って旅をする ("sit and travel on the back of animal, usually while controlling its motions")

        c. 車両で運ばれる、または旅する ("be carried or travel or in a vehicle")

        d. の後ろに乗る ("get up on the back of")

        e. 特定の種類の輸送または特定のルートによって旅行するか、進行する ("travel or go by means of a certain kind of transportation, or a certain route")

        f. 持つまたは取れるように設計された ("be designed to hold or take")

        g. （電車、バス、船、航空機など）に乗り込む ("get on board of (trains, buses, ships, aircraft, etc.)")

        h. 必要な設備により、執行あるいは実行のために準備し供給する ("prepare and supply with the necessary equipment for execution or performance")

---

[2]Accessed through Open Multilingual Wordnet [Bond and Paik, 2012] at http://compling.hss.ntu.edu.sg/omw/, April 18, 2018.

[3]The six verb senses not shown in (38) aren't associated with any lemmas in Japanese, suggesting that perhaps that part of the Japanese wordnet hasn't been completed yet.

[4]Accessed as in footnote 2.

i. 乗り込んだ状態になる ("go on board")

The overall set of sense distinctions can vary from one language to another. In other words, a language may exhibit sense distinctions that speakers of another language wouldn't expect to be lexicalized: for example, the distinction between the senses of the Hebrew words שרפה *sreifa* (meaning "destructive fire") vs. אש *eish* (meaning "fire") is not lexicalized at all in English.

Sets of word senses can be classified according to whether they are productively related to each other (regular polysemy, see #19) or not (homonymy, see #21). The set of possible senses for the words of a language is not fixed. Speakers can and do create new meanings as they talk, sometimes following established patterns [Pustejovsky, 1995], sometimes in more idiosyncratic ways [Garrod and Anderson, 1987]. Understanding the extent to which words can be used with differing meanings, how these differing meanings arise, and how their distributions might vary across different corpora is useful for natural language understanding. For example, one approach is to represent word meaning as a vector, which assigns values to various features of the context in which the word appears (see #25 and #26 for details). But estimating these vectors from one corpus, and then using it to process another corpus within a different domain with no modifications or transfer learning, risks introducing considerable noise into the system. Consequently, there are established techniques for projecting embeddings that are acquired from very large, open domain corpora to a given target domain [e.g., Yang and Eisenstein, 2015].

#19 Regular polysemy describes productively related sense families.

Some words exhibit a range of senses that is largely predictable and even productive [Pustejovsky, 1995]. For example, the English word *book* can refer to the physical object (*that book is on the shelf*) or the abstract content (*that book is about syntax*), and these senses are attested for other English words that denote representational artifacts, e.g., *magazine, newspaper, leaflet*, etc. This kind of predictable sense ambiguity is known as *regular polysemy*.

We call regular polysemy a *productive* process because we see evidence that speakers readily accommodate words used in new senses based on known polysemous patterns, even on first encounter. For example, after having just learned that *porg* refers to a (fictitious) animal by being told something like (40a) one interprets *porg* in (40b) as referring to the edible meat derived from the animal.

(40)   a. Look at that cute porg hopping along the rocks!

       b. Porg is a delicacy on Ahch-To.

This property is shared by all animal terms in English, by and large (we will discuss in #23 why some animal words seem to defy this regularity, e.g., *pig* and *cow*). One type of regular polysemy is *metonymy* [Lakoff and Johnson, 1980]: one can sometimes use an expression to denote something that's *related* to what it normally denotes. Another cross-linguistically common type of regular polysemy the use of a word for a container to denote its contents: *that dish is tasty* and *I drank the whole bottle*.

Regular polysemy is different from *homonymy*. A homonymous ambiguity is when word senses are unrelated and not rooted in some kind of linguistic regularity. An example is the word *mogul*, which can denote a mound of snow or the head of an Indian dynasty. What makes this homonymy rather than regular polysemy is that neither of the senses can be predicted from the other. For more on homonymy, see #21.

There are also cases where one sense can be predicted from another, but the prediction applies to just one word, and not a whole class. This is called simply *polysemy*, and contrasts with both regular polysemy and homonymy. For example, the "popular trend" sense of *bandwagon* has a transparent, commonsense relationship with its "vehicle" sense: one conceptualizes the scene involving the vehicle as one where people gather round the bandwagon enthusiastically, and the "popular trend" sense is a metaphorical extension of this.[5] The senses of *bandwagon* are related, so this isn't homonymy. They're not an example of regular polysemy either: the relation between the senses of *bandwagon* does apply to a class of words—it is specific to *bandwagon*, and it isn't attested for other vehicles.

Regular polysemy is strong evidence that the lexicon exhibits structure [Asher, 2011, Pustejovsky, 1995]: A lexicon conceived of as just a list of words associated with a fixed set of senses, as in a dictionary, would miss generalizations such as those noted above (e.g., that physical representational artifacts all exhibit the physical sense and the abstract content sense that we described earlier). In fact, there are two types of structure to the lexical semantic part of the lexicon [Copestake and Briscoe, 1995]. On the one hand, there is evidence that the lexical semantic representations of some words should have an internal structure that enables quite distinct aspects of their meaning to be picked up as arguments to distinct predicate symbols during semantic composition via linguistic syntax. Evidence for this comes from linguistic data involving *co-predication*. For example, consider again the two senses of book that we mentioned earlier: in (41), the PP selects for the physical sense and the copular VP selects for its abstract content sense, and these senses must be available in a single lexical entry for book, given the syntactic structure of the sentence.

(41)   That book on the shelf is about syntax.

This is an example of what Copestake and Briscoe call *constructional polysemy*, the first of the two kinds of regular polysemy that they identify (the other kind being *sense extension*, which we'll discuss shortly).

The ability to co-predicate distinct senses of a word is a defining characteristic of constructional polysemy (and contrasts with sense extension); we'll discuss that defining characteristic in more detail shortly. But before we do, let's illustrate the idea with further examples, for instance words that can denote towns or the people living in that town:

(42)   Cambridge is in the South East and voted Conservative.

---

[5]Metaphor is in fact a general source of lexical productivity. For further discussion, see #27 and #28.

This phenomenon isn't specific to English but is in fact attested across languages, as illustrated for Japanese, Bulgarian, and Greek in (43)–(45).

(43)   棚　の　上　の　本　は　難しかった。
     Tana no   ue   no   hon   ha   muzukashikat-ta
     Shelf ADN top ADN book NOM difficult-PST

"The book on the shelf is difficult." [jpn]

(44)   Онази   книга   на лавицата   се   отнася   за
     Onzaki   kniga   na lavitsata   se   otnasya   za
     that.FEM.SG book.FEM.SG on shelf.FEM.SG.DEF REFL concern.PRS.3SG for
     синтаксиса.
     sitaksisa
     syntax.MASC.SG.DEF

"That book on the shelf is about syntax." [bul]

(45)   Εκείνο   το   βιβλίο   στο
     Ekino   to   vivlio   sto
     that.NOM.NEUT.SG the.NOM.NEUT.SG book.NOM.NEUT.SG to.the.ACC.NEUT.SG
     ράφι   είναι   για σύνταξη.
     rafi   ine   ja sidaksi
     shelf.ACC.NEUT.SG be.3sg.PRS for syntax.ACC.FEM.SG

"That book on the shelf is about syntax." [ell]

While there probably is considerable overlap in the patterns used in constructional polysemy across languages, it would also not be surprising to find that some patterns are language-specific, or that there is variation in the exact range of the word classes implicated in each constructional polysemy pattern.

In the case of the second type of regular polysemy, *sense extension*, the senses are related, but can't cohabit the same lexical entry. In such cases, Copestake and Briscoe [1995] suggest modeling the relevant structure in the lexicon via *lexical rules* that take as input one lexical entry (consisting of a lemma, syntax, and semantics) and output a distinct lexical entry that's defined in terms of the input. On this view, forms derived via morphological processes like nominalization (see #22) are a kind of regular polysemy,[6] but it also occurs when there is no change in word form nor morphosyntax. In such cases, distinguishing sense extension from constructional polysemy can be subtle.

One way to test for the difference is via co-predications such as those given in (41)–(45). If one can coherently co-predicate the two senses, then this is evidence that they are related via constructional polysemy—one instance of a word is making both senses available within the same sentence and so both should be modeled as belonging to the same lexical entry. In contrast,

---

[6]This is one reason why in Abstract Meaning Representations (AMR) [Banarescu et al., 2013] any nominalization is represented using the verb from which it's is derived, including that verb's semantic roles; see Chapter 5.

co-predicating two senses that are related by sense extension creates *zeugma*, as exhibited for English in (46):

(46) a. Mr. Pickwick took his hat and his leave.

    b. I like mustard on my thighs but Bill prefers sun tan lotion.

    c. You are free to execute your laws and your citizens, as you see fit.

Zeugma is co-predication that, like the examples in (46), has a shocking, dramatic or "word-pun" effect: the examples in (46) are zeugmatic, while (41) is not. On this basis, the (novel) use of *porg* meaning meat mentioned earlier is an example of sense extension:

(47) That porg was happy and tasty.

However, one must be careful in applying the zeugma test for distinguishing constructional polysemy from sense extension. (48) sounds anomalous, but in light of (41) it would be wrong to conclude that the polysemy between the physical and abstract content senses of *book* is an example of sense extension:

(48) Kim's thesis is orange and unreadable.

One must control for *coherence*, a concept we introduced in Chapter 2 and will return to in Chapters 9 and 13. Many claim that coherence is central to pragmatic inference, and furthermore argue that predicates that are introduced by a coordinated VP must be coherently related or the sentence will sound anomalous [Asher et al., 2001, Kehler, 2002, Lascarides et al., 1996b]—for the same reason that non sequiturs in multi-sentence discourse sound anomalous—regardless of whether it is an attempt to co-predicate a single lexical entry or two distinct entries. In (48), there is no obvious semantic relationship between being orange and being unreadable and so it's not a valid test case for distinguishing constructional polysemy from sense extension.

#20 Structured lexical meaning representations can support the analysis of constructional polysemy.

Constructional polysemy is evidence that certain aspects of real-world knowledge about the denotation of a word can get conventionalized and therefore should be understood to be part of our knowledge of our language: for instance, the fact that books are representational artifacts is what justifies treating its semantics as of a complex type, which includes as components a physical object and the abstract content within the book. Pustejovsky [1991] represents these structured meanings using typed feature structures: this not only provides a way to represent meaning as a structured list of features and values, but it also allows one to capture generalizations for whole classes of words via default inheritance (default because lexical generalizations always admit idiosyncratic exceptions). For example, simplifying somewhat, the semantic component of *book* is as follows:

$$(49) \quad \begin{bmatrix} \textbf{book} \\ \text{argstr} : \begin{bmatrix} \text{arg1} : \textbf{x:ind} \\ \text{arg2} : \textbf{y:abstr} \end{bmatrix} \\ \text{qualia} : \begin{bmatrix} \text{agentive} : \textbf{write(e,w,y)} \\ \text{telic} : \textbf{read(e,z,y)} \end{bmatrix} \end{bmatrix}$$

This feature structure gives two types of information. The first is the *argument structure* (argstr), which specifies two possible individuals of distinct type that predicate symbols can select for when they qualify *book*. The second is the *qualia structure* which indicates aspects of the word's meaning drawn from rudimentary world knowledge:[7] what it denotes, what its purpose is, how it was created, and so on.[8]

These complex representations are used to predict how distinct senses get selected for during semantic composition in the grammar. For example, semantically, the word *enjoy* qualifies an event, but syntactically it can take a noun phrase complement and when it does so it (typically) selects for the event in the TELIC component of the qualia of that noun phrase. The TELIC component encodes purpose, so *enjoy the book* means enjoy reading the book, given the qualia structure in (49). The verb *enjoy* can also select for the event in the AGENTIVE component of the qualia: thus *Stephen King enjoyed that book* can mean he enjoyed writing it. This is known as *logical metonymy*: a verb selects semantically for an argument of one type but syntactically can take a complement of a distinct type.

A model of the lexicon that includes this information (rather than leaving it to language-external "world knowledge") accounts for the fact that whether logical metonymy is licensed depends on the specific words used rather than on what they denote. For instance, even if the interlocutors share the knowledge that in the room there is a book being used as a doorstop, *Kim enjoyed that doorstop* sounds distinctly odd (while *Kim enjoyed that book* is fine). Further, representing word meanings via a complex qualia structure accounts for the fact that one can co-predicate: *Sarah picked up and enjoyed her beer*.

While there is ample evidence for representing the lexicon using highly structured and generative devices, all lexical generalizations admit exceptions (see #23 for one type of general case).

#21 Homonymy arises when the senses of a word are not now related to each other, even if they were according to etymology.

Words can have multiple senses that are not related to each other. An oft-cited example of this is the noun *bank*, which can denote a mound of earth or a financial institution (among other

---

[7] *Qualia* derives from the Latin term, meaning the way something seems to us (or is perceived by us). The use of qualia structure in lexical semantics is inspired by Aristotle's theory of explanation, and its take up by Moravcsik [1975] in encoding word meaning.

[8] Asher [2011] captures similar information in a different way, via a system of complex semantic types.

senses).[9] The financial vs. earth mound senses of the noun *bank* are considered unrelated: these two senses aren't licensed as a result of some linguistic regularity of the kind we discussed in #19. When a word can take more than one sense and those senses are unrelated, this is known as *homonymy*.

The difference between homonymy and regular polysemy rests on the vague notion of relatedness and so distinguishing one from the other can be difficult. One might be tempted to use etymology—i.e., the origins and history of words—to make judgments about the distinction between homonymy and regular polysemy. But homonymy can be independent of whether the word senses share a common origin. For example, Lyons [1995, p. 28] claims that the two senses of *bank* did at one time coincide in the evolution of the Italian language (where the word form is *banca*, from which *bank* is derived according to the Merriam Webster dictionary). Italian Renaissance bankers—where the modern banking industry was founded—used to sit on riverbanks when conducting their business, and so to go to the financial institution was tantamount to going to the river's edge. But most modern English speakers are unaware of this common origin to the senses of *bank* and so don't view them as connected.

Given the lack of tests distinguishing homonymy from polysemy, why maintain the distinction? One reason is that unlike regular polysemy, homonymy doesn't indicate systematic patterns. In other words, the relationship between two senses of *bank* discussed here should be expected to turn up in other words or in other languages (except via borrowing). It is beneficial for NLP practitioners to understand the distinction in order to know what to expect in a language's lexicon, *viz.*, systematic polysemy as well as accidental homonymy. Difficult to operationalize as it is, it is not surprising that it is not encoded in broad-coverage lexical semantic resources like wordnets (e.g., Bond and Paik 2012, Fellbaum 1998, Miller 1995; discussed further in #18 above and in #97). Wordnets include other kinds of information about the relationship between senses, including *synonymy* (senses shared by different word forms), *hyponymy/hypernymy* (subtype/supertype relations between senses, e.g., a car is a type of vehicle), and *meronymy* (part-of relations between senses, e.g., a steering wheel is a part of a car). This information is extremely useful for practical NLP, and wordnets (especially the Princeton WordNet of English) have been used extensively in sentence compression [Clarke and Lapata, 2008], summarization [e.g., Barzilay and Elhadad, 1999], discourse parsing [e.g., Marcu, 2000], question answering [e.g., Pasca and Harabagiu, 2001], RTE [e.g., Bos and Markert, 2005], and more.

#22 Derivational morphology can be used to create new words with predictable senses.

#19 above described how productive processes can result in new senses for the same word form. There are also productive processes in language that result in new forms with senses related,

---

[9]The word *bank* also shows categorial ambiguity: it can be used as a noun or a verb and the verb *bank* is sense ambiguous, in ways which are related to the different senses of the noun *bank*. Categorial ambiguity is orthogonal to the distinction between regular polysemy and homonymy.

in predictable ways, to the root forms that they are derived from. This is called *derivational morphology*.[10] For example, *nominalization* describes the derivational morphological processes by which nouns are created from verbs. In nominalization in English, the noun that's derived from the verb can describe the most prominent semantic argument (typically the agent) of the verb (*nominator* in (50a)), the undergoer semantic argument of the verb (*nominee* in (50b)), the result of the action denoted by the verb (*confirmation* in (51a)), or the event itself (*confirmation* in (51b)).

(50) a. The nominator was thorough.

   b. The nominee was controversial.

(51) a. The confirmation of the nominee sparked protests.

   b. The confirmation of the nominee took several weeks.

Another example comes from languages with *morphological causatives*, where the causative affix can be used to derive a verb meaning "to cause to X" from a verb stem meaning "X". This is illustrated in (52) for Japanese, where the single, morphologically complex, word 読ませる *yomaseru* means "cause to read."

(52) a. 山田　が　本　を　読む.
      Yamada ga　hon　wo　yomu
      Yamada NOM book ACC read.NPST

      "Yamada reads a book." [jpn]

   b. 田中　が　山田　に　本　を　読まされた.
      Tanaka ga　Yamada ni　hon　wo　yoma-sare-ta
      Tanaka NOM Yamada DAT book ACC read-CAUS-PST

      "Tanaka made Yamada read a book." [jpn]

An important property of derivational morphology is that it interacts with lexicalization: That is, some derived forms become learned parts of the lexicon in their own right [Alegre and Gordon, 1999, Brinton and Traugott, 2005]. Over time, any established lexical item can see its meaning drift, thereby taking derived forms away from their original predictable senses (see #24).

#23 Word senses that are predicted by productive processes can be blocked by sufficiently high frequency underived words with the same sense.

In #19, we described how the lexicon is generative because there are lexical rules that license generating certain words with certain senses from other words with certain other senses [Copestake

---

[10]See also Bender, 2013, Chapter 2 for discussion of derivational morphology.

and Briscoe, 1995, Pustejovsky, 1991]. An example lexical rule for English is: for each count noun denoting an animal there is also a mass noun denoting the edible substance. This rule is *productive*: it can create novel but understandable meat-denoting words as in (40b) above.

But such lexical rules are in fact *semi*-productive: there are cases where a word satisfies the antecedent of the lexical rule but the derived "word" that the rule predicts is not in fact a part of the language's lexicon. One general cause for semi-productivity is known as *blocking* or *pre-emption by synonymy* [Jackendoff, 1975]: a non-derived word that has the same sense as the derived word you would get from the lexical generalization *blocks* the derived word from being a word of the language. For example, while the mass nouns *cow* and *pig* denoting meat are predicted by the above lexical rule that applies to animal words, they are not words of English because they get blocked by *beef* and *pork*, respectively. This is why the examples in (53) sound highly anomalous.

(53)   a. I ate cow stew.

b. Would you like a pig kebab?

Blocking seems to be a language universal [Jackendoff, 1997]: the productivity of lexical rules in all languages is constrained by it.[11]

Whether one word blocks another word from being derived via a lexical rule depends on the frequency of the blocking word, not on whether it is itself primitive or derived [Rainer, 2005]. For instance, the word *beef* blocks *cow* from meaning meat because *beef* is used to denote the edible substance of a cow sufficiently often. The words that trigger blocking can themselves be derived. For example, one can nominalize a verb in English via suffix *-ee* or *-er*, but *escapee* blocks *escaper*. Because blocking depends on frequency, two words with the same sense, at least one of which is the result of a lexical rule, can co-exist. For instance, *coney* is used in the fur trade for rabbit fur, but that doesn't block *rabbit* from being used for the skin and fur in general use. In fact, *coney* is also an older/dialect term for rabbit in general, including meat and fur, which occurs in *Lord of the Rings* and also in some place names, but it doesn't block *rabbit* from being used to denote meat either. More generally, Briscoe and Copestake [1999] propose that the degree to which a lexical rule is productive can be defined as the ratio of possible input entries and attested output entries one observes in a large open-domain corpus such as the British National Corpus (BNC) [Burnard, 1995]. This makes lexical productivity a matter of knowledge of the language itself and how it's used: the frequency is a property of the word and not just its denotation, since synonymous words can be attested with a radically different frequency (e.g., *rabbit* vs. *coney* and *diet* vs. *legislative assembly*).

A lack of frequency is not the only way to curb blocking. Language users also have the capacity to *unblock* the derivation of a word that is normally blocked. For example, there is

---

[11]Blocking (or pre-emption by synonymy) can limit the productive power of derivational morphology as well. For example, one can turn an adjective into a noun via the suffix *-ity*, e.g., *divine–divinity*, *serene–serenity*, *profane–profanity*, *curious–curiosity*, *domestic–domesticity*, and many more. But *space* blocks *spaciosity* and *glory* blocks *gloriosity* [Aronoff, 1976].

a lexical rule in English that nominalises a verb by adding *-er* such that the resulting word denotes the agent of the verb (e.g., *teach* to *teacher*, *speak* to *speaker*, *talk* to *talker*, and so on). The word *thief* normally blocks *stealer* [Bolinger, 1975], but it's not blocked in contexts where the meaning of *stealer* has been specialized or modified. For instance, it can be used metonymically as in Shakespeare's *the ten stealers* (fingers) or it can be specialized via modification, as in *stealer of hearts* [Bauer, 1983, pp. 87–88]. Copestake and Briscoe [1995] cite the following attested examples of unblocking, which also create particular pragmatic effects:

(54)   a. "Hot sausages, two for a dollar, made of genuine pig, why not buy one for the lady?"
          "Don't you mean pork, sir?" said Carrot warily, eyeing the glistening tubes.
          "Manner of speaking, manner of speaking," said Throat quickly. "Certainly your actual pig products. Genuine pig."
          (Terry Pratchett, 1989. *Guards Guards!*)

       b. There were five thousand extremely loud people on the floor eager to tear into roast cow with both hands and wash it down with bourbon whiskey.
          (Tom Wolfe, 1979. *The Right Stuff*)

These examples show that blocking is not an absolute rule of lexical organization; it's defeasible [Briscoe et al., 1995], meaning it can and does get overridden in highly specific contexts. Thus, when a speaker unblocks a word, interlocutors make sense of it by accommodating into the context the conditions that license unblocking, for instance by specializing the meaning of the derived word. Thus, the interlocutor of (54a) infers that the mass noun *pig* denotes meat derived from a pig, but it is questionable whether the meat is of sufficient quality to warrant being called *pork*. One also infers in (54b) that the speaker is conveying a particular attitude toward the meat denoted by *cow*.

#24 Word senses can change over time.

Just as with all other aspects of linguistic systems, word senses are subject to change over time and synchronic variation (the cotemporaneous use of both old and new senses). Sometimes sense change involves the addition of new senses and sometimes it involves the replacement of old senses by new senses. For an example of sense change, Hamilton et al. [2016] note *awful*, which once had a meaning related to *impressive* and *majestic*, captured by the Oxford English Dictionary (OED)[12] sense I "awe-inspiring," but started moving at some point before 1800 (per OED attestations) toward *disgusting* and *mess*, i.e., OED sense I.4 "Frightful, very ugly, monstrous." For an example of the addition of meanings, they note *call*, which prior to c.1890 did not have the sense of "to contact or attempt to contact by telephone" (OED sense 25a.).

Studies of semantic change have looked at how semantic change is initiated as well as what kinds of semantic changes spread robustly through the speech community. Traugott and

---

[12] *OED online*, http://www.oed.com/, accessed May 8, 2018

Dasher [2001, p. 280] argue that "[semantic] innovations are (i) constrained by context-specific pragmatic enrichment [and] (ii) only minimally different from earlier meanings". Recurring patterns of change that are observed include metaphor (e.g., *broadcast*, originally meaning to cast seeds out; see also #27 and #28), narrowing (e.g., *skyline*, from any horizon to one decorated with skyscrapers), generalization (e.g., brand names coming to stand for any similar product or process, like *hoover*, *kleenex*, and *xerox*), and pejoration (Old English *stincan*, meaning simply "to smell" becoming Modern English *stink*) [*Ibid.*, Bréal, 1964, Jeffers and Lehiste, 1979].

Semantic change, and especially the development of both specific senses and the development of productive polysemous relationships is heavily influenced by culture, communicative practice, and especially the ways that power interacts with communicative practice. McConnell-Ginet [1984] describes in detail how gender roles and associated power imbalances, including in communicative practice, influence the development of English lexical semantics and the prevalence of pejoration in connection with terms denoting women and girls. For example, *buddy* and *sissy* were once simply diminutive forms of *brother* and *sister*, respectively, but developed in quite different directions.

Frermann and Lapata [2016] develop a dynamic Bayesian model of diachronic meaning change, trained on a corpus of texts that were written in 1700–2010. Hamilton et al. [2016] investigate using vector-space representations of lexical semantics (see #25) to explore semantic change at scale. They first verify that vector-space representations can model changes known from careful word-by-word studies and then looked across large corpora for English, German, French, and Chinese and found two major trends in semantic change: (1) higher frequency words change senses more slowly and (2) more polysemous words[13] change senses more quickly (once frequency is controlled for). Rosenfeld and Erk [2018] model word change over time via a deep neural network that treats time as a continuous variable and makes word use a function of time. They also propose a metric for using their model to measure the speed of change in a word's use.

#25 You know the meaning of a word by the company it keeps!

Up to this point, we have been speaking of senses as things that words have (though they may change over time), and talking in terms of the lexicographer's problem (identifying and describing word senses) and issues of how senses are related to each other. An alternative view point (attributed to Wittgenstein[14]) sees word senses as deriving instead from how they are deployed by speakers carrying out communicative intents, without clear boundaries between word senses [Biletzki and Matar, 2018].[15]

---

[13]Hamilton et al. approximate polysemy by measuring the degree to which words appear in diverse contexts.

[14]The title of this item comes from Firth [1957, p. 11], who quotes Wittgenstein as saying in *Philosophical Investigations* that "the meaning of words lies in their use."

[15]The notion that the meaning that is attached to linguistic forms is continually negotiated and either reproduced or altered in practice is also central to the study of socially meaningful linguistic variation [e.g., Eckert and McConnell-Ginet, 1992].

More practically, Harris [1954] suggests (from a structuralist point of view) that distributional analyses (already useful for identifying other linguistic units such as phonemes and morphemes) can provide a method for arriving at, if not representations of meaning, at least analyses of similarity of meanings:

> "[I]f we consider words or morphemes A and B to be more different in meaning than A and C, then we will often find that the distributions of A and B are more different than the distributions of A and C. In other words, difference of meaning correlates with difference of distribution. [...] Though we cannot list all the co-occurrents (selection) of a particular morpheme, or define its meaning fully on the basis of these, we can measure roughly the difference in selection between elements, say something about their difference in meaning, and also (above and §4.1) derive certain structural information." (pp. 156–157)

These ideas have been deployed practically within computational linguistics in the form of *vector space representations* of word meaning, which in turn are used both for investigating lexical semantics and as features or input representations of words in a wide variety of tasks. In vector space representations, a word w is represented by a vector $\vec{w}$ whose parameters reflect the co-occurrence of w with different linguistic categories (e.g., words, POS tags, and grammatical relations) in context in some source corpus.

The representation $\vec{w}$ of a word w is thus dependent on how the parameters of the vector are defined, and how their values are computed from the corpus. Different perspectives on the context are required for different tasks and correspond to different intuitive notions of similarity. For example, $\vec{w}$ could capture word frequencies for all the words in a paragraph or even a document in which w occurs; the similarity relation between words is then roughly one of topical similarity [Clark, 2015]—the similarity between *car* and *engine* may be roughly the same as between *car* and *truck* if the vectors are defined this way. In contrast, for a similarity relation between word vectors corresponding roughly to *synonymy*, then a much smaller context window is needed—perhaps just the two open-class words on either side of the target word w.

The definition of context can also be made more sensitive to linguistic structure. For example, one technique is using *lemmas* rather than word forms as context parameters (so *love, loved, loving*, etc. contribute to the same value in $\vec{w}$). One could also include in the vector counts for the POS tags of words in close proximity to w, or one could include only those words that are in specific syntactic or semantic relationships to the target word w, in which case, one can distinguish within $\overrightarrow{rabbit}$, say, the number of times *rabbit* is the subject of the verb *eat* vs. the object of the verb *eat*, and so on. Including grammatical relations in the vector is useful for capturing *relational* similarities [Budanitsky and Hirst, 2006, Turney, 2006]: for instance, detecting that *mason* is to *stone* as *carpenter* is to *wood*. More generally, since the notion of similarity that the vector space representations of words capture will depend on the model parameters, computational linguists must think carefully about the type of similarity that will be useful for their task, and identify suitable parameters accordingly.

There are several alternative metrics for measuring the distance between two vectors, but the most commonly used one in computational linguistics is the cosine measure:

$$
\begin{aligned}
sim(\vec{w}1.\vec{w}2) = \quad & cosine(\theta) \text{ (where } \theta \text{ is the angle between } \vec{w}1 \text{ and } \vec{w}2) \\
= \quad & \frac{\vec{w}1.\vec{w}2}{|w_1|.|w_2|} \\
= \quad & \frac{\vec{w}1.\vec{w}2}{\sum_i (w1_i)^2 \sum_i (w2_i)^2}
\end{aligned} \tag{4.1}
$$

Thus, if $\vec{w}$ defines word frequencies in a three-word window to the left of w, then the cosine measure quantifies the extent to which the three-word windows to the left of $w1$ vs. those of $w2$ are similar. One would expect $sim(\overrightarrow{cat, dog}) > sim(\overrightarrow{cat, house})$, for instance.

When word meanings are understood to be or represented as a product of actual language use, this includes various societal attitudes, as discussed in #24 above. Practically speaking, this means that NLP systems built with vector-space representations trained on a given corpus may encode and thus reify societal biases in ethically problematic ways. Speer [2017] presents a very nice case study of this, wherein a sentiment analysis system trained to predict ratings in user-generated restaurant reviews based on the review text systematically under-predicted the ratings for Mexican restaurants, because of the negative associations with the word *Mexican* in American political discourse included in the web text that the word vectors were trained on. There is research into "debiasing" word vectors [e.g., Bolukbasi et al., 2016] which can go some way toward mitigating such potential harms. Another complementary approach proposes foregrounding characteristics of training data to facilitate reasoning about when attitudes learned by the system may be harmful [e.g., Bender and Friedman, 2018].

#26 Vector space representations offer a different perspective on word meaning from the set theoretic concepts used in formal semantics.

A vector space representation $\vec{w}$ of a (target) word w defines w's meaning in terms of the contexts in which w is used (see #25). This is a very different perspective on meaning from that of formal semantics. Formal semantics uses set-theoretic models to define meaning, thereby capturing the key intuition that linguistic words and phrases denote objects, properties of objects, relations among them, propositions that can be true or false, and so on. This set-theoretic approach is extremely useful for modeling meaning in terms of inference (see #2), but has no straightforward way to quantify similarity between words like *cat* and *dog*. Instead, formal semantics typically captures their relationship via *meaning postulates* [Carnap, 1952]—rules that impose constraints on the admissible models of the language. For example, a meaning postulate can specify that every cat is an animal, and (likewise) every dog is an animal. Organizing the lexicon into a hierarchical structure of typed feature structures (see #20) offers an alternative to meaning postulates for relating senses [e.g., Copestake and Briscoe, 1995, Pustejovsky, 1991].

Representing words as vectors, on the other hand, allows for convenient and highly intuitive measures of similarity. If $\vec{w}$ represents the contexts in which the word w appears, then on the intuitively compelling assumption that words of similar meaning appear in similar contexts, vector similarity will provide a decent measure of similarity between word meanings. The assumption that words of similar meaning occur in similar contexts is known as the *distributional hypothesis* [Turney and Pantel, 2010].

The notion of lexical similarity that vectors capture isn't represented in formal semantics. Nor is it captured in models that represent lexical generalizations via multiple default inheritance [Copestake and Briscoe, 1995, Pustejovsky, 1991] (see #19) or complex semantic types [Asher, 2011, Pustejovsky, 1995] (see #19). Vector space representations also are able to handle novel word use much more gracefully than hand-constructed lexical resources such as a WordNet (see #18 and #97), because the corpus itself determines a word's meaning, rather than prior knowledge of its conventional use. This is useful—novel word use can easily occur thanks to lexical productivity (see #19). But the symbolic lexical models also have advantages that vector space representations lack. For example, it's a major challenge, though not completely impossible, for the notion of similarity afforded by vector space representation to distinguish synonyms from antonyms [Lin et al., 2003]—*good* and *great* appear in similar contexts, but so do *good* and *bad*; indeed there is no widely accepted approach to deriving distinct word senss from distributional models (but see Peters et al. 2018). But these lexical relationships (and others) are explicitly represented in online resources like WordNet and in symbolic representations of lexical structure that are defined in terms of complex types and inheritance.

#27 Word senses can be extended through metaphor, shifting word meaning in unbounded ways.

All languages allow people to convey information via metaphor. For example, Romeo's utterance from Shakespeare's *Romeo and Juliet*[16] is one where he is not only asserting that Juliet is near her bedroom window, but also that she is beautiful (and other properties associated with the sun):

(55)   What light through yonder window breaks?
        It is the East and Juliet is the sun.

More generally, metaphor is a way of conveying a proposition or referring to an object or concept via a word or phrase that literally denotes some other object or concept, and people use metaphor for particular rhetorical effects.

As we'll discuss further in #28, metaphor is productive and governed by principles that draw on semantic relationships between metaphorical meaning and literal meaning [Lakoff and Johnson, 1980]. For example, (56) all conceive of love as a journey; likewise the lovers correspond to travellers, the relationship is the vehicle, the lovers' common goals their common destination on the journey, and so on.

(56)   a. Our relationship is at a dead end.

---

[16]Line 847–848

b. Look how far we've come.

c. Our marriage has been an uphill struggle.

d. Our relationship has got over the bumpy phase.

e. Our friendship is off track.

In all these cases, computing a metaphorical interpretation involves pragmatic inference, not only with real-world knowledge about the denotations of the literal word meanings and their relationships, but also reasoning about discourse coherence. For instance, the well-known Disraeli quote (57a) in the null discourse context has a perfectly good non-metaphorical interpretation, but the semantic consequences of the *contrast* relation, which is signaled by the cue phrase *but* in an amended version of Disraeli's quote (57b), are satisfiable only if it is assigned a metaphorical interpretation:

(57)   a. I have climbed to the top of that greasy pole.

b. I have always despised politics. But I have climbed to the top of that greasy pole.

Here, the pole is conceived as the career (the higher you are on the pole, the higher you are in your career), the grease is associated with the difficulty of promotion, and so on.

The distinction between metaphor and sense extension (see #19) can be hard to draw. This is partly because sense extensions are productive, and so they are a source of novel but non-metaphorical uses of words (e.g., *Porg is a delicacy on Ahch-To*). The distinction is also hard to draw because frequency or familiarity with the word meaning isn't always a good basis for drawing the distinction. In fact, some metaphors are extremely common (e.g., *enter* as used in *France entered the war*) and when common enough they become conventionalized (see Lakoff and Johnson, 1980 and #29). By and large, the distinction between metaphor vs. sense extension stems from the essential role that context plays in *specifying* the meaning of metaphor rather than simply *identifying* an existing specific meaning. For instance, reasoning involving real-world knowledge of the sun's properties is necessary for interpreting what *sun* corresponds to in (55). From a technical perspective, this difference stems from the fact that while both sense extension and metaphor can be represented with lexical rules, the meaning of the output from a lexical rule representing metaphor is much more vague than the meaning of the output of a lexical rule that represents sense extension [Asher and Lascarides, 1995b].

#28 Metaphorical extensions are nonetheless governed by established word meanings and how they relate to each other.

In #27 we emphasized that metaphorical meanings are productive and related to literal meanings. For example, the metaphorical interpretations of the sentences in (56) is made possible because interlocutors can *generalize* the "literal" senses of words and phrases like *dead end*, *off track*, *bumpy*, etc., while retaining similar relationships among these words as hold between their literal senses. To put this another way, the metaphorical interpretations draw on identifying relationships (or analogies) among inferences that one can draw in the literal domain vs. those one can draw in the domain that's being described by the metaphor: for instance, in the domain of physical movement, when you reach a dead end you have to stop and turn round in order to keep moving vs. in the domain of relationships, if a relationship reaches an impasse one must change or break up.

A word can be interpreted metaphorically in an unbounded number of ways, because the range of discourse contexts in which it can be coherently used metaphorically are unbounded. Nevertheless, metaphorical interpretations are governed by certain constraints, i.e., there are some things that a word can never mean in any context, even metaphorically. For example, Asher and Lascarides [1995a] argue that what distinguishes a change of location verb from other change of location verbs in its literal use must also distinguish it from those verbs in metaphorical use. The literal meanings of change of location verbs are defined in terms of the features of the source of the movement, the goal, and the intermediate path. For instance, the French movement verbs *partir* "to go; to leave" vs. *sortir* "to go out; to come out" differ in that the goal of *sortir* must be in a nearby neighborhood to its source, while this isn't the case for *partir* [Asher and Sablayrolles, 1995]. Thus, to retain this distinction in metaphor, the source and goal arguments to metaphorical *sortir*, while not necessarily spatial locations, have to be associated with a scalar concept that places the goal near the source. This explains why *partir de la guerre* "leave the war" is acceptable while *sortir de la guerre* "go out of the war" is not: *guerre* "war" isn't a scalar concept and so it doesn't support an interpretation where we can identify its near neighborhoods. Likewise, the English verb *enter* requires the goal to have two-dimensional spatial extent, and so metaphorical *enter* requires its argument to have two-dimensional extent—if not in the spatial dimension, then in some other other dimension, such as temporal. So one can *enter a discussion* and *enter an agreement* because discussion and agreements have temporal extent (which is why we can talk of a discussion or an agreement lasting for an extended period of time). On other other hand, one cannot *enter the line of permissible behavior*, but one can *cross* it.

Bulat et al. [2017] show that capturing general relationships among salient attributes of the denotation of words in the source and target domains enhances performance in metaphor classification. This is effectively corpus-based evidence that metaphor understanding is dependent on mappings between attributes and relationships in the source domain vs. the target domain of the metaphor, just as Lakoff and Johnson [1980] claimed in their earlier work.

#29 Metaphorical meanings can be conventionalized.

What might have started as a creative metaphor can, through a familiarity among the language users that's caused by its frequency of use, become conventional [Lakoff and Johnson, 1980]. Arguably, conceiving of time as a resource has now become conventionalized in English (e.g., *time is running out*, *you have plenty of time*), as has conceiving of argument in terms of battle or war (e.g., *Kim won the argument, Sandy was defeated by Kim's claims, they defended their hypothesis,* and so on).

The defining feature of metaphor is that the metaphorical interpretation is dependent on a particular analogy that one must infer between the literal and metaphorical domains, which in turn are of a different type. This contrasts with (productive) sense extension, which we described in #19, e.g., that for each animal count noun the lexicon also licenses a mass noun that denotes the meat. Even for speakers who have never heard *porg* used as a mass noun denoting meat, its use in *Porg is a delicacy on Ahch-To* is not metaphorical, because inferring that *porg* denotes meat does not rely on inferring an analogy between two domains.

One perhaps surprising effect of this is that we cannot distinguish metaphor from sense extension via frequency of use. *Fox* denoting meat is very rare but it's a literal sense of the mass noun *fox* thanks to a productive lexical rule of English; in contrast, *fox* meaning cunning or sexy is metaphorical, and arguably through frequency of use these metaphorical meanings are now established in English.

#30 Words can have surprising nonce uses through meaning transfer.

Meaning transfer is the linguistic process by which a property or relation denoting term takes on a new sense just in case there is some salient connection between the term's existing senses and the new one [Nunberg, 2004]. This is exemplified by the examples in (58):[17]

(58)   a. We are parked out back.

   b. I am parked out back and have been waiting for 15 minutes.

   c. *I am parked out back and may not start.

   d. Ringo squeezed himself into a narrow space.

   e. Yeats did not like to hear himself read in an English accent.

   f. The ham sandwich and salad at table 7 is getting impatient.

Nunberg argues that the transfer in (58a) is not on the pronoun *we*, but rather on the predicate *parked out back*. That is because there is a salient relationship between cars and people who are looking for them for the purpose of driving them/riding in them. Nunberg notes that the plural pronoun refers to more than one person (who are sharing a single car), and not more than one car (driven by a single person). The analysis of the predicate undergoing meaning transfer is further supported by the examples in (58b–c), which show that *parked out back* in this sense can be coordinated with another predicate that describes the person denoted by the subject but not with one that describes the car which mediates the meaning transfer.[18] The examples involving reflexives in (58d–e) similarly are more easily accommodated into a compositional

---

[17](58a–e) are from Nunberg 2004 and (58f) from Nunberg 1995.

[18]If the meaning transfer in these examples involved the sense of the subject, we'd expect the opposite grammaticality judgments.

semantic analysis if we consider the predicates to have undergone meaning transfer rather than the subjects. In (58d), *squeeze ... into a narrow space* denotes something about the person (what they do to park a car) and both *Ringo* and the reflexive *himself* refer to a person. Finally, meaning transfer can apply to predicates denoting properties which are used as part of noun phrases. This is seen in (58f), where *ham sandwich and salad* refers to the person who has the property of having ordered that meal. Noteworthy in this example is that the actual food items might still be in preparation (i.e., not *at table 7*) and that the verb takes singular agreement (reflecting the person) not plural as would be expected for the coordinated NP.

To the extent that this phenomenon is common in training texts, it will introduce noise into any distributional semantic models. Furthermore, in meaning-sensitive tasks (such as inference) failing to detect meaning transfer can lead to errors. Accordingly, it is useful to be aware of this phenomenon when undertaking error analysis.

#31 Word senses comprise different dimensions and some of those are marked as defeasible in the lexicon.

It is common to think of words as introducing a single predicate that takes one or more variables as arguments (see #32 below). However, there are further dimensions to lexical meaning: some lexical entries carry information about default interpretations of their arguments while others carry information about how they should be interpreted in contexts that require, e.g., an event rather than an individual. In both cases, we see that this information is both lexically specific and defeasible.

Examples of English verbs with default interpretations for their arguments include *cook*, *bake*, *eat*, and *drink*, which can all be syntactically intransitive as well as transitive. Semantically, the intransitive verb still entails there's a patient (in contrast to the intransitive verb *talk*, for instance). Furthermore, as pointed out by Fillmore [1986] and Lascarides et al. [1996a], their intransitive use may have a specific default interpretation of the linguistically implicit object. For instance, *Have you eaten?* can (normally) be paraphrased as *Have you eaten a meal?* (not just something edible), *I drank all night* defaults to meaning *I drank alcohol* (as opposed to liquid generally), and *The kids will bake tomorrow afternoon* defaults to meaning they will bake a flour-based product such as cake or bread, as opposed to a natural object like potatoes.

This (defeasible) information about meaning seems to be a property of the verb itself rather than a product of commonsense inference about events of drinking, eating, etc., since synonyms or near synonyms don't abide by these default interpretations concerning the (linguistically implicit) patient. For example, when *sip* is used intransitively, it doesn't default to the implicit argument being alcohol. Thus, one needs to specify these default values for implicit objects within the lexicon. This can be done symbolically (for instance, via default typed feature structures and default unification [Lascarides and Copestake, 1999]) or probabilistically (as in e.g., Briscoe and Copestake, 1999).

The example in (59) shows that these default values should remain defeasible when computing a discourse interpretation, because they can be overridden in specific discourse contexts with arbitrary background information. That is, it's not the case that once the object is dropped its interpretation is necessarily fixed by the information in the lexical entry.

(59)   Kirk has some symptoms of diabetes. For instance, he drinks all the time.

The second type of defeasible semantic information that should be recorded in the lexicon is illustrated by logical metonymy. As we saw in #20, logical metonymy involves predicates that select syntactically for a noun phrase but semantically for an event associated with the semantics of that noun phrase. Which event that is is lexically specific, as illustrated in (60):

(60)   a. Kim enjoyed the book.

       b. Kim enjoyed the latte.

The generalization is that the event that's enjoyed is the purpose or *telic role* of the NP: so (60a) means Kim enjoyed reading the book, while (60b) means Kim enjoyed drinking the latte [Pustejovsky, 1991, 1995]. We see evidence that these are lexically specified in the anomaly of examples like (61), which sounds odd even if both the speaker and the interlocutor share the knowledge that the denotation of *doorstop* is a book.

(61)   Kim enjoyed the doorstop.

However, these interpretations of *enjoy*+NP are default interpretations that can be overridden by arbitrary sources of background pragmatic information:

(62)   My goat eats anything. He really enjoyed your books.

Tracking these defeasible aspects of verb meaning, and inferring they apply and when they are overridden, can be important to natural language understanding. Doing so will require lexical resources that encode this information.

CHAPTER 5

Semantic Roles

#32 Word meanings are sometimes best represented as predicate symbols that take multiple arguments.

So far we have talked about word meanings as senses which pick out properties of referents. But many words are better understood as representing relations among referents, including both indvidiuals and events (see #15 and Davidson, 1980) This is clear for (non-intransitive) verbs: *Kim saw Sandy* is true just in case the referents of *Kim* and *Sandy* stand in the *see* relation to each other. Alternatively, one can conceive of this as a tripartite relation between an event *e* of seeing, and the referents of *Kim* and *Sandy*. The relations can be among much larger lists of arguments, where *bet* for example takes up to five, each set off by brackets in (63):

(63)   [Kim] bet [Sandy] [$5] [to three donuts] [that Chris would win].

It's not just verbs that can express relations between multiple arguments. Multi-argument predicates can also be expressed by other parts of speech, including subordinators like *because*, which expresses a relation between the content of two clauses:

(64)   Kim left because Sandy stayed.

We also find examples of relational nouns as in (65):

(65)   a. A friend of Sandy's arrived.

     b. Kim's cousin arrived.

     c. The fact that Kim won surprised Sandy.

     d. Pat denied the rumor that Chris cheated.

     e. The destruction of the wall by the termites was unfortunate.

In (65a), *friend* expresses a relation between Sandy and the person who is Sandy's friend, while also denoting that friend. Similarly *cousin* expresses a relation between the cousin and Kim. The relational nouns in (65c-d) are more abstract; here the relation is between the abstract fact or rumor and its content. Finally, (65e) is an example of a deverbal noun whose argument structure is quite similar to the verb it is derived from: *destruction* describes a relation between the termites and the wall, while also denoting the event they all participated in.

In all of these examples of relational nouns, one of the arguments is denoted by the noun itself. Similarly, non-relational nouns like *fork* in *Kim lost the fork* are one-place relations taking the item which has the property of being, e.g., the fork as their arguments. While it is perhaps more obvious for nouns, verbs also have such an intrinsic argument, viz. the event described by the verb. Thus, weather predicates like *rain* are one-place predicates, predicated of a raining event. And *bet* in (63) above actually has six semantic arguments, including the betting event.[1]

On the other hand, there are words that don't represent semantic predicates at all. On some analyses, this includes personal pronouns (which denote variables that are arguments to other predicates). Less controversially, there are expletives like *it* in (66) and various kinds of "syntactic glue" such as infinitival *to*, certain uses of prepositions, and the complementizer *that*.

(66)   It bothers Kim that Sandy left.

For more on semantically empty syntactic elements, see Bender 2013, #88–89.

#33 Semantic arguments are differentiated by their role with respect to the predicate.

When predicates take multiple arguments, it is typically the case that the roles the arguments play with respect to the event or situation denoted by the verb differ. For example, in (63) above, Kim is placing a bet against Sandy; the value of Kim's bet is \$5 whereas Sandy's is three donuts, and the predicted outcome that Kim is betting on is that Chris wins. Kim and Sandy play similar roles, as do the dollars and donuts, but these roles are very different to each other and to the expected outcome role. In the most common case, the roles for a given predicate are sharply distinct, as in (67a–b), but we also find cases where they seem quite similar, as in *bet* above and (67c) [Dowty, 1991].

(67)   a. Kim saw Sandy.

   b. Kim kissed Sandy.

   c. Kim resembled Sandy.

A further class of exceptions to distinct roles comes from collective verbs like *meet*: the following sentences are paraphrases of each other.[2]

(68)   a. Kim met Sandy.

   b. Kim and Sandy met.

   c. Sandy met Kim.

Syntax plays an important role in indicating which semantic roles which constituents participate in and with respect to which predicates (see #47), but it is not the case that syntactic roles such as "subject" or "object" map consistently onto semantic roles. This is true both across predicates and for the same predicate in different syntactic constructions. Consider (69), where

---

[1]This approach is due to Davidson [1980]. See also footnote 1 on p. 31.
[2]VerbNet [Palmer et al., 2017] (see #34) solves this by having Theme and Co-Theme.

the semantic role of *Kim* in (69a) is more like that of *Chris* in (69b) than that of *Pat*, even though both *Kim* and *Pat* are subjects.[3] The passive examples in (69c–d) show that the passive construction can alter the mapping between syntactic and semantic roles for a predicate. For more on the mapping of syntactic to semantic roles, see Bender 2013, Ch. 8.

(69) a. Kim fears Sandy.

      b. Pat scares Chris.

      c. Kim is feared by Sandy.

      d. Pat is scared by Chris.

#34 Semantic roles can be analyzed at varying degrees of granularity.

There is a long history of attempting to categorize the roles played by semantic arguments of a predicate into a small set of types of roles that recur across predicates—arguably going back as far as Pāṇini's (6th century BCE) concept of *kārakas* [Dowty, 1989]. However, as Dowty [1991] and Baker et al. [1998] argue, the fine details of lexical semantics preclude the creation of any such set with reliably operationalized definitions.

There are several different approaches that have been taken in light of this observation. On the one hand, there is the approach of FrameNet [Baker et al., 1998, Ruppenhofer et al., 2016], which groups predicates into *frames*, with each frame defining frame-specific roles (called *frame elements*). A frame is "a script-like conceptual structure that describes a particular type of situation, object, or event along with its participants and props" [Ruppenhofer et al., 2016, p. 7]. Any given frame can include multiple predicates (called *lexical units*), but there is no expectation that the fine-grained frame elements will be shared across larger sets of predicates.[4] An example is given in Figure 5.1.[5] At the same time, linguistic generalizations are captured by arranging both frames and frame elements into a hierarchy that supports monotonic, default and multiple inheritance. For example, the Creating_Physical_Artwork frame in Figure 5.1 inherits from the Intentionially_Create frame (which covers verbs like *create*, *develop*, *make*, and *produce*).

In contrast to FrameNet, there is the approach of PropBank [Palmer et al., 2005] and also the English Resource Grammar (ERG) [Flickinger, 2000, 2011], which both reuse role names (ARG0, ARG1, etc.) across predicates while positing that their interpretation is predicate-specific. For the ERG, the argument roles are numbered in order of syntactic obliqueness. For PropBank, ARG0 is aligned with Dowty's [1991] notion of Proto-Agent and ARG1 with his Proto-Patient, but no further cross-predicate similarity is claimed. Dowty's claim is that complete predicate-specificity is going too far and that there should be a notion of proto-roles that allows for the roles as used by individual predicates to vary from the prototype.

---

[3]And in cases like (67c), two different syntactic roles are mapping onto the same semantic role.

[4]In English FrameNet version 1.7, the frame with the most lexical units ("Emotion_directed") has 182; the average frame has 11.1 lexical units (Nathan Schneider, pc, December 17, 2018).

[5]From https://framenet2.icsi.berkeley.edu/fnReports/data/frameIndex.xml?frame=Create_physical_artwork, accessed June 17, 2019

Definition: A Creator creates an artefact that is typically an iconic Representation of an actual or imagined entity or event. The Representation may also be evocative of an idea while not based on resemblance.

Examples: Diagrams must be clearly <u>drawn</u> on construction paper.

I <u>took</u> the picture of that building to prove that you can find the internet Café.

Frame Elements: Core: creator, representation

Non-Core: manner, location_of_representation, purpose, reference, time, place.

Lexical Units: *artist.n, cast.v, draw.v, paint.v, sculpt.v, take [picture].v*

Figure 5.1: The FrameNet frame for Create_physical_artwork.

The English VerbNet project takes a practical middle ground. The initial set of VerbNet annotations made use of a heterogeneous set of semantic role labels. Some were general in that they were expected to occur across verb classes (e.g., Agent, Theme) others specific to particular verb classes (e.g., the role Topic is specific to verbs of communication, and Experiencer to verbs that denote feelings or attitudes), and still others more syntactically motivated (e.g., Predicate, which is used for verb classes with predicative complements) [Palmer et al., 2017]. In a recent revision to the role set, VerbNet has proposed a hierarchy of roles, where the most general types map fairly closely to the very general LIRICS roles,[6] and the more fine-grained ones to FrameNet Frame Elements [*Ibid.*].

Aside from determining what labels to use when annotating semantic roles, there is an additional question of determining which dependents to assign a semantic role at all. That is, given a word and its syntactic dependents, some syntactic dependents will correspond to semantic dependents and so qualify for being assigned a semantic role; but others might be semantically empty [see Bender, 2013, #88], and there are also syntactic dependents that might be analyzed semantically as predicates that take the word whose syntactic dependent they are as a semantic argument. This latter set are sometimes called "adjuncts" or "modifiers." For example, the phrases *today, in the garden, at dusk,* and *with a lantern* in (70) all fall into this category.

(70)   Kim met Sandy today in the garden at dusk with a lantern.

In PropBank, they are annotated with the ARGM role. In FrameNet, they are represented by non-core Frame Elements. In the ERG, adjuncts are treated as semantic predicates in their own right (and not semantic dependents). VerbNet doesn't annotate adjuncts, because it follows Levin [1995] in focusing on argument structure alternations. For discussion of the difficulty of drawing this distinction, see Przepiórkowski and Patejuk 2018.

---

[6]LIRICS was a project working toward ISO standards for various kinds of linguistic annotation. For more information, see http://lirics.loria.fr/.

Understanding the granularity of a semantic-role labeling scheme is important for understanding how to make optimal use of the labels it provides. For example, generally speaking, the bleached role labels meant to have predicate-specific interpretations (ARG0 et al. from PropBank or the ERG) are probably not useful for guiding back-off in cases of data sparsity.

The set of words that get associated with semantic roles differs between resources: FrameNet includes verbs, event nominals, a wide variety of content words and even some function words. PropBank includes semantic roles for verbs, event nouns and some adjectives, with derivational variants being assigned the same set of roles (e.g., *destroy* and *destruction*). VerbNet remains limited to verbs. Thus, *destruction* in (65e) would be considered a predicate with semantic roles in FrameNet and PropBank, but not VerbNet.

#35 Selectional restrictions are soft constraints on the type of argument expected to fill each semantic role.

For many predicates, there are generalizations which can be found in corpora [e.g., Resnik, 1996, Ribas, 1995] or elicited from the intuitions of native speakers [e.g., Brockmann and Lapata, 2003, Lapata et al., 1999, Resnik, 1996] about which kinds of arguments are likely to appear with which kinds of predicates. These generalizations are called selectional restrictions. For example, (71a–b) are odd, while (71c) is unremarkable.

(71)   a. The teapot danced.

        b. The idea danced.

        c. The child danced.

The generalization here is that the argument of *dance* should be animate. These are soft constraints, in that they can be overridden by context. (71a) is a perfectly fine description of a scene from *Beauty and the Beast*,[7] and even (71b) is fine in a metaphorical sense (see #27 and #28):

(72)   The idea danced through the conversations at the party.

Selectional restrictions can pertain to various properties of possible arguments—*drink* selects for something that is liquid (and preferably a beverage), *blue* and other color terms select for physical entities, etc.—but for the most part these properties do not correlate with anything that's grammaticized in languages. One big exception is the property of *animacy*. The verb *dance* (like many others) displays a soft selectional restriction for an animate argument, but animacy is related to hard grammatical constraints in many languages [de Swart et al., 2008]. Among the examples cited by de Swart et al. are the following: In Malayalam, animate, but not inanimate, direct objects must be marked with accusative case as in (73) [Asher and Kumari, 1997] and in Japanese active transitive verbs reject inanimate subjects [Kuno, 1973], as in (74):

---

[7]An animated film in which enchanted household items are able to talk, move, and dance

(73)   a.   അവൻ   ഒരു   പശുവിനെ   വാങ്ങി
            Awan   oru   paʃu-wine   waaŋŋ-i.
            he.NOM INDEF.SG female.cow-ACC buy-PST

       "He bought a cow." [mal]

       b.   അവൻ   പുസ്തകം   വായിച്ചു
            Awan   pustakam waayicch-u.
            he.NOM book   read-PST

       "He read the book." [mal] [Asher and Kumari, 1997, 203]

(74)   *台風   が   窓   を   壊した。
       *taihuu ga   mado   wo kawashi-ta
       typhoon NOM window ACC break-PST

       Intended: "The typhoon broke the window." [jpn] [Kuno, 1973, 30]

#36 When an argument is not overtly expressed, the semantic predicate still carries a role for it.

Semantic roles describe relations between predicates and their arguments, but they are inherent to the predicates.[8] There are several grammatical means by which arguments can be unexpressed in the string, but the semantic role is still carried by the predicate. In what is called "Constructional Null Instantiation" in FrameNet [Baker et al., 1998, Fillmore and Petruck, 2003], the grammatical structure of a sentence licenses the absence of an overt argument and constrains its interpretation. This includes phenomena such as passive voice and imperatives as illustrated for English in (75a–b): here the INGESTOR role, which is one of the frame elements for *eat*, is not directly realized and yet is still present in the semantics.

(75)   a.   The cake was eaten.

       b.   Eat the cake!

Further, these distinct syntactic constructions impose different (semantic) constraints on the ingestor role that's present in semantics. In the passive example in (75a), the ingestor is constrained to be left indefinite. That is, (75a) entails that someone is the ingestor, but the speaker is not committed to any claim about who that is, nor does the form of the sentence indicate that the hearer should necessarily know. In contrast, in the imperative (75b), the unexpressed INGESTOR is interpreted as the addressee of the command.

Further, the frame element to a predicate may be "non-local," thanks to control and raising verbs, as illustrated in (76a–b):

(76)   a.   Kim tried to eat the cake.

[8]See also Bender 2013, #96–97.

  b. We ordered Kim to eat the cake.

In (76a), the subject control verb *try* is lexically specified to require that the missing subject of the verb in its complement be interpreted as the same as the subject of *try* itself, and so the subject *Kim* of *try* is annotated with the ingestor role for *eat*. Similarly in (76b), the object control verb *order* is specified to require that its object is the same as the subject of the verb in its complement, so again *Kim* is marked as the ingestor for *eat*.

In English, outside of Constructional Null Instantiation, subjects are generally not left unexpressed. Non-subject arguments of some predicates can be dropped, but whether or not this is possible and how the dropped arguments are interpreted are properties of particular lexical items [Fillmore, 1986]. For example, *eat* but not *devour* can appear without its object and the missing argument is interpreted as indefinite (and also defeasibly interpreted as a meal; see #31 and Fillmore [1986]):

(77)   a. I ate.

  b. *I devoured.

The verb *tell* can appear with no overt expression of its message argument, but in this case, the interpretation is definite:

(78)   Kim already told Sandy.

Here, the hearer is expected to know what it is that Kim told Sandy.

In other languages, either subjects (as in Spanish) or all arguments (Japanese, Mandarin) can be omitted when they are sufficiently salient in context. This use of dropped arguments is very similar to the use of unstressed pronouns in English:

(79)   Com-í   pizza.
       eat-PST.1SG pizza

       "I ate pizza." [spa]

(80)   あげた。
       Age-ta.
       Give-PST

       "(They) gave (it) to (them)." [jpn]

In the Spanish example, the verb's inflection gives person and number information about the subject, i.e., as much information as the pronoun *I* does in English. In Japanese, the verbal morphology gives no such clues, but there are other kinds of interacting linguistic systems that give partial information, including the presence or absence of subject-oriented honorifics and, for lexical items like あげる *ageru* "give" in (80), lexical semantic information about whether the giver or the recipient is relatively closer socially to the speaker (see #9).[9]

---

[9]The English pronouns in the translation of (80) are chosen arbitrarily; many other combinations are possible, depending on the discourse context. However, because of the lexical constraints about in-group membership, it would not ever be translatable as "You gave it to me."

Finally, in yet other languages, the interpretation of a dropped argument as definite or indefinite is dependent on the presence or absence of an agreement marker on the verb. This is the case in Chicheŵa [Bresnan and Mchombo, 1987], as exemplified in (81):

(81) a. ndi-a-dya (kale).
          1SM-PF-eat (already)

          "I have eaten (already)." [nya]

      b. ndi-a-i-dya.
          1SM-PF-OM-eat

          "I have eaten it." [nya]

These examples differ in their felicity conditions: (81a) can be used in response to a question such as *Are you hungry?* where (81b) is appropriate in response to a question like *What happened to the cake?*.

Practically speaking, reference resolution for dropped arguments is a very difficult task. Gerber and Chai [2010], Ruppenhofer et al. [2010], and Moor et al. [2013] present English corpora annotated for dropped arguments and baseline results. Supervised methods have achieved F-measures in the mid-40s on the Gerber and Chai 2010 data set [Do et al., 2017, Laparra and Rigau, 2013]. Schenk and Chiarcos [2016] and Cheng and Erk [2018] develop methods that don't rely on hand-labeled training data to attempt this problem; Cheng and Erk's [2018] system achieves high-40s F-measure on the Gerber and Chai 2010 dataset. Despite the difficulty of this task, it's valuable to be aware, in designing NLP and NLU systems, of the phenomenon of unexpressed arguments and in particular in the ways it varies across languages (see, e.g., Sikos et al. 2016 on differences in implicit arguments between English and German and Deng and Xue 2017 for differences between English and Chinese).

CHAPTER 6

Collocations and Other Multiword Expressions

#37 Multiword expressions (MWEs) straddle the boundary between lexical and compositional semantics.

Multiword expressions (MWEs) are collections of words which co-occur and are idiosyncratic in one or more aspects of their form or meaning [Sag et al., 2002, Baldwin and Kim, 2010]. The idiosyncrasy could be simply statistical, where words co-occur with a frequency much greater than chance (e.g., *sperm whale*) (see #38 below, and Cruse, 1986, Sag et al., 2002); syntactic, where the form of the MWE departs from typical syntactic rules for the language (e.g., *long time no see*) [Bauer, 1983, Chafe, 1968]; semantic, where the meaning of the full expression is not predictable on the basis of its component words (e.g., *kick the bucket*) [Bauer, 1983, Chafe, 1968]; or pragmatic, where the MWE is associated with a particular set of situations in which it is typically uttered (e.g., *all aboard, good morning*) [Jackendoff, 1997, Kastovsky, 1982]. All of these dimensions are gradable, with some MWEs being completely idiosyncratic and others much closer to predictable (see #44 and #45). Our focus here will be primarily on the semantic properties of MWEs.

In many ways, MWEs behave like individual words: they can have multiple different senses (see #41); there are patterns for generating new MWEs (akin to derivational morphology, see #42); and, like with derived words, MWEs' senses can drift from what the productive pattern would predict (see #43). MWEs are also like individual words in being extremely numerous: it is estimated that the number of MWEs in a language is on the same order of magnitude as the number of simplex lexical items [Bannard, 2006, Jackendoff, 1997, Pauwels, 2000, Tschichold, 1998]. The ubiquity of MWEs, their language-specific nature and their idiosyncratic behavior combine to present a major challenge to a wide range of NLP tasks, but especially semantic parsing and machine translation, for which shared tasks in multilingual MWE detection and processing have formed a focus of research (e.g., the PARSEME project; Sailer and Markantonatou, 2018).

#38 Collocations are dependent on word form and not just word senses.

A collocation is a sequence of two or more words that appear together more than would be expected by chance, i.e., with a greater frequency than their individual frequencies would predict:

for example, *coffee filter*, *take a risk*. In the terms introduced in #37 above, collocations are MWEs which are only statistically idiosyncratic; in other respects they conform with the general rules of the language for syntactic well-formedness and semantic compositionality.

Collocations do not arise simply because speakers frequently want to refer to what they denote [Lin, 1988]. Rather, collocations are dependent on the word forms, not just their denotations. In fact, a defining characteristic of collocations is that substituting a word in a collocation with a synonym produces something that sounds odd or even anomalous:

(82)	emotional baggage	?emotional luggage
	strong tea	?powerful tea
	make progress	?do progress
	do homework	?make homework
	center divider	?middle separator
	in my opinion	?from my opinion
	from my point of view	?in my point of view

Collocations also vary across dialects of the same language [Sag et al., 2002], e.g., *telephone box* is a collocation of British English, while *telephone booth* is the corresponding item in American English, but neither dialect accepts *telephone closet*.

The sensitivity of collocations to substitution with synonymy, combined with the fact that many of them are relatively infrequent, makes them a major challenge for language learners and for machine translation.

#39 Collocations are often less ambiguous than the words taken in isolation.

According to WordNet (Miller et al., 1990; see also Chapter 14), the English adjective *heavy* has 27 different senses. As well as the sense "of comparatively great weight," there are also the senses "prodigious," "of great intensity" and "deep and complete," among others. But in the collocations *heavy smoker*, *heavy blow*, and *heavy sleeper*, the word *heavy* is assigned the last three distinct senses, respectively [Asher, 2011, Pustejovsky, 1991]: *heavy sleeper* as a collocation does not mean "a sleeper of comparatively great weight." Similarly, so-called light verbs like *make* are highly sense ambiguous (49 distinct senses in WordNet), but less ambiguous in the collocations *make a cake* and *make a mistake*.

The fact that a word in a collocation isn't as ambiguous as the individual words on their own is a special case of a more general phenomenon: a word is often less ambiguous in its linguistic context than it is in isolation of any context, thanks to knowledge about preferred linguistic forms and preferred meanings. The fact that context drives the resolution of ambiguity is a central focus of Chapters 9 and 13.

#40 The strength of a collocation is not equivalent to its frequency.

One cannot estimate the strength of a collocation via an n-gram language model, such as a bigram or a trigram. For example, *warm day* will be a relatively frequent bigram, but so are *sunny day*, *cold day*, *warm week*, and so on. *Bat your eyelashes*, on the other hand, is relatively infrequent, but intuitively it's a strong collocation because substituting the words with synonyms produces a phrase that's anomalous (e.g., *hit your eyelashes*, *tap your eyelashes*).

Table 6.1 presents the ranked list of highest frequency bigrams in Moby Dick. The highest frequency bigram consisting only of open-class words is *sperm whale*, at number 27. Those above it are not collocations, but rather artifacts of the higher overall frequency of function words. Even if we remove bigrams that contain closed class words (and so sacrifice detecting collocations that include closed class words, such as *in my opinion* vs. *??from my opinion* and *from my point of view* vs. *??in my point of view*), the highest frequency bigrams still aren't uniformly collocations. For instance, removing bigrams with closed class words from *Moby Dick* yields the following top five bigrams: *sperm whale*, *white whale*, *Moby Dick*, *old man*, *Captain Ahab*. Intuitively, *old man* is not a collocation—in general English usage, *elderly man* and *old gentleman* are perfectly acceptable.

Mutual Information (MI) is a better metric than ngram frequency for predicting word collocations. Take a two word phrase XY: MI measures the (joint) probability $P(XY)$ of seeing

Table 6.1: Top bigrams in *Moby Dick*

Rank	Bigram	Count
1	of the	1,879
2	in the	1,182
3	to the	731
4	from the	440
5	the whale	407
6	of his	373
7	and the	370
8	on the	359
9	of a	334
10	at the	330
...	...	...
27	sperm whale	182

the phrase XY against the probabilities of seeing the individual words:

$$MI(XY) = log_2(\frac{P(X,Y)}{P(X)P(Y)})$$ (6.1)

The MI of *old man* will be relatively small if *old* is just as likely to appear with other nouns as it is with *man* (and likewise *man* is just as likely to appear with other adjectives as with *old*). But an accurate measure relies on having a very large open-domain corpus. For example, in Moby Dick the MI for *of the*, *sperm whale*, and *old man* are, respectively: 2.2, 7.3, 6.6. In other words, because of what the book *Moby Dick* is about, using MI to predict collocations makes *old man* almost as much of a collocation as *sperm whale*.

#41 Like individual words, MWEs can have sense ambiguity.

Just as individual words can bear a range of senses (see #18), so can multiword expressions. For example, English WordNet [Miller et al., 1990] lists four senses for the MWE *pull up* used as a verb: "straighten oneself" (*I pulled my rib cage up*), "come to a halt after driving somewhere" (*The chauffeur pulled up to the kerb*), "remove, usually with some force or effort" (*I pulled the weeds up*), and "cause (a vehicle) to stop" (*I pulled up the car in front of the hotel*). Also as with individual words, MWEs exhibit predictable and productive sense extensions. The collocation *instruction manual* (cf. *??direction manual*), like the simple word *book*, can refer to both the physical object and the abstract content. (83) uses the co-predication test to show that, and that both of these senses must cohabit the same lexical entry (see #19):

(83)   The instruction manual for the printer is in that box.

In this case, the collocation exhibits the same (predictable) sense ambiguities as the individual head noun *manual*. So while some collocations select for specific word senses (see #39), others (such as *instruction manual*) exhibit the same regular polysemy as its individual words do.

Other cases of multiple senses for the same MWE do not seem to belong to any productive pattern, and thus would likely be better classified as homonymy (see #21). For example, WordNet lists 10 senses for the MWE *make out*, including "detect with the senses" (84a) and "make out and issue" (84b).

(84)   a. Kim strained to make out the lettering on the sign.

          b. Make the check out to Acme Linguistic Services.

There is no clear general pattern that relates these two senses.

We also find metaphorical sense extensions (see #27) in multiword expressions. Consider the Japanese compound verb 引き抜く *hikinuku*, with component verbs 引く *hiku* "to draw, to pull" and 抜く *nuku* "to extract." Japanese WordNet [Isahara et al., 2008][1] lists four senses for

---

[1]Accessed through Open Multilingual WordNet [Bond and Paik, 2012] at http://compling.hss.ntu.edu.sg/omw/, August 14, 2018.

this MWE: "pull or pull out sharply," "rip off violently and forcefully," "remove, usually with some force or effort," and "bring, take, or pull out of a container or from under a cover." Breen and Baldwin [2009] note that it is also used to mean "to head hunt" and "to lure away."

#42 Like derivational morphology, there are patterns for generating new MWEs.

While many MWEs are idiosyncratic (i.e., not reflective of productive patterns), some MWEs arise via patterns, in which a word that has an entrenched or idiosyncratic meaning in one MWE is attested in another MWE that shares the same syntactic constructions. For example, Jackendoff [2002] finds several patterns for English verb-particle MWEs that apply seemingly productively to broad classes of verbs to create new MWEs. These include verbs with directional particles (85a), aspectual particles including completive *up* (85b), continuative *away* and *on* (85c,d), and the curious "time-away" construction where the MWE not only involves the combination of the verb plus the particle *away*, but also an alteration to the verb's valence frame (expected complements) to make room for a selected NP expressing a duration (85e).[2]

(85)   a. Beth {tossed/took/put/carried} the food (right) {up/in/away/back}.

   b. Hilary packed up the suitcase.

   c. Bill sneezed away.

   d. Bill wrote on.

   e. Pat programmed three whole weeks away.

In fact, not only do some MWEs follow productive or semi-productive patterns like derivational morphology (see #22), there are cases where the resulting lexical item is sometimes a MWE and sometimes a single word form, as in Germanic separable prefix verbs, illustrated here with data from Dutch in (86).

(86)   a. Jan zegt   dat hij   morgen   zijn   moeder opbelt.
      Jan say.3SG.PRS that 3SG.MASC tomorrow 3SG.POSS mother up.ring.3SG.PRS

      "Jan says that he will phone his mother tomorrow" [nld]

   b. Jan belt   zijn   moeder morgen   op.
      Jan ring.3SG.PRS 3SG.POSS mother tomorrow up

      "Jan will phone his mother tomorrow" [nld] [Kemenade and Los, 2003, p. 80]

Here the verb *bellen* "ring" combines with *op* "up," either as a prefix or as a separate word, depending on the syntactic context. The meaning of the combination ("phone") is the same in both cases and in both cases is not purely predictable from the meaning of the two parts. This hybrid behavior of formatives like *op* poses additional problems for NLP systems above and beyond

[2]All examples from Jackendoff [2002, pp. 76–81].

those already introduce by MWEs: accurate processing will need to be able to recognize *opbellen* as the same lexical item in both configurations.

#43 Like derived words, the sense of an MWE can drift from what the productive pattern would predict.

Because MWEs are idiosyncratic in some respect (see #37 above), they must be learned as additional lexical items. Two prominent ways for new MWEs to be added to the lexicon are *grammaticalization* and *idiomatization* [Ishizaki, 2012; see also Brinton and Traugott, 2005]. In grammaticalization, a form takes on less concrete semantics and generalizes the contexts in which it may appear. Thus, the development of aspectual particles (like *away* in the "time-away" construction mentioned in #42 and (87) and (88) below, out of the directional adverb *away*) is an example of grammaticalization.

In idiomatization, a form takes on a new meaning that is typically not as abstract as the meanings encoded with grammaticalization and also typically fixed to one or a few specific forms. Thus, where grammaticalization gives us the general patterns of MWEs described in #42, idiomatiziation gives us more idiosyncratic uses. This can be illustrated with *give away*, which starts close to the grammaticalized usage of V *away* but then also gives rise to multiple idiosyncratic senses. The OED[3] dates the usage *give away* in the sense of "to dispose of as a present" (as in (87)) to approximately 1400 CE. This sense is quite close to the aspectual use of *away* in verb-particle constructions, where it conveys perfectivity, i.e., the giving is completed. Similarly, the sense "to sacrifice (another's interests or rights)" is both close to the aspectual use and relatively early, with the first citation listed in the OED from 1548 (88).

(87)   Thou hase giffene thi part of bothe away. (*Sir Perceval* 1983)

(88)   Yea, said the capitain, so that you geve away no mannes right, but his, whose aucthoritie you have. (*Hall's Vnion: Henry VI* 155 b)

Other, more idiosyncratic senses (again per the OED) come in later, including "to perform the ceremony of handing over (a bride) to the bridegroom at marriage" with a first citation in 1719 (89), "to betray, expose to detection or ridicule, to let slip (a secret), esp. through carelessness or stupidity" with a first citation in 1878 (90), and "to abandon, give up, stop" in 1949 (91).[4]

(89)   I was Father at the Altar..and gave her away. (D. Defoe *Farther Adventures of Robinson Crusoe* 191)

(90)   Ye went back on her, and shook her, and played off on her, and gave her away—dead away! (*Scribner's Monthly* **15** 812/1)

---

[3] *OED online*, http://www.oed.com/, accessed September 5, 2018.
[4] These latter two senses are listed as U.S. slang and Australian slang, respectively.

(91)   It's about time you mugs woke up to yourself. You're not in the race to get in without a ticket. Why don't you give the game away? (L. Glassop *Lucky Palmer* iii. 37)

The senses in (89)–(91), although related to the grammaticalization of *away* signaling the perfective, are idiosyncratic and more concrete. Hence these senses of *give away* are examples of idiomatiziation.

#44 MWEs vary in their syntactic flexibility.

The term *idiom* is sometimes used interchangeably with *fixed phrase*, but Nunberg et al. [1994] argue that in fact among multi-word expressions with semantic idiosyncrasy, we find both *idiomatic phrases* such as those in (92) where the order of the words is fixed and *idiomatically combining expressions* such as (93) which show quite a bit of flexibility.

(92)   a.   Kim kicked the bucket. ("Kim died.")

       b.   Kim and Sandy shot the breeze. ("Kim and Sandy had a chat.")

       c.   Kim sawed logs all day long. ("Kim slept all day long.")

(93)   a.   The FBI kept tabs on Jane Fonda. ("The FBI kept Jane Fonda under surveillance.")

       b.   Kim spilled the beans. ("Kim revealed the information.")

Idiomatically combining expressions allow both meaning preserving alternations like passive (94a) and relativization (94b) as well as interacting with other syntactic phenomena that show that their components must be available for semantic composition (see #45 below).

(94)   a.   Close tabs were kept on Jane Fonda by the FBI.

       b.   I was worried that the beans might be spilled by one of the assistants.

Idiomatic phrases, on the other hand, allow no such modifications. While the examples in (95) are grammatical, they do not carry the idiomatic meaning associated with (92).

(95)   a.   The bucket was kicked by Kim.

       b.   The breeze was shot by Kim and Sandy.

Phrases such as *kick the bucket* and *shoot the breeze* do however allow for inflectional morphology (marking tense and subject agreement) on the verb.

Fully accurate parsing requires recognizing idioms even when they are not in their canonical form (for a detailed survey of parsing and MWEs, see Constant et al., 2017). Conversely, fully adequate generation requires avoiding generating variants on fixed expressions.

#45 MWEs vary in their compositionality.

As noted in #37, multi-word expressions need not be semantically idiosyncratic, so long as they are idiosyncratic in some other way. Thus, some MWEs, including collocations like *coffee filter* (see #38), are completely semantically transparent. Among verb-particle constructions (VPCs), Bannard [2006] finds cases which appear to use both the sense of the verb and of the particle compositionally (e.g., *push down*), ones that are only compositional on the verb (e.g., *finish up*, where *up* is completive rather than directional), ones that are compositional only on the particle (e.g., *make away (with)* "steal") and non-compositional (e.g., both the "see" and "sexual" senses of *make out*).

Even among those that are more strikingly semantically idiosyncratic, however, we find variation in compositionality. Nunberg et al. [1994] argue that syntactic flexibility (see #44) correlates with whether or not speakers can divvy up the meaning of the idiom and apportion the meaning onto its parts. They adduce a variety of evidence for this quasi-compositionality of idioms based on how idiom parts interact with other semantic phenomena, including internal modification (96a), information structure (96b), pronominal reference (96c), ellipsis (96d), and even coordination with non-idiomatic elements (96e).[5]

(96)   a. The team left no legal stone unturned.

   b. Those strings, he wouldn't pull for you.

   c. We worried that Pat might spill the beans, but it was Chris who finally spilled them.

   d. My goose is cooked, but yours isn't.

   e. Reinventing and Tilting At the Federal Windmill

In (96a), the intended reading is one in which all legal options are explored (so that *legal* only modifies the part of the idiomatic reading assigned to *stone*), and not, for example that it was legal to try all methods. Similarly, what is focused in (96b) is just part of the idiom (both in the syntax and the semantics) and so that part must be available in the semantics as well as the syntax for being focused.[6] (96c) and (96d) both involve coreference resolution, where the antecedents of the pronoun *them*, the unexpressed possessed element implied by *yours* and the dropped verb phrase (after *isn't*) must all be found in parts of the idiom given earlier in the clause. Finally, in (96e), the complement (*At the Federal Windmill*) is shared between the two coordinated transitive verbs, so some portion of the idiom's meaning must be available to fill the semantic role required by *Reinventing*.

The phenomenon of idiomatically combining expressions, with idiosyncratic meaning that is nonetheless distributed amongst the parts, is not confined to English. The example in (97) illustrates with pronominal reference the fact that similar effects can be found in Italian.

(97)   Andreotti ha   tenuto   le   fil-a   fino al   '92, e   poi le
       Andreotti have.PRS.3SG hold.PSTP DEF.FEM.PL line-PL until INDEF '92, and then 3.FEM.PL
       ha   tenute   Craxi.
       have.PRS.3SG hold.PSTP Craxi.

---

[5]Examples are all from Nunberg et al. [1994, pp. 500–502], in some cases modified to make them complete sentences. (96e) is an attested example which Nunberg et al. [1994] attribute to *The Washington Post Weekly* of September 13–18, 1993.

[6]On focus, see #85.

"Andreotti held the lines (i.e., ran things from behind the scenes) until 92, and then Craxi held them." [ita] [Nunberg et al., 1994, p. 503]

#46 It's challenging to represent the relationship between the meaning of an idiom and the meanings of its parts.

As noted in #45, MWEs (including verb-particle constructions and idioms) vary in the extent to which they are compositional. Partial compositionality presents problems for semantic representations: How do we capture both the idiosyncratic meaning and the relationship to the "ordinary" meaning of the component words in cases like *make away with*, where *away* presumably has its ordinary sense? How do we capture the idiosyncratic meaning as well as its allocation to the idiom parts in idiomatically combining expressions like *spill the beans*?

To make this concrete, consider the verb-particle construction *put up* as in (98a). To capture the fact that (98a) means that Kim puts the picture somewhere and that as a consequence of this event the picture was up, we might choose to represent it as (98b):

(98) a. Kim put the picture up.

  b. $put(e, x, y) \wedge name(x, kim) \wedge picture(y) \wedge up(e, y)$

But there is more to the verb particle construction (VPC) *put up* than this. Its meaning is essentially more specific than the meaning of *put* and of the particle *up*, because it entails that the picture is supported on some entity that is a solid vertical plane, and not just that the picture ends up higher at the end of the event than it was at the beginning. This is a very specific sense of *up* (let's call it the "hanging-up" sense), which can be used in a copular construction (*The picture is up*) and in the VPC *hang up*, but in no other context. So if one were to include in the grammar's lexicon the "hanging-up" sense of the particle *up* as a separate lexical item, then one would face the challenge of constraining its syntactic use appropriately.[7]

The VPC *put on* presents similar challenges: the meaning of (99) has something to do with the meaning of *put* and of *on*, but it's more specific because it means that Kim ends up *wearing* the jacket, rather than the jacket ending up lying on Kim's head:

(99) Kim put the jacket on.

One could assume within a grammar a particular lexical entry for *on* whose predicate symbol corresponds to wearing, but like *up* in *put up*, it is a particle that can be used in only a few syntactic combinations (e.g., *my shoes are on* and *I have my t-shirt on the wrong way round* but not *I placed my ring on*, meaning "I placed it on my finger").

Similar problems arise with the idiomatically combining expressions. As noted in #45, examples like (96c) show that the parts of the idiom have to be able to interact compositionally

---

[7]Note, incidentally, that VPCs can themselves be part of larger collocations (see #38): *Hang your jacket up* is perfectly natural, but *put your jacket up* is anomalous, and refers to the rather odd situation in which one displays the jacket by attaching it to a vertical plane, rather than putting it on a hanger on a rail, or putting it on a peg.

with other parts of the grammar—here *the beans* has to be available as an antecedent of *them*, and the second occurrence of *spill* has to be able to combine with the pronoun *them* (rather than the idiomatic *the beans*).

(96c)   We worried that Pat might spill the beans, but it was Chris who finally spilled them.

In both of these cases, the fundamental problem is that if we associate parts of the idiomatic meaning with parts of the idiomatic form (i.e., the separate words), then the grammar has to also ensure that those idiomatic words don't appear (and thus insert their idiomatic meaning) where they are not licensed. One solution to this is proposed by Riehemann [2001], where the predicate symbols of idiomatic words are flagged as such and the grammar includes a series of entries for idioms enumerating the permitted semantic configurations involving idiomatic predicate symbols. The pronominal examples like (96c) show that the check for permitted idiomatic predicates must also take coreference resolution into account.

CHAPTER 7

Compositional Semantics

#47 Compositional semantics is largely about working out who did what to whom, where, when, how, and why.

As noted in Bender [2013, p. 2], "[m]orphosyntax is the difference between a sentence and a bag of words." In other words, the meaning of a sentence isn't just the amalgamation of the meaning of its component words. Rather, the semantic contributions of the words combine with each other in a structured way that is dependent on the morphosyntactic scaffolding and on the semantic argument structures provided by each word (see #32 and #33). The description of this semantic structure (often called *predicate-argument structure*) and of mechanisms for deriving it, given syntactic analyses, is the heart of compositional semantics.

Across different theories of compositional semantics, we find that "who did what to whom" is represented via a Boolean combination of "atomic" formulae, each consisting of a predicate symbol with variables and/or constants as arguments. Some predicate symbols express the "doing what," in which case its arguments identify the individuals that are the "who" and the "whom." Other predicate symbols express properties (and indeed relations) among those individuals—identity among the arguments to these predicate symbols is what ensures that the semantic representation as a whole ascribes particular properties (and relations) to the who and the whom that are doing the what. These atomic formulae are expressed in a particular Boolean combination in the semantic representation, which is dependent on the presence, or absence, of "logical" words like negation. Thus, (100a) can be represented as (100b) and (100c) as (100d):[1]

(100)   a. Cats chase dogs.

   b. $chase(e, x, y) \wedge cat(x) \wedge dog(y)$

   c. Cats don't chase dogs.

   d. $\neg(chase(e, x, y) \wedge cat(x) \wedge dog(y))$

In the semantic representation, each predicate is associated with an intrinsic variable: e stands for the chasing event, x for the cats, and y for the dogs. This is because formal semantics exploits set theory to represent meaning (see #2): the meaning of the predicate symbol *cat* is the set of things that are cats and the meaning of *chase* is a set where each element is a triple consisting of

---

[1]In this example we abstract away from things like number (the plural marking on both *cats* and *dogs*) and tense (see #60), which are also in the purview of compositional semantics. We are also abstracting away, for now, from quantifiers (see #51–#53).

the chasing event, the chaser and the chasee. Thus, the representation in (100b) is true just in case the event e is a chasing event where the chaser is a member of the set of cats and the chasee is a member of the set of dogs (this ignores the meaning of (100a) that's derived from the fact that the noun phrases are bare plurals; we'll return to the content of quantifiers in #51–#53). The representation (100d) is true just in case (100b) is false.

The same mechanism can be used to represent the meaning of modifiers, of both events and event participants, as in (101) (once again, ignoring for now in our simplified representation (101b) the meaning of bare plurals):

(101)   a. Sleek cats chase fluffy dogs through the park at midnight.

   b. $chase(e, x, y) \wedge cat(x) \wedge sleek(x) \wedge dog(y) \wedge fluffy(y) \wedge through(e, p) \wedge park(p) \wedge$
   $at(e, m) \wedge midnight(m)$

Here, the event being described now involves entities that are at the intersection of things that are cats and things that are sleek, events that are chasing events and events that happen at midnight and through a park, etc.

This kind of representation immediately captures intuitively compelling entailments among natural language utterances. This is thanks to an axiom of classical logic that is called *wedge elimination* [Gamut, 1991a, p. 129], which is represented as follows: $p \wedge q \vdash p$, $p \wedge q \vdash q$.[2] In words, this means that the formula $p \wedge q$ entails p and it also entails q, i.e., what remains when the wedge ($\wedge$) plus one of its arguments is removed. Thanks to wedge elimination, the representation in (101b) predicts that any sentence whose compositional semantic representation is just like (101b) except that one or more conjuncts are missing (or suppressed) is entailed by (101a).[3] So (101a) entails (100a) and all of the sentences in (102a)–(104a) and many more. That is, if (101a) is true, then all of the following must be as well:[4]

(102)   a. Cats chase fluffy dogs through the park at midnight.

   b. $chase(e, x, y) \wedge cat(x) \wedge dog(y) \wedge fluffy(y) \wedge through(e, p) \wedge park(p) \wedge at(e, m) \wedge$
   $midnight(m)$

(103)   a. Sleek cats chase fluffy dogs at midnight.

   b. $chase(e, x, y) \wedge cat(x) \wedge sleek(x) \wedge dog(y) \wedge fluffy(y) \wedge at(e, m) \wedge midnight(m)$

(104)   a. Sleek cats chase fluffy dogs through the park.

   b. $chase(e, x, y) \wedge cat(x) \wedge sleek(x) \wedge dog(y) \wedge fluffy(y) \wedge through(e, p) \wedge park(p)$

---

[2]The symbol $\vdash$ indicates the entailment relation.

[3]This fact was Davidson's [1980] main motivation for including an event argument in predicate symbols corresponding to verbs—the so-called Davidsonian or neo-Davidsonian semantics.

[4]Not all applications of wedge elimination yield a formula that represents the semantics of a well-formed natural language sentence, however. For example, it is logically valid, via wedge elimination, to drop *park(p)* from (101b). But the result doesn't match the semantic representation of any English sentence, since *through* requires its complement in syntax. Likewise, if we drop just *through*, then the semantic representation is disconnected and similarly wouldn't correspond to any English sentence.

Wedge elimination is just one axiom among several in classical logic; in and of itself it does not form a complete theory of entailment. And, indeed, depending on how we express the logical forms of natural language sentences in a formal language, we may fail to validate intuitively compelling entailments. For example intuitively, (101a) entails (105a), but if we represent (105a) as (105b), then classical logical fails to predict this entailment (via wedge elimination or any of its other axioms):

(105)   a.   Sleek cats chased something at midnight.

   b. $chase(e, x, y) \wedge cat(x) \wedge sleek(x) \wedge something(y) \wedge at(e, m) \wedge midnight(m)$

The problem here is the treatment of *something* as a (non-logical) predicate symbol. To model the entailment between (101a) and (105a), given their semantic representations (101b) and (105b), one would need to add the following axiom to the logic: $dog(x) \rightarrow something(x)$. But this misses a very important generalization: it's not just chasing *dogs* that imply chasing *something*; chasing anything is an instance of chasing something! Even more generally than that, loving anything, giving anything etc. is an instance of loving something, giving something etc. There is an alternative, and much more elegant way, of capturing the entailment that captures this generalization: namely, represent *something* as a *quantifier* in the formal language (see #51). This illustrates the mutual dependence in modeling semantics between decisions about appropriate notions of entailment and validity and decisions about how one expresses semantic representations of linguistic words and constructions.

Compositional semantic representations also help us get a handle on several kinds of ambiguity (see #10). In most theories, (23a) will be associated with two different syntactic analyses, which provide scaffolding for the two different compositional semantic representations shown in (23b–c), which differ only in the first argument of *with*:

(23)   a.   I saw a kid with a telescope.

   b. $see(e, x, y) \wedge I(x) \wedge kid(y) \wedge with(e, t) \wedge telescope(t)$

   c. $see(e, x, y) \wedge I(x) \wedge kid(y) \wedge with(y, t) \wedge telescope(t)$

This is not to say that syntactic and semantic representations stand in a one-to-one relationship. For instance, as discussed in #53 below, syntactic structure does not (fully) constrain quantifier scope. Conversely, there are cases where any sufficiently broad-coverage grammar of a language finds multiple different syntactic structures that correspond to the same semantic representation. This is true for the English Resource Grammar [Flickinger, 2000, 2011] for sentences like (106), where syntactically the adverb *tomorrow* can combine with the VP *go to school*, the VP *will go to school* or the S *I will go to school*, but in all cases, semantically it is predicated of the going event.

(106)   I will go to school tomorrow.

#48 Compositional semantic representations can be constructed for strings, with and without types and with and without explicit syntax.

There are many different systems, across a range of frameworks, for arriving at compositional semantic representations for input natural language strings. One approach uses *semantic typing* to specify a very transparent and general relationship between the syntactic categorization of a word (that is, the list of specifiers and complements that it combines with in syntax) and the semantic type of the predicate symbol it's associated with in semantics. This transparent relationship is represented explicitly in Montague Grammar [Dowty et al., 1981], Combinatory Categorial Grammar (CCG) [Steedman, 2000], and grammars that combine Dynamic Syntax [Kempson et al., 2000] with a semantic component written within Type Theory with Records (TTRs) [Purver et al., 2011].

In the case of CCG, this tight link between lexical syntactic categories and semantic types has enabled researchers to extend with minimal manual effort an existing wide-coverage CCG parser for English [Clark and Curran, 2004] to include a semantic component; this results in a wide coverage parser that maps natural language strings to logical forms [Bos et al., 2004]. More recently, the tight link between lexical syntax and semantic types has proved useful in two further areas of NLP. The first is the task of learning a mapping from natural language strings to logical form based on training data consisting of pairs of natural language strings and associated logical forms but no information about their syntax [Cheng et al., 2019, Kwiatkowski et al., 2010, Zettlemoyer and Collins, 2007].[5] The second is grounded language acquisition [Dobnik et al., 2012, Yu et al., 2016], which is the task where the machine learns from images that are annotated with descriptions how to classify (in the test phase) whether a description of an (unseen) visual scene is true, or not.

Another approach to broad coverage parsing uses semantic representations that allow certain aspects of meaning of a natural language string to be underspecified. Such representations are motivated by the assumption that some semantic ambiguities can persist even when all syntactic ambiguity is resolved. On this conceptualization, linguistic syntax doesn't produce a complete logical form that gets evaluated against a model of the world, but rather it yields a *partial description* of such a logical form. Minimal Recursion Semantics (MRS) [Copestake et al., 2005], Hole Semantics [Bos, 1995], and Dominance Constraints [Koller et al., 2000] all take this approach, but vary in the algorithms one can use to enumerate the specific and complete logical forms that are satisfied by the partial or underspecified semantic representation that's produced within the grammar.

These formal languages are not typed, but the complete logical forms that they partially describe can be viewed in one of several ways: they can be typed or untyped; first-order (e.g.,

---

[5]The term "semantic parsing" has come to denote this specific body of work where the model learns from pairs of natural language strings and their semantic representations. But of course any parsing algorithm that uses a grammar with a semantic component that produces a semantic representation from each syntax tree that it licenses is also effectively an algorithm for parsing natural language strings into semantics!

representing *fake gun* as *fake*(*x*) ∧ *gun*(*x*)), or higher-order (e.g., *fake*[*gun*](*x*)); and the complete logical forms could receive a static interpretation (of the kind used in Montague Grammar, say) or a dynamic interpretation [Groenendijk and Stokhof, 1991] (see also #69).

#49 Comparatives express the degree to which an entity has some gradable property in relation to some standard of comparison.

All languages have means for expressing *comparatives*—that is, constructions which indicate the extent to which an entity has some gradable property [Kennedy, 2005, Stassen, 1985]. These expressions always involve three components in their semantics: the gradable property, the entity bearing the property, and a standard of comparison. In (107), these are the property of being blue, the sky, and the extent to which the sea is blue.

(107)   The sky is bluer than the sea.

Not all properties are gradable; adjectives expressing non-gradable properties are infelicitous in comparatives, as illustrated in the following examples.[6]

(108)   a. ??Giordano Bruno is more dead than Galileo.

       b. ??Carter is as former a president as Ford.

When the standard of comparison is overt, it can be expressed in many different ways, each involving semantic composition supported by syntactic structure. These include: an expression indicating a separate entity that also has the property (109a); an expression indicating a different property held by the same entity, where the standard of comparison is the degree to which that other property holds (109b); an expression indicating a different property held by a different entity, where the standard of comparison is the degree to which that other property holds (109c); an expression indicating an anticipated value for the degree (109d); and an expression indicating some other state of affairs that is enabled or prevented because the entity holds the gradable property to a sufficient degree (109e). Furthermore, the difference between the standard of comparison and the degree to which the property holds can be measured explicitly, as in (109f).

(109)   a. The Mars Pathfinder mission was less expensive than previous missions to Mars.

       b. More meteorites vaporize in the atmosphere than fall to the ground.

       c. The crater was deeper than a 50-story building is tall.

       d. The flight to Jupiter did not take as long as we expected.

       e. The equipment is too old to be of much use to us.

       f. Mercury is .26 AUs closer to the sun than Venus.

---

[6]Examples (108)–(109) are from Kennedy 2005.

When the standard of comparison is left implicit, its interpretation must be resolved to something in the context:

(110)   This mission is more expensive.

Although all languages have means of expressing comparatives, there is variation in the forms that they use to do so. Stassen [1985] reports several axes of variation. First, some languages (including English) mark the expression of the gradable property as being part of a comparative. In (109), this is done with the adverbs *less* and *more*, the affix *-er*, and the comparative markers *as* and *too*. Other languages allow comparatives without an explicit marker on the expression of the gradable property. This is illustrated for Japanese and Mundari in (111)–(112), where in both cases the only marker of comparison (*yori* and *-ete*, respectively) is associated with the standard of comparison only.

(111)   日本語　は　ドイ語　より 難しい。
      Nihongo ha   doitsugo yori muzukashi-i
      Japanese TOP German than difficult-NPST

      "Japanese is more difficult than German." [jpn] [Stassen, 1985, p. 39]

(112)   Sadom-ete hati   mananga-i.
      horse-from elephant big-3SG.PRS

      "The elephant is bigger than the horse." [unr] [Hoffmann, 1903, p. 110]

In all of the examples above, the point of comparison is expressed as a subconstituent of the main clause. Stassen [1985] also notes languages where comparisons involve conjoined clauses, including Sika and Hixkaryana, as illustrated in (113) and (114):

(113)   Dzarang tica gahar, dzarang rei kesik.
      Horse   that big,   horse   this small

      "That horse is bigger than this horse." [ski] [Arndt, 1931]

(114)   Kaw-ohra naha   Waraka kaw naha   Kaywerye.
      tall-NEG   be.3SG.PRS Waraka tall be.3SG.PRS Kaywerye

      "Kaywerye is taller than Waraka." [hix] [Derbyshire, 1985, p. 86]

#50 Coordinate constructions can be understood in terms of pluralities of entities and events.

The most transparent kind of coordination is the coordination of two sentences, where the truth value of the coordinated sentence is dependent on the truth value of the constituent sentences and the truth conditions of the connective—*but* and *and* require both constituents sentences to be true, while *or* requires one of them to be true:

(115) The bird swooped {and/but/or} the wolf howled.

However, coordination of subsentential constituents is also ubiquitous, and here the syntax-semantics interface requires more care. For example, in (116a), there are two verbs both understood as predicated of the same subject; in (116b) there are two adjectives both understood as predicated of the same head noun; and in (116c) and (116d), there are coordianted NPs which serve as the subject or object of a verb, respectively:

(116) a. The bird swooped and soared.

   b. The big and hungry wolf howled.

   c. The bird and the wolf left.

   d. Kim saw the bird and the wolf.

(116a) and (116b) are relatively straightforward, as the relevant semantic argument can just be shared. The ones with coordinated NPs are trickier. Early accounts [e.g., Partee and Rooth, 1983] treated them as reduced forms of coordinated sentences, so that (116c) is interpreted the same way as (117a), and (116d) the same as (117b):

(117) a. The bird left and the wolf left.

   b. Kim saw the bird and Kim saw the wolf.

However, as Chaves [2007] and others argue, that's not the right approach. Rather, coordinated NPs are plurality denoting constituents, which, like other plural NPs, can combine with both distributive and collective predicates. In (118) and (119), the a examples involve a distributive reading (each kid/each of Kim and Sandy are individually asleep), the b examples a collective reading (the kids/Kim and Sandy met each other), and the c examples are ambiguous between the two. Furthremore, in the d examples, the relative clause *who met* requires a collective interpretation while the main predicate *smiled* a distributive one, on the same NP.

(118) a. The kids are asleep.

   b. The kids met.

   c. The kids weigh 90 kg.

   d. The kids who met smiled.

(119) a. Kim and Sandy are asleep.

   b. Kim and Sandy met.

   c. Kim and Sandy weigh 90 kg.

   d. The actor and the musician who met smiled.

Chaves, following Oehrle [1987] and Lasersohn [1995], further points out that coordinated verbs and adjectives are also best understood as denoting pluralities. In (120a) and (120b), *often* describes the frequency of the joint event types and not of each component event type individually.[7] Similarly, in (120c), *alternately* only makes sense when predicated of the complex state of being sometimes fearful and sometimes angry.

(120) a. Often, Kim goes to the beach and Sue goes to the city.

b. Kim often sang and danced.

c. Kim became alternately fearful and angry.

Note that in (120b) and (120c), even while the predicates are composed into a plurality of events or properties, they both take the same entity (here, *Kim*) as their subject, for the individual events or properties.

Finally, there are coordination constructions which can only be assimilated to the above analysis if they are interpreted as also being instances of ellipsis, as in (121) [Chaves, 2007]:

(121) a. The difference between being an interesting teacher and a tedious teacher is this.

b. This is both the only journal and the last journal ever published by the university.

c. Kim bought a magazine yesterday and bought a newspaper today.

d. Every mother and every father came to the party.

Natural language understanding systems faced with coordination in the data (including not only *and* coordination as discussed here, but also structures with other conjunctions such as *or* and *but*) will need to be prepared to handle the above subtleties in intepretation.

#51 Quantifiers express relations between sets described by predicate-argument structure.

Consider the following two sentences:

(122) a. A dog barked.

b. Every dog barked.

As we explained in #47, formal semantics is built on set theory. It represents the meaning of open-class words as predicate symbols, which in turn denote sets. Quantifiers denote *relations* among sets: intuitively, (122a) is true just in case the intersection of the set of dogs and the set of things that bark is non-empty; and (122b) is true just in case the set of dogs is a subset of the set of things that bark.

Let D be the universe of things. Then abstracting away from dogs and barking (and in particular ignoring the fact that *bark* might be represented as a two-place predicate symbol whose first argument is an event), we can replace them with two sets of individuals X and Y (so $X, Y \subseteq D$), and so produce the following meanings of *a* and *every* [Mostowski, 1957]:

---

[7]There is another reading of (120b) in which *often* attaches low, to *sang* only. That reading is not directly relevant here.

(123)   a. $a_D(X, Y) \longleftrightarrow X \cap Y \neq \emptyset$

   b. $every_D(X, Y) \longleftrightarrow X \subseteq Y$

Other quantifiers can be defined as relations between sets as well, as illustrated in (125) which gives representations for the quantifiers used in (124):

(124)   a. More than two dogs barked.

   b. Neither dog barked.

   c. More than half of the dogs barked.

   d. Only dogs bark.

   e. All but one of the dogs barked.

(125)   a.   more than $2_D(X, Y)$ $\longleftrightarrow$ $|X \cap Y| \geq 2$

   b. $neither_D(X, Y)$ $\longleftrightarrow$ $|X| = 2$ and $X \cap Y = \emptyset$

   c.   more than $half_D(X, Y)$ $\longleftrightarrow$ $|X \cap Y| > \frac{|X|}{2}$

   d. $only_D(X, Y)$ $\longleftrightarrow$ $X \cap Y \neq \emptyset$ and $(D \setminus X) \cap Y = \emptyset$

   e.   all but $one_D(X, Y)$ $\longleftrightarrow$ $|X \cap Y| = |X| - 1$ and
$|X \cap (D \setminus Y)| = 1$

The theory of generalized quantifiers (see #52) builds on this idea that the meaning of a quantifier is a relation between sets. It explicitly represents the *variable* that is bound by the quantifier, and that appears as a free variable in the formulae that denote the sets X and Y in the above definitions (known as the restrictor and body of the quantifier, respectively). A good introduction to the theory of generalized quantifiers is given in Westerståhl 1989.

#52 The semantics of natural language determiners can be represented as generalized quantifiers.

In traditional formal logic, the syntax of the formal language is defined so that a quantifier combines with a variable (which it is said to "bind" for reasons we'll see shortly) and a (single) formula to form a well-formed formula, as in (126) from Gamut [1991a]:

(126)   If ϕ is a well formed formula (wff) and x is a variable, then $\exists x \phi$ and $\forall x \phi$ are also wffs.

In such a logic, the relationship between the sets conveyed by natural language expressions modeled with logical quantifiers ends up being expressed as part of the formula ϕ that the quantifier combines with. This is illustrated in (122) for two English examples:

(122)   a. A dog barked.
$\exists x (dog(x) \wedge bark(x))$

   b. Every dog barked.
$\forall x (dog(x) \rightarrow bark(x))$

Note the presence of different logical connectives, $\wedge$ and $\rightarrow$, in these semantic representations. The reason for this becomes clear by considering how one can (or cannot) paraphrase the two English sentences. Sentence (122a) can be paraphrased as *there is something which is a dog and it barks* but not *there is something such that if it's a dog, then it barks*; on the other hand, (122b) can be paraphrased as *for all things, if it's a dog then it barks*, but not *for all things, it's a dog and it barks*. See also the set relations denoted by these quantifiers in #51; roughly put, conjunction corresponds to set intersection and the conditional to set inclusion. While it is perfectly feasible to compose these distinct formulae compositionally off a syntax tree for English, it rapidly becomes cumbersome to do so in practice. Generalized quantifiers provide a means to ignore this task during semantic composition in the grammar, and instead define the semantics of the quantifiers (i.e., the specific relations between sets) purely via the model theory of the formal language (and hence externally to the grammar and the task of semantic composition).

Specifically, this can be accomplished by introducing quantifiers into well-formed formulae (wffs) as in (127) instead of (126):[8]

(127)   If ϕ and ψ are wffs in which the variable x is free, and Q is a quantifier, then $Qx(\phi, \psi)$ is a wff.

With this revised syntax in the formal language, the logical forms of (122a,b) become (128a,b), respectively:

(128)   a. $\exists x(dog(x), bark(x))$

        b. $\forall x(dog(x), bark(x))$

The next step is to define a model theoretic semantics for the generalized quantifiers so that expressions like (128) can be evaluated against a model to determine their truth values according to the model. As with any model theory, these definitions should be recursive. Furthermore, to adequately represent the meaning of quantifiers, they should determine the Boolean relationship between the truth of the first formula (known as the *restrictor*) and that of the second (known as the *body*). For example, where M is a model (see #2), g is a *variable assignment function* (a function which maps each variable to an individual in the model's domain D) and $g[x/d]$ is the variable assignment function that is the same as g in all respects save that $g[x/d](x) = d$, the truth conditions for the universal and existential quantifiers are as follows (where D is the set of individuals in the model M):

(129) $\llbracket \forall x(\phi, \psi) \rrbracket^{M,g}$ is true iff for all $d \in D$, if $\llbracket \phi \rrbracket^{M,g[x/d]}$ is true then so is $\llbracket \psi \rrbracket^{M,g[x/d]}$.

(130) $\llbracket \exists x(\phi, \psi) \rrbracket^{M,g}$ is true iff there is a $d \in D$ such that $\llbracket \phi \rrbracket^{M,g[x/d]}$ and $\llbracket \psi \rrbracket^{M,g[x/d]}$ are both true.

---

[8]In fact, Q can be viewed as a relation between two lambda terms: e.g., $every(\lambda x(fluffy(x) \wedge dog(x)), \lambda z\, bark(e, z))$, but it is very convenient to use the convention of including a variable x that the quantifier Q binds, and replace the lambda terms with formulae where the lambda-abstracted variable is replaced with a (free) variable x, i.e., $every_x(fluffy(x) \wedge dog(x), bark(e, x))$.

The purpose of having the variable assignment function g be a part of the context of evaluation for the formulae is to allow for the formulae ϕ and ψ to feature other free variables, aside from the one that the quantifier is directly concerning itself with, while ensuring that those free variables are assigned to the same individual in all variable assignments $g[x/d]$ on which the truth of the quantified formula $Qx(\phi, \psi)$ depends. This property of g vs. $g[x/d]$ is needed for getting the right semantics for formulae that feature more than one quantifier. For example, it ensures that (131b), which is one interpretation of (131a), is true only if every dog chased the same cat (we'll talk more about quantifier scope ambiguity of (131) in #53):[9]

(131) a. Every dog chased a cat.

   b. $\exists x(cat(x), \forall y(dog(y), chase(e, x, y)))$

Treating quantifiers this way looks like a small change, both syntactically and semantically. But it enables one to introduce many quantifiers Q into the formal language, each one with its own unique model theoretic interpretation, as required by the range and complexity of natural language expressions whose semantics is best modeled with quantifiers: the Boolean relationship between the restrictor and body can get quite elaborate, as required for expressions like *all but one* or *more than three but less than fifteen*). Indeed, as *all but one* suggests, one should ideally be able to compose a generalized quantifier from its component generalized quantifiers (here, *all* and *one*), as suggested by Westerståhl [1989]. But this is largely still an open (and under-researched) problem.

An additional benefit of generalized quantifiers as a theoretical device is that they make it possible to formalize several observations about the behavior of natural language [Keenan and Westerståhl, 1997, Westerståhl, 1989]. For example, from a logical perspective, it is quite natural to distinguish upwardly monotonic from downwardly monotonic quantifiers:

Upwardly Monotonic: If $[\![Qx(\phi, \psi)]\!]^{M,g}$ is true and $[\![\lambda x\psi]\!]^{M,g} \subseteq [\![\lambda x\psi']\!]^{M,g}$, then $[\![Qx(\phi, \psi')]\!]^{M,g}$ is also true.

Downwardly Monotonic: If $[\![Qx(\phi, \psi)]\!]^{M,g}$ is true and $[\![\lambda x\psi']\!]^{M,g} \subseteq [\![\lambda x\psi]\!]^{M,g}$, then $[\![Qx(\phi, \psi')]\!]^{M,g}$ is also true.

And these definitions turn out to be useful for expressing generalizations about natural language. In this case, they help capture a generalization about negative polarity items. Negative polarity items are a class of words (like English *any*) whose distribution is restricted as follows: they can appear in the scope of a downwardly monotonic quantifier, but not an upwardly monotonic one [Ladusaw, 1980].

(132) No dog chased any cat.

(133) *Every dog chased any cat.

---

[9]Using a variable assignment function g to interpret quantified formulae is common to all formal languages that feature quantifiers, whether they are generalized quantifiers or of the more classical form featured in (126).

This is an important generalization to capture in some applications of NLP, particularly natural language generation and machine translation.

#53 Quantifier scope ambiguity is not fully resolved by syntactic ambiguity resolution.

In sentences with more than one quantifier, we find quantifier scope ambiguities. That is, (134a) can mean either that there is one book that all of the students read or that every student read a book, but not necessarily the same one. The first of these is captured by the representation in (134b), where the universal quantifier shows up inside the *body* (aka *scope*) of the existential. The second reading corresponds to (134c), where the scopal relation is reversed.

(134)　　a.　Every student saw a teacher.

　　　　　b.　$\exists y (teacher(y), \forall x (student(x), see(e, x, y)))$

　　　　　c.　$\forall x (student(x), \exists y (teacher(y), see(e, x, y)))$

One might wonder whether this ambiguity matters: given that (134b) entails (134c), why not just take a conservative position and represent (134a) with (134c)? However, while these two readings are in an entailment relation, only the reading in (134b) licenses the use of the pronoun in a subsequent utterance *I think she was Ms. Smith*. Thus, defining adequate constraints on anaphoric dependencies in discourse requires capturing (and resolving) this semantic scope ambiguity (see #74).

　　　In most theories of grammar (Montague Grammar and CCG being two notable exceptions [Montague, 1974, Steedman, 2000]), there is no syntactic structural ambiguity that the grammar ascribes to (134a) that corresponds to the ambiguity in meaning that's represented by (134b) and (134c).[10] This means that one and the same syntactic structure corresponds to multiple semantic representations. One way to resolve this dilemma is to have each syntactic structure correspond to one underspecified semantic representation. This representation should: (a) capture everything that is common between (134a) and (134b) (e.g., that the bodies of both quantifiers feature the *read* predication as a part); (b) abstract away from the difference in relative semantic scope in the two specific representations; and (c) ensure that this underspecified representation can be further enriched, to arrive at these two fully specified representations. This is the motivation behind systems of underspecified semantic representations such as Minimal Recursion Semantics (MRS) [Copestake et al., 2005], Hole Semantics [Bos, 1995], Underspecified Discourse Representation Theory (UDRT) [Reyle, 1993], and the Constraint Language for Lambda Structures (CLLS) [Egg et al., 2001].

---

[10]Theories of syntax in the transformational tradition, including the current Minimalist Program [Chomsky, 1995] do not make a clear distinction between syntactic and semantic representations, instead positing a series of structures, related by movement or other transformations, that include both a structure for the surface string and a structure that represents the logical form. In such theories, there are multiple different logical form structures for examples like this, but we argue these are still semantic, not syntactic, representations.

For example, MRS gives (135) as the underspecified representation that generalizes over (134a) and (134b). The h variables label each of the pieces of the representation[11] and the last line of this representation is a set of *handle constraints* that give partial information about quantifier scope.

(135) $h0{:}read(e, x, y), h1 : \exists(x, h2, h3), h4 : student(x), h5 : \forall(y, h6, h7), h8 : book(y)$
         $h2 =_q h4, h6 =_q h8$

One gets a fully scoped semantic representation from (135) by equating each h argument in a predication with the label of another, unique predication, while satisfying the handle constraints and ensuring that every instance of a variable is bound by its quantifier. In (135) there are two alternative ways of doing this: $h2 = h4, h3 = h5, h6 = h8$, and $h7 = h0$ yields (134b); and $h2 = h4, h3 = h0, h6 = h8$, and $h7 = h1$ yields (134c).

The idea of enabling a disambiguated syntax to produce an underspecified semantic representation leads to the following question: to what extent does syntactic structure constrain quantifier scope?[12] The mainstream transformational syntax literature argues for quite a few syntactic configurations that constrain quantifier scope, but Hofmeister and Sag [2010] argue that many such constraints are actually due to processing factors rather than rules of grammar. Those that are still seen as grammatical constraints include the constraint that the material inside a noun phrase can only belong to the restrictor, not body, of the quantifier associated with its determiner. Copestake et al. [2005, p. 296] illustrate this with (136), which can mean that there is some famous politician all of whose nephews run, or that anyone who is the nephew of any famous politician runs. In both of these readings, the *nephew* predication is interpreted as part of the restrictor of $\forall$, i.e., the smaller set in the subset relation. Readings where it is in the body (the larger set) are not possible: the sentence cannot be used to mean, for example, that everyone who runs is the nephew of some famous politician.

(136)   Every nephew of some famous politician runs.

In MRS, these facts are captured with partial constraints on quantifier scope that describe where in the scope tree any given predicate can appear. The $=_q$ constraints in (135) indicate that the semantic contribution of *student* and *book* must each appear within the restrictor of their associated quantifiers.

Another example of partially constrained quantifier scope is given in (137):

(137)   All bassoonists and all violinists hate a saxophone player.

Steedman [2012] observes that this sentence can mean that there's one saxophone player hated by all bassoonists and all violinists, or that each bassoonist or violinist hates some saxophone player but not necessarily the same one. However, it can't be used to mean that all the bassoonists

---

[11]Informally, they denote a scopal position in a fully scope-resolved semantic representation.

[12]Of course, it's a separate issue whether resolving quantifier scope is important for NLP; see #55 for a brief discussion.

hate one and the same saxophone player but all violinists potentially different ones.[13] Steedman develops a CCG that rules out the latter reading, but he does so by eschewing all indefinite quantifiers, and instead he uses skolemization to represent all indefinite noun phrases (for an introduction to skolemization, consult Gamut 1991a).

Underspecified logical forms (ULFs) like the one shown in (135) simplify processing by delaying decisions that cannot be made with syntax alone to later steps. For many NLP applications, these underspecified representations are sufficient. However, as we explained in #2, formal semantics is designed to supply semantic representations for which you can define *truth conditions* with respect to a model that is an abstract representation of the state of the world. And while fully specific logical forms can be directly evaluated against such models, the interpretation of ULFs is one step removed from this. A typical approach is to interpret each ULF as a partial description of a fully specific logical form [Egg et al., 2001]. For example, the ULF in (135) is a partial description of both (134b) and (134c) and conversely (134b) and (134c) both *satisfy* (135). To put this another way, the models against which one interprets ULFs do not represent the state of the world, but rather each model corresponds to a unique formula in the langauge in which one represents fully specific logical forms (which in turn is used to evaluate truth against the actual state of affairs).

This approach to interpreting ULFs provides some flexibility, in that it allows us to distinguish the inferences we need in order to construct from linguistic syntax a (semantic) representation of what was said vs. the inferences we need to evaluate whether what was said is true, given the current state of affairs. To put this more technically, the ULFs that a grammar composes afford some flexibility in exactly what theory of fully specific formal semantic representations one adopts for defining the truth conditions of utterances in context [Asher and Lascarides, 2003]. In other words, ULFs produced compositionally by a grammar can be seen as partial descriptions of formulae in a wide range of different formal languages: for instance, one might choose the formal language in which fully specific logical forms is expressed to be that of classical first-order logic, Discourse Representation Theory (DRT) [Kamp and Reyle, 1993] or a language that admits higher types (see #48). Further, making the interpretation of a ULF independent of the model theory one uses to interpret the fully specific logical forms means that the latter can be static or it could be dynamic (see #69).

#54 The relative scope of other scopal operators, however, is resolved by syntactic structure.

Languages also have scopal operators other than quantifiers. These can be detected because they interact scopally with quantifiers. They include negation, (other) scopal adverbs like *probably*, modals like *should*, and clause-embedding verbs such as *believe*, as illustrated in (138a–d):

(138)   a. Kim didn't read three books.

---

[13]The MRS representations produced by the ERG don't capture this restriction.

    b. Kim probably read three books.

    c. Kim should read three books.

    d. Kim believes a unicorn was in the park.

In (138a), the two readings are: "there are three books that Kim didn't read" and "it is not the case that there are three books that Kim read." Similarly, (138b) and (138c) can mean either "there are three books that Kim probably read/should read" (i.e., for each of those three books, it is probable that Kim read them/Kim should read them) or "it is probably/should be the case that Kim read three books." Finally, in (138d), the existential quantifier expressed by *a* can be inside the scope of *believe*, such that the speaker is not asserting the existence of a unicorn, or outside, where the speaker is.[14]

    Some predicates, including connectives like *because* embed two clausal arguments, and both show interactions with quantifiers:

(139)   a. Every student passed the exam because it was (too) easy.

       b. Their parents celebrated because every student passed the exam.

The differences between these readings are subtle, but (139a) can mean either that for each student it was the case that they passed the exam because it was (too) easy or that it was because it was too easy that the whole group of student passed. Similarly, (139b) can mean that there were separate celebrations for each student inspired by their passing or that the parents were collectively celebrating the fact that all the students passed.

    These facts lead semanticists to model all of these elements as scope-taking, like quantifiers. However, unlike quantifiers, the scope of these elements is generally fixed by the morphosyntax, and the ambiguity in the examples above can be attributed to the fact that the quantifiers have freedom in where they take scope. The fixed scope of non-quantificational scopal operators can be seen when they co-occur as illustrated for English and Japanese in (140):

(140)   a. Kim probably believes that Sandy saw a unicorn.

       b. サンディー が　ユニコーン を　見た　　と　キム は　多分　　思う。
          Sandii　　ga　yunikoon　wo mi-ta　to　Kimu ha tabun　omo-u
          Sandy　　NOM unicorn　ACC see-PST COMP Kim　TOP probably think-NPST

       "Kim probably believes that Sandy saw a unicorn." [jpn]

These can only mean that it's probably the case that Kim holds that belief, and not that the speaker is certain that Kim believes Sandy probably saw a unicorn.

    In some cases, the grammatical rules fixing the scope can be quite subtle, as is the case with English modal auxiliaries and scopal adverbs they combine with. Note that (141a–b) share truth conditions, even though the adverb and the modal appear in different orders.

---

[14]In fact, the situation is more complicated than this (see the infamous Hobb-Nob example in Geach 1962), but we gloss over this here.

(141) a. Kim probably should read the book.

   b. Kim should probably read the book.

This is related to the fact that the relative scope of post-modal adverbs is controlled by the modal and lexically specific. This is particularly clear with negation, as shown in the following examples from Kim and Sag [2002] [see also Warner, 2000]:

(142) a. Paul could not have worked as hard, could he?

   b. Paul must not accept the offer.

In (142a), negation takes wide scope over the modal ("it's not the case that Paul could have worked as hard") whereas in (142b) the modal must have wide scope ("It must be the case that Paul doesn't accept.").

   We observe some cross-linguistic variation on this point, in particular in languages where negation is expressed morphologically on the main verb. Bender and Lascarides [2013, pp. 112–114] note the following examples from Turkish and Inuktitut, where the former allows either ordering of the two scopal operators (negation and causative) whereas in the latter it's fixed by their order in the word.[15]

(143) Ebeveyn-ler çocuk-lar-ına meyve yedir-t-me-di-ler.
   Parent-PL child-PL-DAT fruit eat-CAUS-NEG-PST-3PL

   a. "The parents did not make (or force) the kids to eat the fruit."

   b. "The parents made the kids not eat the fruit." [tur]

(144) a. ᐊᓂᖕᒋᑦᑎᑕᕋ
      ani-nngit-tit-tara.
      go.out-NEG-CAUS-1SG.3SG.TR

      "I cause him/her not to go out." [ike]

   b. ᐊᓂᑎᑦᖕᒋᑕᕋ
      ani-tit-nngit-tara.
      go.out-CAUS-NEG-1SG.3SG.TR

      "I did not make him/her go out." [ike]

#55 The importance of correctly representing scopal operators depends on the NLP application.

Correctly identifying elements negation and other scopal adverbs and/or their relative semantic scope may be unimportant for some NLP tasks, such as information retrieval, where a page can still be relevant to a search query even if the relevant sentence is negated. For example, (145) may be highly relevant to a user seeking information about Pokémon popularity:

[15]Bender and Lascarides credit Elke Nowak, pc, for the examples in (144).

(145)   Pikachu is not the most popular Pokémon anymore.

Other NLP tasks, however, are highly sensitive to both the presence of negation and its relative scope to other scope-bearing elements. A clear example is the task of classifying patient records for presence or absence of a condition: a proper understanding of negation and markers of uncertainty are critical to correct classification, as illustrated in (146a) and (146b), from Vincze et al. [2008]. This has motivated the development of the BioScope corpus [Vincze et al., 2008], as well as a number of shared tasks [e.g., Farkas et al., 2010, Kim et al., 2009, Morante and Blanco, 2012].

(146)   a.   There is no primary impairment of glucocorticoid metabolism in the asthmatics.

     b.   Slightly increased perihilar lung markings may indicate early reactive airways disease.

Correct handling of negation is critical for translation adequacy in machine translation (an effect not well measured by BLEU; Wetzel and Bond, 2012). On the other hand, machine translation is not particularly sensitive to quantifier scope ambiguity—this was one of the original motivations for the development of the underspecified semantic representations mentioned in #53 [Alshawi et al., 1991, Wahlster, 2000]. The situation is complex, however, because of examples of cross linguistic differences that mean fully accurate machine translation requires resolving quantifier scope ambiguities. For example, according to Scontras et al. [2017, p. 5], Mandarin Chinese does not have a single sentence that represents both readings of English (147a), so a translation system would need to determine which is intended in order to make the correct choice between (147b) and (147c).[16]

(147)   a.   Every shark attacked a pirate.

     b.   每一条　　　鲨鱼 都 攻击了　一个　　　海盗.
       Měi-yì-tiáo　　shāyú dōu gōngjí-le　yī-gè　　　hǎidào.
       every-one-NUMCL shark all　attack-PST one-NUMCL pirate

       "Every shark attacked a/one pirate." ($\forall > \exists$ only) [cmn]

     c.   有　一个　　　海盗　被　　　　　　　每一条　　　鲨鱼 都 袭击了.
       Yǒu　yī-gè　　hǎidào bèi　　　　　měi-yī-tiáo shāyú dōu gōngjí-le.
       Exist one-NUMCL pirate　every-one-NUMCL PASS　　　shark all　attack-PST

       "There's one pirate that's been attacked by every shark." ($\exists > \forall$ only) [cmn]

Quantifier scope ambiguities are by and large unproblematic for question answering systems—in practice, assuming that the relative scope of the quantifiers matches their textual order does no harm to the overall performance of the system (Johan Bos, personal communication). It has also been argued that human language processors resolve ambiguity only when it's needed for the current purposes of the conversation [Clark, 1992]. In particular, people don't always resolve semantic scope ambiguities [e.g., Sanford and Graesser, 2006, Sanford and Sturt, 2002]. Hobbs [1983] illustrates the phenomenon with (148):

---

[16](147c) is not directly from Scontras et al. 2017, but rather added to show the contrast to (147b).

(148)   In most democratic countries, most politicians can fool most of the people on almost every issue most of the time.

Under some theories of grammar, there are 120 ways of resolving the relative scope of the quantifiers, all of which have distinct truth conditions (in other words, for any pair of readings among the 120 possibilities, there is a model that satisfies one but not the other; see #2 and #51). However, it is intuitively clear that people understand this sentence, in some sense at least, without having to resolve this ambiguity; they may never identify which of those 120 readings the speaker intended. Hobbs proposed a treatment of quantifiers which is then generalized in theories of semantic underspecification (see #53, Bos, 1995, Reyle, 1993, and Copestake et al., 2005).

While fully resolving quantifier scope may be unnecessary in many contexts, there are linguistic phenomena that are conditioned on how it gets resolved. One of them is pronouns in discourse (see Chapter 10): specifically, which elements in the discourse context are available as antecedents to the pronoun in the current utterance? The answer to this question depends on the relative semantic scope of the quantifiers in that discourse context:

(149)   a. A person gets run over on Princes Street every day.

        b. He's getting really pissed off about it.

Given real-world knowledge, the most natural interpretation of (149a) is one where *every* semantically outscopes *a*. But the continuation of this discourse in (149b) is one where an interpretation of the pronoun *he* is possible only if *a* outscopes *every* (i.e., it's the same man that gets run over every day): this is the only way to identify an available referent in the context that *he* can denote [Kamp and Reyle, 1993].

#56 Compositional semantics interacts with word sense.

In Chapter 4, we discussed constructional polysemy and co-predication (see especially #19). In that discussion, we appealed to co-predication examples like (41) to illustrate the way that different predicates can pick out different component parts of a structured denotation:

(41)   That book on the shelf is about syntax.

Having now introduced the notion of predicate-argument structure and logical form representations which relate predicates to each other using variables, we are in a position to make that notion of selection more concrete. Pustejovsky [1991, 1995] calls the phenomenon where a predicate selects for the component part of a structured semantic representation of complex semantic type *semantic co-composition*. Rich lexical entries like (49), repeated here from #20, provide multiple different variables that can serve as arguments, and these in turn are typed: for example, **x:ind** means that x denotes a physical individual; and **y:abstr** means that y denotes an abstract individual. Only structures where predicates take variables of the right type are semantically well-formed.

(49)
$$
\begin{bmatrix}
\textbf{book} \\
\text{argstr} : \begin{bmatrix} \text{arg1} : \textbf{x:ind} \\ \text{arg2} : \textbf{y:abstr} \end{bmatrix} \\
\text{qualia} : \begin{bmatrix} \text{agentive} : \textbf{write(e,w,y)} \\ \text{telic} : \textbf{read(e,z,y)} \end{bmatrix}
\end{bmatrix}
$$

If *book* in (49) is the argument of *read*, then *read* takes the variable y as its argument (because *read* is restricted to taking variables of type **abstr** as its argument). If instead it's the argument of *move*, then *move* takes the variable x as its argument. Thus, word sense interacts with semantic composition on the syntax tree, because word senses are structured and of complex semantic types.

Note that this specialization of senses will also interact with quantification: For example *every book in the library* can refer to the physical objects (the 1000 physical books that are in the library, say) or the abstract content (in which case there may be less than 1000 instances in the same library, because there may be multiple physical copies of the same book). The verb *read* selects for abstract content and *move* selects for the physical object, and thus the domains quantified over in (150) are different [Asher, 2011], and their truth conditions are different:

(150)   a.   Kim read every book in the library.

      b.   Kim moved every book in the library.

For instance, (150a) can be true even when Kim hasn't read every physical copy of *War and Peace* that's in the library: reading one copy of *War and Peace* will do, and it doesn't even have to be a copy of that book that has ever been in the library in question! But (150b) is true only if Kim moves every physical copy of *War and Peace* that's in the library.

#57 The semantics of a phrase that's derived by composing distributional models of its words is highly sensitive to how the vectors are composed.

This chapter has focused so far on the formal semantic approach to composing meaning representations. Formal semantic representations are defined in terms of truth and reference, and they are designed to predict logical relationships (see #2): for instance, that (151a) entails (151b) but contradicts (151c).

(151)   a.   A philanthropist gave cash to a charity.

      b.   A philanthropist gave something.

      c.   No philanthropist gave anything.

      d.   A philanthropist donated money to a charity.

      e.   A charity donated money to a philanthropist.

But the discrete symbols in the semantic representation and their set-theoretic interpretations are not particularly suited to reasoning quantitatively about semantic similarity, e.g., to predict that (151a) is semantically similar to (151d), while (151e) is not.

Distributional models of meaning offer a different perspective (see #25 and #26). A word is represented as a vector, which captures information about the contexts in which the word is used. Distributional models of words can be constructed very easily from large open-domain corpora, and quantitative measures of semantic similarity are easily defined, for instance in terms of the cosine measure (see Equation (4.1) on page 48). These models are designed to predict the similarity between *give* and *donate*, and between *cash* and *money*. So to capture semantic similarity among phrases, and not just words, researchers have recently focused on methods for composing the distributional models of words into a semantic representation for a phrase.

The commonest method for combining vectors is to average them. In distributional models of word meaning, vector averaging has proved useful in some NLP applications, like essay grading [Landauer and Dumais, 1997]. But it is insensitive to word order and so it cannot capture the correct relationships between (151a) and (151b) or (151c) [Mitchell and Lapata, 2008]. In effect, vector averaging doesn't fully capture the principle of compositionality. Specifically, it ignores that part of the principle that says that the syntax rule that combines the components into a phrase influences semantic composition: i.e., the formal semantic principle is that the semantic representation of a phrase p is a function of not only of the semantics of its parts (q and r, say) but also the syntax rule that combines q and r to form p (Montague, 1974; see also #2).

Mitchell and Lapata [2008] introduce a general framework for studying how various ways of doing vector composition impact the task of measuring semantic similarity among phrases. They show, via correlations with human judgments on semantic similarity, that composition based on multiplication, as given in (7.1) where C is a fixed parameter, works better than composition based on addition, as given in (7.2), where A and B are fixed parameters:

$$\vec{p} = C\vec{q}.\vec{r} \tag{7.1}$$

$$\vec{p} = A\vec{q} + B\vec{r} \tag{7.2}$$

They argue that this is because addition simply lumps the content of the two vectors together, while multiplication picks out the content relevant to their combination, scaling each component of one vector with the strength of the corresponding component of the other. This operation for composition offers a decent approximation of human judgments on semantic similarity on small phrases, such as *hard problem* vs. *hard cheese*. But Baroni et al. [2014, p. 265] argue that it is also quite limited: it highly appealing to compose the meaning of a phrase like *hard problem* as a mixture of features that have been observed in the corpus for *hard* things and for *problems*. But this doesn't seem an appropriate way to compose phrases that include grammatical words like *some*. Furthermore, while the parameter C can work as a proxy for the contribution of syntax to semantic composition when focused on a particular type of syntactic phrase (e.g., adjective noun combinations), one would need a different factor C for other syntactic combinations.

A second approach, therefore, retains more of the standard methods of composition that's familiar from formal semantics, using grammars like HPSG [Pollard and Sag, 1994] or CCG [Steedman, 2000]. The aim is to retain the formal semantic analysis of function words, while enhancing the interpretation of predicate symbols corresponding to open-class words with distributional information. Coecke et al. [2010] use tensor products to compose distributional models in a way that's sensitive to predicate-argument structure: nouns are vectors, intransitive verbs are matrices (mapping noun vectors to sentence vectors), transitive verbs are third-order tensor products, and so on. But this method of composition cannot handle quantifiers [Grefenstette, 2013].

Lewis and Steedman [2013] use CCG to construct logical forms and they use distributional information in a large corpus to induce relational constants for open-class words, where each constant is associated (via distributional clustering) with probability distributions over semantic types of the entities involved: for example, *suit* is associated with a probability distribution, where it denotes *clothes* with probability 0.6, *legal* with probability 0.3, and so on. When the logical form of a phrase z is composed via function application on the lambda-terms of its constituent parts x and y, the updated probabilities on the types of denotations are the product of the type distributions for x and y:

$$p_z(t) = \frac{p_x(t) p_y(t)}{\sum'_t P_x(t') p_y(t')} \tag{7.3}$$

Thus, *file a suit* will disambiguate to be about legal matters, even though both *file* and *suit* are ambiguous, while *wear a suit* will disambiguate to be about clothes. This method of composition exploits distributional models to produce the clustering and probability distributions over semantic types and it is shown to be useful for resolving semantic ambiguity, but the semantic representations so produced don't support quantitative metrics of semantic similarity in the way that vectors do.

A further grammar-driven approach to composition is proposed by Emerson [2018] [see also Emerson and Copestake, 2016]. A logical form, featuring predicate symbols and their arguments, is constructed via a grammar in the usual way. But the interpretation of atomic formulae, like $give(e, x, y)$, is generalized to be a probability, rather than simply true or false. The idea is that for each entity in the logical form (e.g., e, x, and y), one can ask which predicates are likely to be true of it. If the situation is one where a philanthropist gives cash to a charity, then it is highly likely that e is a donating event, x is a rich person and y is an organization, and highly unlikely that e is a voting event, x is a table and y is democracy. These probabilities are estimated via a feedforward neural network that associates each predicate c with a vector of weights that determines the strength of association of c with each dimension of the semantic space—i.e., with other predicate symbols corresponding to other open-class words. Thus, it addresses directly the task of estimating semantic similarity among phrases, while being able to retain the formal semantic approach to both semantic composition and the treatment of function words.

CHAPTER 8

Compositional Semantics beyond Predicate-Argument Structure

#58 Compositional semantics includes grammaticized concepts, such as tense, aspect, evidentials, presupposition triggers, or politeness.

The previous chapter focused on predicate-argument structure and the representation of quantifiers and other scope-bearing elements like negation, which together form the heart of compositional semantics. However, if we see "compositional semantics" as concerning all aspects of natural language meanings that are constrained or scaffolded by the grammar of the language, including both morphology and syntax [Bender et al., 2015], then it includes quite a bit more. In this chapter, we will briefly describe several facets of natural language meaning that share this property, including tense (#60), aspect (#61), evidentials (#62), and politeness (#63–#65). Syntax and morphology also provide at least partial constraints on presuppositions (see Chapter 11) and information status and information structure (see Chapter 12).

#59 The concepts that are grammaticized and how they are grammaticized vary from language to language.

All languages have words which express argument-taking semantic predicates and grammatical means of associating syntactic arguments to semantic ones. In some languages, like English and Mandarin, word order is the primary means of signaling which argument is which. Accordingly, the sentence pairs in (152) and (153) are not paraphrases of each other:

(152)   a. The tiger saw the dog.

        b. The dog saw the tiger.

(153)   a. 老虎　看见了　　狗.
           lǎohǔ kànjiàn-le gǒu
           tiger see-PF   dog

           "The tiger saw the dog." [cmn]

b. 狗 看见了 老虎.
gǒu kànjiàn-le lǎohǔ
dog see-PF   tiger

"The dog saw the tiger." [cmn]

In languages like Japanese and German, word order is more flexible, and case marking is key to argument linking. In (154) and (155), the a and b examples are paraphrases (although contrasting in their information structure; see #84), but the c examples contrast in their meaning.

(154) a. 虎　が　犬　を　見た。
tora ga inu wo mi-ta
tiger NOM dog ACC see-PST

"The tiger saw the dog." [jpn]

b. 犬　を　虎　が　見た。
inu wo tora ga mi-ta
dog ACC tiger NOM see-PST

"The tiger saw the dog." [jpn]

c. 犬　が　虎　を　見た。
inu ga tora wo mi-ta
dog NOM tiger ACC see-PST

"The dog saw the tiger." [jpn]

(155) a. Der   Tiger hat   den   Hund ge-seh-en.
the.MASC.NOM tiger have.3SG the.MASC.ACC dog   PTCP-see-PTCP

"The tiger saw the dog." [deu]

b. Den   Hund hat   der   Tiger ge-seh-en.
the.MASC.ACC dog have.3SG the.MASC.NOM tiger PTCP-see-PTCP

"The tiger saw the dog." [deu]

c. Der   Hund hat   den   Tiger ge-seh-en.
the.MASC.NOM dog have.3SG the.MASC.ACC tiger PTCP-see-PTCP

"The dog saw the tiger." [deu]

Still other languages make primary use of agreement markers on the verb to differentiate arguments. This is illustrated in (156) for Tzutujil (a Mayan language of Guatemala).

(156) jar aak'aalaa7 x-Ø-kee-k'aq   aab'aj pa rwi7 ja jaay.
the boy.PL   COMP-3SG-3PL-throw rock   on top.of the house

"The boys threw rock(s) on top of the house." [tzj] [Dayley, 1985, p. 282]

Nichols [1986] develops the general notions of *head marking* and *dependent marking* to describe where (if anywhere) the relationship between a dependent and a head is marked. Nichols and Bickel [2013] survey the marking patient-like arguments in 236 languages for their chapter in *The World Atlas of Language Structures Online* (WALS) [Dryer and Haspelmath, 2013]. They find a fairly even spread between head-marking (71 languages), dependent-marking (68), double-marking (58), and no marking (42), plus 2 languages categorized as "other."

Beyond predicate-argument structure, however, there is great variation in what is grammaticized—that is, which concepts have dedicated grammatical systems for their expression. Again turning to surveys in WALS, we find that 88 of the 222 languages surveyed had no marking of a past/non-past tense distinction [Dahl and Velupillai, 2013a], and 121 of 222 had no marking of a perfective/imperfective aspect distinction [Dahl and Velupillai, 2013b]. Similarly, de Haan [2013] finds that 181 of 418 languages lack grammatical evidentials (see #62); of the remaining 237, 131 use verbal affixes or clitics to express these concepts. Aspects of meaning that seem utterly essential from the perspective of English, such as the singular/plural distinction on nouns, can be marked only optionally or not at all in other languages. Conversely, English is relatively impoverished when it comes to aspect and evidentials, both of which are frequently sites of rich grammatical elaboration in other languages.

#60 Tense encodes the three-way relationship between speech time, event time, and an anaphorically determined reference time.

Prior [1957] proposed a treatment of tense in modal logic. The past tense, for instance, is represented with a modal operator $\mathcal{P}$, where $\mathcal{P}\phi$ is true now just in case ϕ is true at some time before now. More formally, a model $\mathcal{M}$ that is used to interpret $\mathcal{P}\phi$ includes a set of times in a total order, and the truth conditions of $\mathcal{P}\phi$ are evaluated against $\mathcal{M}$ and a time t that intuitively is "now" or the time of speech:

(157) $[\![\mathcal{P}\phi]\!]^{\langle \mathcal{M}, t \rangle}$ iff there is a time $t' \prec t$ in M such that $[\![\phi]\!]^{\langle \mathcal{M}, t' \rangle}$

Prior never claimed that his modal tense logic is an adequate representation of natural language tense. Nevertheless, it gained traction in early formal semantic frameworks [e.g., Montague, 1974], in spite of the fact that Reichenbach [1947] observes properties of natural language tense that aren't definable within the above modal logic scheme. Specifically, Reichenbach claims that when a speaker utters a sentence in the English past tense, they aren't asserting that the event happened at some indefinite time in the past (as $\mathcal{P}\phi$ captures); rather, they are asserting that it happened at a particular past time, and that particular time is context specific. (This is true of the past tense in other languages that mark it as well.) For instance, imagine that you're in the car, about to leave the house to go to the theater. Suddenly you say (158):

(158)   I left the oven on!

Under a Priorean interpretation, this is almost certainly true: there is bound to be at least one time in the past when the oven was on and you left it on! But that's not what you mean here: what you mean is that just before you got into the car you left the oven on. In other words, you are asserting that at a particular past time you left the oven on, and you are relying on your interlocutor's ability to identify the particular past time you have in mind from the context in which you uttered the sentence.

The semantics of Prior's [1957] modal tense operators are defined in terms of a relation between two times: i.e., the time of speech and a time at which the (tenseless) proposition is true—this latter time is known as the *event time* because it is conceived of as the time at which the event that's described by the sentence occurs. In contrast, Reichenbach [1947] proposes that tense should be defined in terms of a relation between three times: the time of speech, the event time and an anaphorically determined *reference time*. The reference time is anaphoric in the sense that its referent is determined by context (much like the referents for pronouns are determined by context); in (158), the reference time would be the time interval just before the speaker got into the car.

Having a reference time, in addition to an event time and speech time, captures the intuition that (158) is a claim about what happened at a particular past time: the reference time is a specific time that is identified in virtue of the context of the utterance, and the semantics of the past tense is satisfied only if the event time is identical to this reference time, which in turn is before now. Thus, simply having left the oven on be true of some past time is no longer a sufficient condition for the past tense sentence to be true: leaving the oven on must be true of the specific, and contextually determined, (past) reference time. Intuitively, the reference time provides a temporal perspective from which we look at the time of the event itself.

Arguably, to define the past tense, one could (in principle at least) do away with the reference time and impose its anaphoric properties onto the event time, thereby preserving the semantics of the past tense as a binary temporal relationship. But to do this misses important linguistic generalizations across the different tenses in natural language. The three-way relationship among times provides the basis for distinguishing the different tenses in English, for instance. The perfect sentence *I have left* and the past tense sentence *I left* both entail that the event time E is before the time of speech S; their difference lies in the temporal relationship between the reference time R and these other times. For the perfect tense,[1] $E \prec R = S$—or to put this another way, the speaker is viewing a past event from the perspective of now. For the past tense, $R = E \prec S$—the perspective from which the event is viewed is in the past. The overall proposed tense system for English is given in (159), where E is the event time, R is the reference time and S is the time of speech:

---

[1]Some authors [e.g., Moens and Steedman, 1988] argue that perfects aren't tenses; for simplicity we follow Reichenbach's [1947] classification here.

(159)
$$\begin{array}{rl} \text{present } (\textit{Kim leaves}): & E, R, S \\ \text{simple past } (\textit{Kim left}): & E, R \prec S \\ \text{pluperfect, also called past perfect } (\textit{Kim had left}): & E \prec R \prec S \\ \text{simple future } (\textit{Kim will leave}): & S \prec E, R \\ \text{present perfect } (\textit{Kim has left}): & E \prec R, S \\ \text{present future } (\textit{Kim leaves next week}): & S, R \prec E \\ \text{future perfect } (\textit{Kim will have left}): & S \prec E \prec R \end{array}$$

This notion of the temporal perspective from which an event is viewed, as illustrated by the different relationship between E and R in the simple past vs. perfect sentences in English, is also relevant for grammatical systems marking *aspect*. We discuss this in more detail in #61.

#61 Aspect encodes the description of the internal temporal properties of the event and how it's viewed.

Where tense systems (#60) are grammaticized means of encoding the location in time of an event, aspect systems are grammaticized means of encoding the temporal properties of the event itself. Broadly speaking, these break down into two types of systems [see, e.g., Smith, 1991]: those relating to inherent temporal properties of an event (known as situation aspect or Aktionsart) and those relating to how the event is viewed, e.g., as completed or on-going (known as viewpoint aspect).

Situation aspect is usually described in terms of a small number of situation types. Vendler [1957] posits four: statives, activities, achievements, and accomplishments. Statives describe situations which extend over time and are static throughout their duration. These include predicates such as *know* or *be happy*. Activities are like statives, except they are dynamic rather than static: *run, row, draw*. Achievements describe instantaneous changes of state, such as *arrive, win,* or *die*. Finally, accomplishments describe an activity and its culminating change of state: *fill* or *dissolve*.

Situation aspect is both lexical and compositional [Moens and Steedman, 1988, Pustejovsky, 1995]. It is lexical in the sense that it is part of the lexical semantics of particular words, i.e., how those words conceptualize part of the world. For example, *sneeze* is categorized as an achievement—an instantaneous event—on the grounds that it passes the standard linguistic tests for achievements (e.g., *Kim is sneezing* normally has an iterative interpretation); but in actual fact a single sneeze occurs over a non-instantaneous time interval. It is compositional in the sense that the situation aspect of a verb phrase or a sentence can depend not only on the verb but also its complements and modifiers. For example, the sentences in (160) (adapted from Poulson, 2011) all involve the same main verb but vary between activities and accomplishments:[2]

---

[2]Note that the modifier *in an hour*, diagnostic of change of state, is incompatible with *read* without an overt object, or unless there is a contextually salient object that is being read: **Kim read in an hour* [Dowty, 1979].

(160)   a. Kim read. (Activity)

      b. Kim read the book. (Accomplishment)

      c. Kim read the book for an hour. (Activity)

      d. Kim read the book in an hour. (Accomplishment)

And of course the lexical and compositional properties of situation aspect interact: Kiparsky [1998] finds that a small class of Finnish verbs are underspecified for situation aspect but the case marking on their complement resolves it. For example, the verb illustrated in (161) denotes an activity if the complement has partitive case and an accomplishment if the complement has accusative case. This is reflected in the translation of the verb as either "shoot at" (161a) or "shoot" (161b).

(161)   a. Ammu-i-n   karhu-a.
        shoot-PST-1SG bear-PART

        "I shot at the/a bear." [fin]

      b. Ammu-i-n   karhu-n.
        shoot-PST-1SG bear-ACC

        "I shot the/a bear." [fin]

While situation aspect relates to how a particular set of lexical choices describes the temporal properties of a situation, viewpoint aspect is the grammatical means by which languages allow speakers to describe a particular temporal viewpoint on the situation. The primary contrast here is between *perfective* aspects, which view a situation or event as completed or including its end point and *imperfective* aspects which view it "from the inside," i.e., without its end points. Mainstream U.S. and UK English are relatively impoverished when it comes to viewpoint aspect, but they do have a progressive aspect, which is a kind of imperfective. Thus, the progressive sentence in (162) views the event of reading a book (an accomplishment with an inherent end point) as incomplete/in progress:

(162)   Kim was reading the book when Sandy arrived.

Languages can have quite rich aspectual systems, with specific grammatical forms for such viewpoints as the end of a situation (*cessative aspect*, as in (163), from Sonora Yaqui) or the habitual occurrence of a situation (*habitual aspect*, as in (164) from African American English or (165) from Wambaya).

(163)   ču'u 'ıntok čai-yaate-k 'a'a nok-hıkkaha-ka-i.
      dog and   yell-stop-PF him talk-hear-PPL-STAT

      "The dog stopped barking when he heard him talking." [yaq] [Dedrick and Casad, 1999, p. 322]

(164)   Leontyne always be singing new songs.
      "Leontyne always sings new songs/a new song." [Green, 1993, p. 43]

(165)   Manku nga-ny-ala   girra.
         hear   1.SG.A-2.O-HAB.NPST 2.PL.ACC

         "I will always be thinking about you." [wmb] [Nordlinger, 1998, p. 147]

The expression of viewpoint aspect is often tightly bound up with that of tense (and also mood). For example, in (165), the suffix *-ala* marks both habitual aspect and non-past tense.

#62 Evidentials encode the source a speaker credits the information to and/or the degree of certainty the speaker feels about it.

Another kind of meaning that some but not all languages provide specific grammatical formatives for involves both the source of the information a speaker is conveying (in a declarative) and the speaker's degree of certainty regarding that information. English does not grammaticize this, but these meanings can of course be expressed with longer phrases, as in (166):

(166)   a. *Apparently*, Kim is the winner.

         b. *I've heard that* Kim won.

         c. *It looks like* it's raining.

In languages where these contrasts are grammaticized, they form systems of opposing *terms* that carve up the possible meaning space in different ways. Aikhenvald [2004] provides a typology of these systems, categorizing them on the basis of the specific inventory of terms and the number of terms.

For example, two-term systems may involve contrasts between: (a) firsthand and non-firsthand information; (b) non-firsthand information and everything else (where everything else includes underspecification of the information source); or (c) reported (the information was reported to the speaker) and everything else. Systems with more terms may have specific markers for direct or visual evidence, non-visual sensory evidence, inferred information, and assumed information in addition to the above categories.

An example of a particularly elaborate evidentiality system that Aikhenvald [2004] cites is the six-term system of Foe (Papua New Guinea), described by Rule [1977]. This system distinguishes participatory, visual, non-visual sensory, deductive, inference based on visible evidence, and inference based on previous evidence. These are illustrated in the following examples, from Rule [1977, pp. 71–74]:

(167)   a. na mini wa-bugege.
             I   today come-PRS.PARTICIPATORY.EV

             "I am coming today." [foi]

         b. aiya bare wa-boba'ae.
             air   plane come-VIS.EV

             "An airplane is coming" (can see it) [foi]

c. aiya bare   wa-bida'ae.
    air   plane come-NONVIS.EV

    "An airplane is coming" (can only hear it) [foi]

d. Kabe Irabo wa-ada'ae.
    Mr   Irabo come-DEDUCTIVE.EV

    "Mr Irabo is coming" (can hear him speaking and can recognize his voice) [foi]

e. Agu amena wa-boba'ae.
    Agu men   come-VIS.EVIDENCE.EV

    "The Agu men are coming" (can see the smoke rising on the Agu track) [foi]

f. Kabe Maduane minage wa-bubege.
    Mr   Maduane still   come-PREVIOUS.EVIDENCE.EV

    "Mr Maduane is still coming" (both left together, but the speaker came faster than Maduane, and so he knows he's still on the way) [foi]

Evidential systems can be intertwined with other systems, as is the case in Turkish and other Turkic languages where there is a distinction between evidential and non-evidential past tense markers, as shown in (168) from Göksel and Kerslake [2004, p. 356]:

(168) a. (Ali, to Gül):

           Bahçe-ye   bir meşe ağac-ı   dik-ti-m.
           garden-DAT an oak   tree-NC plant-PF-1SG

           "I've planted an oak tree in the garden." [tur]

       b. (Gül, to Orhan):

           Ali bahçe-sin-e   bir meşe ağac-ı   dik-miş.
           Ali garden-3SG.POSS-DAT an oak   tree-NC plant-EV/PF

           "Ali has apparently planted an oak tree in the garden." [tur]

#63 Politeness markers can encode relative status of or social distance between speaker and referent or speaker and addressee.

Many of the world's languages provide grammaticized means of encoding information about social status or social distance. These, in turn, are used in expressing politeness or solidarity [Brown and Levinson, 1978]. One strategy that is prominent among European languages in particular is distinctions among second-person pronouns. For example, German [deu] distinguishes three second-person pronouns: *du* (singular, familiar), *ihr* (plural, familiar), and *Sie* (number unspecified, honorific). French [fra] has two: *tu* (singular, familiar) and *vous* (singular, honorific or plural, politeness unspecified). In many such languages, if there is also agreement between a verb and its arguments, the verb's inflection will also reflect the choice of second-person pronoun, as illustrated in (169). In some cases, like (169d), the verbal inflection is the only indication of the choice of form of address.

(169) a. Tu   as   raison.
           2SG.FAM have.PRS.2SG.FAM reason.

           "You are correct." [fra]

       b. Vous   avez   raison.
           2PL.FAM|2SG.HON have.PRS.2PL.FAM|2SG.HON reason.

           "You are correct." [fra]

       c. *Vous   as   raison.
           2PL.FAM|2SG.HON have.PRS.2SG.FAM reason.

           Intended: "You are correct." [fra]

       d. Ecoutes!
           listen.2SG.FAM.IMP

           "Listen!" [fra]

Helmbrecht [2013] surveyed 207 languages for politeness distinctions in their second-person pronouns. The majority (136) do not encode politeness in this way, but the remaining 71 languages do, either a binary distinction (49), a system with more distinctions (15), or through second-person pronoun avoidance to express politeness (7).

Grammaticized politeness is not restricted to pronoun choice. Japanese and Korean, for example, also have verbal inflections which mark solidarity or distance to the addressee:[3]

(170) a. 田中   さん を 待つ.
           Tanaka san wo matsu
           Tanaka HON ACC wait.AHON:−

           "(I) wait for Mr/Ms Tanaka." [jpn]

       b. 田中   さん を 待ちます.
           Tanaka san wo machi-masu
           Tanaka HON ACC wait-AHON:+

           "(I) wait for Mr/Ms Tanaka." [jpn] [Siegel et al., 2016, p. 211]

(171) a. 박씨를   기다린다.
           Park-ssi-lul   kitali-n-ta
           Park-HON-ACC wait.for-PRS-DECL

           "(I) wait for Mr/Ms Park." [kor]

       b. 박씨를   기다립니다.
           Park-ssi-lul   kitali-pni-ta.
           Park-HON-ACC wait.for-HON-DECL

           "(I) wait for Mr/Ms Park." [kor]

[3]In (170), AHON stands for "addressee honorific."

The only difference in these pairs of examples is in the inflection on the verb. Furthermore, the sentences have the same truth conditions. The difference in meaning has to do with whether the speaker is signaling social distance to the addressee/formality of situation or not.

Across languages, the choice use politeness markers is not in fact dictated by the circumstances but rather serves to help construct social relationships [McCready, 2019]. Furthermore, the import of pronoun choices varies by language and speech community: Helmbrecht [2013] notes that in Russian speakers can move back and forth between using the polite and familiar forms of address (and the change brings in pragmatic effects), while in German speaking communities this generally isn't done.

#64 Politeness strategies can also mitigate face-threats by softening commands to requests, etc.

In addition to morphological means of expressing politeness described in #63 above, we find politeness markers at various other levels of grammar. On the one hand, there are specific words like English *please* whose function is to mark a polite request. On the other, there are pragmatic strategies of phrasing commands as requests or requests as queries for information. Compare the following, arranged in terms of politeness:

(172)   a. Tell me the time.

b. Please tell me the time.

c. Could you tell me the time?

d. Could you please tell me the time?

e. I was wondering if you could tell me the time.

Brown and Levinson [1978] theorize politeness in terms of mitigating threats to positive and negative "face." Positive face involves a person's self image in the world and it is threatened when the interlocutor doesn't align with the person's wants. Negative face involves a person's freedom of action and is threatened when that freedom of action is impeded. "Softening" commands and requests involves mitigating threats to freedom of action (the requestee can refuse) while also indicating understanding of the requestee's wants in the situation.

#65 Politeness markers can be a useful source of information for reference resolution, especially of dropped arguments.

In #63, we discussed addressee-oriented politeness markers, including distinctions in second-person pronouns and in specific verbal morphology signaling politeness toward the addressee. Other markers of politeness that instead index social relationships between the speaker and individuals referred to in the sentence. These markers of politeness can be very useful for reference resolution, especially when the referring expressions in question are minimal (e.g., pronouns) or even dropped.

For example, Japanese has another system of honorifics (orthogonal to its addressee honorifics) which involve changes in verb form marking the subject as either honored or humble, as illustrated in (173) [Makino and Tsutsui, 1986, pp. 358–362].[4]

(173)   a. お電話　　　　なさいました。
             O-denwa　　　　nasai-mashi-ta.
             HON-telephone do.SHON:+-AHON:+-PST

             "(They) telephoned." [jpn]

    b. 電話　　　しました。
             Denwa　　　shi-mashi-ta.
             Telephone do-AHON:+-PST

             "(They) telephoned." [jpn]

    c. お電話　　　　いたしました。
             O-denwa　　　　itashi-mashi-ta.
             HON-telephone do.SHON:−-AHON:+-PST

             "(I) telephoned." [jpn]

All three of these examples share the truth conditions that someone made a telephone call. They are differentiated in the verb form, which signals something about the relationship between the speaker and the person who made the call. In (173a), the speaker is speaking of the subject as someone in a higher social position, meriting honorific usage. In (173c), the speaker is speaking of the subject in a humble form. Finally, (173b) doesn't say anything in particular about the status of the subject, but in contexts where one of the other forms is expected, choosing (173b) instead would definitely convey information.

Given societal norms in Japan that honorific forms are never used to refer to oneself, it's clear how modeling honorific usage can help with the resolution of dropped arguments in examples like (173). Deeper understanding of the system provides even more information. Wetzel [1988] describes how honorific usage interacts with the cultural notions of *uti* (in-group) and *soto* (out-group) in Japan: The humble forms can be used to describe the actions of anyone in the speaker's in-group. Similarly, honorific forms construct the subject as being relatively out-group. Furthermore, the contextually salient notions of in-group and out-group can change even in a given situation with a fixed set of participants: Wetzel [1988] analyzes the transcript of a cooking show and finds that the announcers deploy the honorifics (and other forms indexing in-group/out-group in Japanesesuch as the verbs of giving) variably, sometimes construing the cooking instructor as in their in-group (and the audience as out-group) and other times construing the audience as in their in-group and the instructor as out-group.

---

[4]All of these examples are presented in the addressee honorific form (AHON:+), but this is independent of the choice of subject honorific (SHON:+ or SHON:−).

CHAPTER 9

Beyond Sentences

#66 Understanding meaning in discourse involves some kind of function of discourse update, using a representation of discourse context and a representation of what's just been said.

In the preceding chapters, we have discussed the meanings of words (and multiword expressions) and how they combine given the scaffolding of morphology and syntax to yield meanings of sentences. The meanings of sentences (and sentence fragments) in context combine with each other and with commonsense reasoning to yield the meanings of discourse. To see how this goes beyond what a sentence alone carries, consider (174), from Hobbs [1979, p. 101]:

(174) John took a train from Paris to Istanbul. He has family there.

On hearing the mini discourse in (174), a listener is likely to conclude that *he* is John (not someone else); that *there* is Istanbul, not Paris; that the second sentence *explains* the first (see #67); that therefore John's family lived in Istanbul in the past; and that additionally John's family still lives there now (signaled by the present tense *has*).

Formal models that construct a representation of the content of discourse, capturing information such as the above observations about the meaning of the simple discourse (174), typically view a discourse $D_{1:n}$ as a sequence of minimal discourse units $u_1 \dots u_n$ (where the u_i are typically clauses). Computing the semantic representation $R(D_{1:n})$ of discourse $D_{1:n}$ is achieved by sequentially applying an *update function* to its minimal units $u_1 \dots u_n$ [e.g., Kamp and Reyle, 1993]. There is an enormous body of work exploring different approaches to that discourse function. We provide a brief overview in Appendix A. We aim in this book to be as theory neutral as possible, but fix some parameters in order to allow concrete discussions of phenomena.

First, we'll assume a coherence-based model of discourse [Asher and Lascarides, 2003, Hobbs, 1979, Kehler, 2002]: the semantic representation $R(D)$ of a discourse D constitutes a *discourse structure* of coherently related segments (see #67). We also assume that this semantic representation $R(D)$ captures content that is a matter of public record about the messages that the dialogue participants exchanged: it represents each dialogue participant's *public commitments* [Hamblin, 1970], given what they said and the context in which they said it. What's a matter of public record is distinct from the perlocutionary effects that these meanings trigger (see #5). For instance, a speaker asserting *It's cold in here* may be sufficient for the interlocutor to infer that the speaker wants her to shut the window, but intuitively the utterance doesn't publicly commit the speaker to that desire. So this desire is not a part of $R(D)$, though it may be inferred separately as a part of the representation of the cognitive state of the speaker.

We do assume, however, that speakers publicly commit to coherent interpretations, i.e., they commit to a particular coherence relation between their current contribution to the conversation and some prior contribution. This view is (partly) motivated by naturally occurring data on agreement and denial (see Lascarides and Asher, 2009 for details). For instance in (10), discussed in #4 and repeated here, B agrees with everything A says except for the linguistically implicit explanation relation that connects the content of the sentences in A's contribution to the dialogue:

(10)   A: John went to jail. He embezzled the company funds.
       B: No. He embezzled the funds but he went to jail because he was convicted of tax
       evasion.

Following Kamp and Reyle [1993], Grosz and Sidner [1986], and others, we take anaphoric reference as a test for what is part of the semantic representation $R(D)$ at the time of the utterance of the anaphoric expression. *No* is anaphoric in the sense that it must identify the content it is denying in the context. In (10), the only way to make sense of *no* is for it to be negating the (implicated) *explanation* relation. It follows that the *explanation* relation, though implicit, is part of $R(D)$.

Since we assume that $R(D)$ features coherence relations among the contents of discourse segments (see also #67), we must also assume that the discourse update function is *nonmonotonic*: coherence relations are inferred defeasibly, because they are dependent on hidden contextual information like real-world knowledge and cognitive states. Accordingly, we assume the discourse update function has at least some access to the semantic contents of the prior discourse and non-linguistic information like real-world knowledge—for inferring a coherence relation is the product of commonsense reasoning—though we stay neutral about the extent of that access (i.e., whether it's unlimited following Hobbs et al. [1993] or limited following Asher and Lascarides [2003]). We also stay neutral on whether the axiomatization of the discourse update function is symbolic or statistical. In the remainder of this chapter, we will explore further how to arrive at meaning beyond the sentence, including how those meanings feature coherence relations that structure the discourse (#67), the interaction of lexical processing and discourse processing (#68), how a dynamic approach to discourse meaning facilitates modeling how interpretation unfolds (#69) and what can be assumed about speaker knowledge of possible signals in processing discourse (#70).

#67 Discourse is structured by coherence relations between contents of discourse segments.

We argued in #7 that each coherence relation (e.g., *explanation*, *elaboration*, *contrast*, *answer*, etc.) is a type of relational speech act. Like actions generally, when speakers elaborate something, or continue a narrative, they change the context: in particular, they change what is salient (or "being talked about now"), which in turn constrains how the discourse can proceed and what things they can refer to with (subsequent) anaphoric expressions like pronouns. Coherence-based theories of discourse structure model these effects on what's salient.

To illustrate the idea, consider (175), taken from Asher 1993:

(175)   a. One plaintiff was passed over for promotion three times.

     b. Another didn't get a raise for five years.

     c. A third plaintiff was given a lower wage compared to males who were doing the same work.

     d. But the jury didn't believe this.

The cue phrase *but* in (175d) signals a *contrast*, in this case between a claim and the fact that this claim wasn't believed. But which claim—that is, what does *this* in (175d) refer to? Well, that depends on which proposition (175d) forms a *contrast* with. So technically, contrast is a relation, interpreting (175d) involves identifying the first argument to that relation, and doing that is logically co-dependent on deciding what *this* refers to.

Importantly, some referents that have been introduced in the discourse context aren't available as antecedents to *this* in (175d). Specifically, *this* can refer to the third plaintiff's claim, described in (175c), or to *all* the claims, described in (175a–c). It cannot refer to the second plaintiff's claim alone (i.e., to (175b)), the first plaintiff's claim alone (i.e., (175a)), or a combination of these (i.e., (175a–b)). Likewise, the *contrast* that *but* signals can be a *contrast* with the content of (175c) or the whole prior discourse, but not a *contrast* with (175a), or with (175b).

Coherence-based theories of discourse explain this observation via a combination of three principles [Asher and Lascarides, 2003, Hobbs, 1985, Kehler, 2002, Webber, 1991]: (i) coherence relations impose structure on a discourse; (ii) that structure constrains how the discourse can coherently progress; and (iii) antecedents to anaphoric expressions must be introduced in units that are coherently related to the units containing the anaphoric expressions.

Coherence relations structure discourse in two ways: First, an argument to a coherence relation can itself be a discourse segment consisting of coherently related sub-segments, thereby generating a hierarchical structure. Second, each coherence relation is either *coordinating* (e.g., *narration, contrast*) or *subordinating* (e.g., *explanation, elaboration, background*). Which it is depends on its semantics [Asher and Vieu, 2002, Hobbs, 1985]—intuitively, with subordinating relations the first argument to the relation remains a salient topic of the conversation, even though the second argument to the relation is said more recently. In contrast, two discourse units that are connected with a coordinating relation have a common topic, but that topic is not the first argument to the relation: it is either distinct from either of the two units, or it is the second unit (i.e., the most recently said unit). For instance, the discourse topic that the segment (175a–c) elaborates on is that three plaintiffs make three claims that they are ill-treated. This linguistically implicit topic "ties" the segment (175a–c) into a coherent whole; the fact that we can identify this common topic is what distinguishes the coherence of (175a–c) from incoherent non-sequiturs—e.g., compare (175a) followed by *Kim's hair is black.* with (175a–b).

The discourse structure for (175a–c) is shown in (176) (ignoring for now the semantic representations of the individual discourse units).

(176)

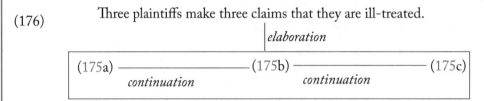

Three plaintiffs make three claims that they are ill-treated.

elaboration

(175a) ——————————— (175b) ——————————— (175c)

continuation   *continuation*

This representation uses the graphical conventions that discourse units related by a subordinating or part-whole relation are arranged vertically, while units related by coordinating relations proceed left to right (i.e., matching the textual order of the utterances they connect). (176) shows how the common topic for (175a–c), while linguistically implicit, gets accommodated into the semantic representation of the discourse so as to satisfy the semantics of *continuation* because two arguments are connected by *continuation* only if they have a common, distinct topic that they both elaborate on.

Such structures are used in coherence-based theories to model constraints on how the discourse can proceed, so as to capture the intuition that a coherent move in discourse must relate to what's currently salient or being "talked about." These theories posit a *right frontier constraint*: the current utterance must connect to a prior discourse unit that is on the discourse structure's *right frontier* [Asher and Lascarides, 2003, Grosz and Sidner, 1986, Hobbs, 1985, Webber, 1991].[1] For example, given the structure (176) for (175a–c), the utterance (175d) must connect (with contrast, signaled by its cue phrase *but*) to (175c), to the (extended) segment (175a–c) or to this segment's common topic—these are the units that are on the right frontier of (176), while (175b) and (175a) are not on the right frontier. This predicts that speakers cannot talk about the first claim or the second claim further without reintroducing them explicitly into the discourse, for instance with a definite referring expression, e.g., *The second plaintiff's claim was more plausible than the others.*

Finally, coherence constrains antecedents to surface anaphors—in particular, pronouns and elided constructions like VP ellipsis. Specifically, if a discourse unit *u* contains an anaphor, then its antecedent must be in *u* or in a prior discourse unit *u'* to which *u* is coherently related. Thus, the anaphoric expression *this* in (175d) must refer to something salient, because (175d) must be coherently related to something salient (i.e., on the right frontier), as determined by how the coherence relations in the context structure that prior discourse. In this example, if (175d) is interpreted as related (with *contrast*) to (175c), then *this* must be the claim referred to in (175c). The extended segment has no accessible referent, because the claims are introduced

---

[1]Theories differ in the finer details of these structures. However, generally speaking, what is on the right frontier of the structure licensed by a theory is the theory's predictions about what is currently salient.

in units that are a part of that segment, and not introduced by the segment itself. So *this* would be uninterpretable in this case. Finally, if (175d) is connected to the topic, then *this* must denote the three claims.

Now let's change (175) by inserting between (175c) and (175d) a clause which expresses the topic of the segment (175a–c):

(177) a. One plaintiff was passed over for promotion three times.

b. Another didn't get a raise for five years.

c. A third plaintiff was given a lower wage compared to males who were doing the same work.

d. In summary, three plaintiffs made three claims.

e. But the jury didn't believe this.

The added sentence is implicated by the original (175a–c), but even so, making it linguistically explicit after (175c) affects salience and hence what *this* can refer to. It cannot be the claim (175c) any more, but rather it is all three claims. Again, the right frontier constraint accounts for this intuition: (177d) attaches to the extended segment (177a–c) with the coordinating relation *summary*. *Summary* is coordinating because the second argument to the relation is its topic (unlike *elaboration* where the first argument is the topic, making that first argument remain salient even though the second argument is said more recently). Thus, (177d) is the only unit on the right frontier. This distinction between (175) and (177) shows that interpreting anaphora is dependent not only on what propositions are communicated, but also on how those propositions are communicated (in particular, their textual order). We touched on this issue briefly in #66, and we'll return to it again in #74, in the context of a broader discussion of constraints on interpretation of anaphoric elements in Chapter 10.

Different theories of coherence relations have different inventories as to what the set of coherence relations are. For instance, Segmented Discourse Representation Theory (SDRT) [Asher and Lascarides, 2003] uses an inventory of around 30 relations, categorized as to whether their semantics is defined as veridical (the relation holds only if the contents of the discourse units it connects are true), the types of contents it relates (question vs. request vs. assertion), and whether the semantic consequences are defined in terms of the domain or cognitive states. In contrast, Rhetorical Structure Theory (RST) [Mann and Thompson, 1986] has an inventory of over 200 relations, partly because they take the meaning of discourse content to include more than public commitments (and so coherence relations must discriminate among the fine-grained options this affords). There is also work that builds the inventory of coherence relations from cue phrases like *but*, *otherwise*, and *because* [Knott, 1995, Webber et al., 2003] or from fundamental domain-level concepts such as causation [Sanders, 1997].

#68 Lexical processing and discourse processing interact.

As we saw in Chapter 4, the semantic representation of words can incorporate relatively rich information about what causes the word's denotation, the telicity or purpose of that denotation, the substance that the word's denotation is made up of, and so on: having such information encoded or conventionalized within the lexicon helps to capture linguistic generalizations about the word's syntactic behavior and its (largely) predictable range of word senses. In addition, we argue here that this lexical information is also a useful for inferring coherence relations in text; indeed, on some occasions it is an indispensable source of information. On the other hand, the flow of information during discourse interpretation can go the other way, from coherence relations to resolving lexical meanings, i.e., one's choice of coherence relation can resolve lexical sense ambiguities.

To see the effect of conventionalized lexical semantics on coherence relations, consider the VPs *sink* and *go to the bottom of the sea*, which are close paraphrases. However, closer inspection highlights some differences. Both sinking events and going to the bottom of the sea events have causes. But *sink* can undergo the causative/inchoative alternation, licensing an expression of the causer as an argument of the same verb, while *go to the bottom of the sea* can't:

(178)   a. The ship sank.

     b. The torpedo sank the ship.

     c. The ship went to the bottom of the sea.

     d. #The torpedo went the ship to the bottom of the sea.

This suggests that the causal information associated with sinking is linguistically encoded—i.e., it is conventionalized or *lexicalized*—for *sink*, but not for its near-paraphrase.

In multi-sentence discourse, this conventional or lexical information about causation proffers relevant information for computing discourse structure. For example, we can use it to validate the inference that the contents of the clauses in (179) are connected with the relation *explanation*:

(179)   The ship sank. The enemy torpedoed it.

Specifically, the content of the second sentence in (179) can bind to the cause that is already introduced linguistically into the semantic representation of the verb *sink*. In this example, the *explanation* relation could also have been inferred on the basis of real-world knowledge; that's why replacing the first sentence in (179) with the sentence (178c) retains the (implied) *explanation* relation between the contents of the sentences. But in some cases, the conventional linguistic knowledge is indispensable [Asher and Lascarides, 2003, Rohde and Kehler, 2014]. For example, psych verbs such as *scare*, *annoy*, and *surprise* lead to a very strong expectation that the next sentence will be an *explanation* for the emotion (if an *explanation* hasn't already been given):

(180)   a. Mary is annoyed. Sandy calls her all the time.

    b. Mary is annoyed. Sandy never calls.

    c. Mary is annoyed. Sandy called her last night.

    d. Mary is annoyed. Sandy ate soup last night.

It's simply not plausible to assume as part of real-world knowledge that eating soup is likely to cause annoyance. The justification for inferring *explanation* in these examples is not real-world knowledge about relationships between eating soup and being annoyed, or calling and being annoyed. Rather, it stems from lexical information; specifically, that there is an event that causes the annoying event is conventionally encoded in the lexical semantics of the verb *annoy*, as evidenced by the fact that it licenses the following alternations [Levin, 1995, p. 190]:

(181)   a. *PRO-Arb Object Alternation:*
        Sandy eating soup never fails to annoy Kim.
        Sandy eating soup never fails to annoy.

      b. *Possessor-Subject Possessor-Attribute Alternation:*
        Sandy annoyed Kim with his soup eating.
        Sandy's eating soup annoyed Kim.

The event that's described by the content of the subsequent sentence can then bind to this antecedent causal event, much like anaphoric expressions bind to antecedents [Asher and Lascarides, 2003, Asher, 2011]. Thus, lexical meaning can encode information that is not only sufficient but also essential for inferring a coherent discourse interpretation.

    Going the other way, resolving lexical ambiguity depends on discourse structure. Consider the following example, adapted from Asher and Lascarides 1995a:

(182)   a. The judge demanded to know where the defendant was.

      b. The barrister apologized and said that he was last seen by the harbor.

      c. The court bailiff found him asleep at the dock.

      c′ But the court bailiff found him asleep at the dock.

The noun *dock* is sense ambiguous between (at least) a harbor vs. courtroom sense. But it is not ambiguous in (182abc), where it gets its harbor sense; nor in (182abc′), where it gets its courtroom sense. The only difference between these sentences is the presence of *but*, signaling *contrast*. Current models of word sense disambiguation estimate the sense s of a word w, given some (restricted) representation of w's context C, by maximizing $Pr(sense(w) = s|C)$ (for a good survey of the various approaches to the task, consult Navigli 2009). There are many words in the context that (according to distributional models) make the courtroom sense of *dock* relatively likely—e.g., *judge, courtroom, barrister, bailiff*. There's also one word which intuitively favors its harbor sense—i.e., *harbor*. Any model that makes the right prediction for (182abc) is highly unlikely to also predict the right answer for (182abc′) (and *vice versa*), unless it can account for the particular contribution of *but*.

#69 The semantic representation of discourse should be dynamically interpreted.

Barring a few notable exceptions—e.g., Dynamic Syntax [Kempson et al., 2000] and DLTAG [Webber et al., 2003]—grammars that compose logical forms from linguistic syntax do so in a way that's independent from the prior sentences in the discourse. This is insufficient, however, to model anaphoric dependencies that cross sentence boundaries. A simple example is given in (183).

(183)   Kim bought a table. It was expensive.

In classical (non-dynamic) approaches, the representation of these two sentences is one where the scope of the quantifier in the first sentence is limited to that sentence and the pronoun *it* in the second sentence corresponds to a free variable:

(184) $\exists x (buy(k, y) \wedge name(k, kim) \wedge table(x))$
        $expensive(y)$

Crucially, classical logic imposes no constraints on the assignment function one uses to interpret the free variable y in the second sentence, and so these formulae are satisfiable in a model where the individual y that is expensive is different from the table x that Kim bought. But this is not how the English discourse in (184) is interpreted. Barring any further contextual information, *it* is interpreted as coreferential with *a table*. This phenomenon is not specific to English, but is attested in other languages as well. Here we illustrate with Spanish, Russian, Mandarin, and Urdu. Note that in Spanish (185a), Mandarin (185c), and Urdu (185d) the variable in the second sentence that is interpreted as coreferential with an expression from the first sentence is an implicit (dropped) argument (see #36). Despite this, we observe the same phenomenon.

(185)   a. Un   hombre camin-ó.   Habl-ó.
           INDEF.MASC.SG man   walk-3SG.PST. Talk-3SG.PST.

           "A man walked. He talked." [spa]

        b. Шёл   человек.   Он   говорил.
           Shyol   chelovek.   On   govoril.
           walk.PST.SG.MASC person.MASC.NOM.SG. 3SG.MASC.NOM speak.PST.SG.MASC

           "A person walked. He talked." [rus]

        c. 一个   人   走了   过去。说了   一句   话。
           Yī-ge   rén   zǒu-le   guòqù. Shuō-le yī-jù   huà.
           One-NUMCL person walk-PF over.   Speak-PF one-NUMCL speech.

           "A person walked over. He said something." [cmn]

        d. ‏ایک آدمی چلتا تھا۔ بولتا تھا۔‏

eːk aːdmi tʃəl-t-a   θʰ-a. bol-t-a   θʰ-a.
one man   walk-IMPF-M PST-M talk-IMPF-M PST-M

"A man walked. He talked." [urd]

In essence, the interpretation of logical forms like (184) fails to reflect the constraints that context imposes on the way the current utterance is interpreted, especially its anaphoric expressions.

It doesn't help, within classical logic at least, to replace y in (184) with x. The result is still one where x is a free variable, because it's (syntactically) outside the scope of the existential quantifier $\exists x$. Alternatively, perhaps one could simply get rid of the quantifier $\exists x$ in the first sentence, and have both sentences feature the free variable x, and one could join them with the conjunction $\wedge$. This way, the individual that's a table and the individual that's expensive are the same. But the interpretation of free variables in classical first-order logic doesn't provide the correct truth conditions of the indefinite noun phrase *a table* in this case: the truth value of a sentence featuring a free variable x is dependent entirely on the particular assignment function g' that is a part of the index of evaluation—the logical form will be *false* if $g'(x)$ is not a table that Kim bought—but intuitively, the first sentence should be true so long as there is some variable assignment function g such that $g(x)$ is a table that Kim bought. One further option would be to allow the logical form of the second sentence to feature the variable x and to place it within the semantic scope of the existential quantifier $\exists x$ that's a part of the logical form of the first entence. But this breaks the standard approach to semantic composition via linguistic syntax (see Chapter 7).

Another potential strategy to deal with this shortcoming in classical logic is to think of pronouns as disguised definite descriptions: Evans [1977] proposes that the pronoun *it* in (183) is equivalent to the description *the table that Kim bought*. Computing which definite description a given pronoun stands for is a matter of contextual reasoning and outside the province of truth conditional semantics. But this assigns the right truth conditions only if there's one and only one table that Kim bought, and there are well-known counterexamples from Heim [1982]:

(186)   I bought a sage plant yesterday. I bought seven others with it.

Consider now the difference between (187a)—where the pronoun successfully refers to the ball not in the bag—and (187b)—where it doesn't.[2]

(187)   a. Exactly one of the ten balls is not in the bag. It's under the sofa.

    b. Exactly nine of the ten balls are in the bag. #It's under the sofa.

According to classical logic, the first sentences in both these discourses mean the same thing: they are satisfied by exactly the same models or states of affairs. However, (187) shows they are not the same in terms of the way the discourse can progress: (187a) makes the ball that's not in the bag available as an antecedent to the pronoun *it* in the next sentence. (187b), which

___

[2]Stalnaker [1996] attributes these examples to Barbara Partee.

like (187a) entails that there's exactly one ball not in the bag, blocks this ball from being an antecedent.

This observation holds cross-linguistically. We illustrate with examples from Spanish, Russian, and Mandarin:

(188)   a.   Exactamente una   de las   diez   pelota-s no   está en
             Exactly   one.FEM.SG of DEF.FEM.PL ball-PL NEG   be.PRS.3SG in   DEF.FEM.SG
             la   bolsa.   Está   bajo   el   sillón.
             bag. Be.PRS.3SG below DEF.MASC.SG sofa.

             "Exactly one of the ten balls is not in the bag. It's under the sofa." [spa]

        b.   Exactamente nueve de las   diez pelota-s están   en la   bolsa.
             Exactly   nine of DEF.FEM.PL ten ball-PL be.PRS.3PL in DEF.FEM.SG bag.
             #Está   bajo   el   sillón.
             Be.PRS.3SG below DEF.MASC.SG sofa.

             Intended: "Exactly nine of the ten balls are in the bag. It's under the sofa." [spa]

(189)   a.   Ровно один   из   десяти шаров   не лежит   в мешке.
             Rovno odin   iz   desyati sharov   ne lezhit   v meshke.
             exactly one.SG.MASC.NOM out.of ten.GEN ball.PL.GEN not lie.PRS.3SG in bag.SG.PREP
             Он   лежит   под   диваном.
             On   lezhit   pod   divanom.
             3SG.NOM lie.PRS.3SG under sofa.SG.INSTR

             "Exactly one of the ten balls is not in the bag. It's under the sofa." [rus]

        b.   Ровно девять   из   десяти шаров   лежат   в мешке.   #Он
             Rovno devyat'   iz   desyati sharov   lezhat   v meshke.   #On
             exactly nine.NOM out.of ten.GEN ball.PL.GEN lie.PRS.3SG in bag.SG.PREP   3SG.NOM
             лежит   под   диваном.
             lezhit   pod   divanom.
             lie.PRS.3SG under sofa.SG.INSTR

             Intended: "Exactly nine of the ten balls is in the bag. It's under the sofa." [rus]

(190)   a.   十个   球 中   正好   有   一个   不 在 那个   袋子 里。
             Shí-ge   qiú zhōng zhènghǎo yǒu yī-ge   bú zài nà-gé   dàizi lǐ.
             Ten-NUMCL ball among happen.to exist one-NUMCL NEG be.at that-NUMCL bag in.
             它 在   沙发 底下。
             Tā zài   shāfā dǐxia.
             It be.at sofa under.

             "Exactly one of the ten balls is not in that bag. It's under the sofa." [cmn]

b.
十个	球	中	正好	有	九个	在	那个	袋子 里。	#它
Shí-ge	qiú	zhōng	zhènghǎo	yǒu	jiǔ-ge	zài	nà-gè	dàizi lǐ.	#Tā
Ten-NUMCL	ball	among	happen.to	exist	nine-NUMCL	be.at	that-NUMCL	bag in.	It

在 沙发 底下。
zài shāfā dǐxia.
be.at sofa under.

Intended: "Exactly nine of the ten balls are in that bag. It's under the sofa." [cmn]

Anaphoric dependencies across sentence boundaries are not restricted to pronouns. The most natural interpretation of (191) is one where *but* and indeed *think* both semantically outscope *or*, which syntactically is a part of a different sentence. In other words, the missing first disjunct of *or* is resolved to be *he missed the bus*, and the full disjunction (*he missed the bus or his car broke down*) serves as the propositional argument of the attitude verb *think*:

(191)   John tried to attend the meeting but I think he missed the bus. Or his car broke down.

As with (183), the semantic scope of a scope-bearing operator, quantifier or relation that's introduced in a prior sentence needs to dynamically change to take within its scope the content of subsequent sentences (in this case, the scope of the relation *but* and propositional attitude verb *think* must do this).

Examples such as (183)–(185) and (187)–(191) show that to adequately characterize the content of discourse, we must not only define the states of affairs in which the discourse is true, but also define how it makes available certain referents for subsequent anaphoric reference, while blocking other referents from being available. Or to put this another way, the content of the discourse must not only define what's true, but also define what's salient. *Dynamic semantics* [Groenendijk and Stokhof, 1991, Heim, 1982, Kamp and Reyle, 1993] is designed with this purpose in mind.

In a dynamic semantics, the interpretation of the current sentence takes an input context and produces a different output one—uttering something is an action, and like actions generally, it changes the current state of the affairs. The representation of these contexts of interpretation vary from one theory to another, but a typical example is that the context consists of a set of *world-assignment pairs* (w, f), where w is a possible world and f is a partial function that assigns variables their referents. As the discourse progresses, the partial variable assignment functions f keep track of what's been made salient in the discourse.

In dynamic semantics, predications like $table(x)$, negated formulae $\neg\phi$ and universally quantified formulae $\forall x \phi$ are tests on the input context: these formulae eliminate any pair (w, f) from the input context for which the formula is false. In contrast, the existential quantifier $\exists x$ changes the variable assignment function: the partial function f in any world-assignment pair (w, f) that's in the input context gets extended to be defined for the variable x. Thus, any free variable x in a subsequent predication is assigned the same referent, regardless of whether it was syntactically within the scope of $\exists x$ or not, so long as certain other constraints are met.[3] To put this another way, the following formulae all have the same meaning:[4]

(192)   a. $\exists x (buy(k, x) \wedge table(x) \wedge expensive(x))$

   b. $\exists x (buy(k, x) \wedge table(x)) \wedge expensive(x)$

   c. $\exists x \wedge buy(k, x) \wedge table(x) \wedge expensive(x)$

Dynamic semantics thereby explains the difference between the a and b discourses in (187)–(190). Interpreting the first sentence of all these discourses yields an output context where the possible world w in any of its world-assignment pairs (w, f) is one where nine of the ten balls are in the bag, and one of them isn't. But the output variable assignment functions differ: in the a discourses, they provide a mapping from a variable x to the ball that's not in the bag, thanks to the dynamic interpretation of $\exists x$ that we mentioned earlier; in the b discourses they don't. And since the grammar assigns to pronouns a semantics that introduces a free variable, which must be made equal to some already defined variable, the b discourses are correctly predicted to be anomalous.

Traditional dynamic semantics [Groenendijk and Stokhof, 1991, Kamp and Reyle, 1993] focuses on examples like (187)–(190), where there is an intersentential anaphoric dependency involving an individual. Segmented Discourse Representation Theory (SDRT) [Asher and Lascarides, 2003] provides a dynamic semantics where antecedents can be propositions, expressed by things other than nominal constituents (in this case, a sentence, see also #72). This is designed to handle cases like (191).[5]

#70 Discourse understanding and dialogue generation seem amenable to game-theoretic modeling, but discourse is too open-ended to assume the requisite complete knowledge.

Formal game theory's definition of rational behavior—i.e., that an agent's actions are an optimal trade off between what they prefer and what they think they can achieve [Savage, 1954]—seems a natural fit for the tasks of discourse understanding [e.g., Franke et al., 2012, Wang et al., 2016] and dialogue generation [e.g., Rieser and Lemon, 2011, Williams and Young, 2007]. An interpreter who wants to understand a speaker's signal needs to identify the (hidden) message that's an optimal trade off between what the speaker and the interpreter herself prefer and think they can achieve. Similarly, someone who wants to communicate needs to identify a message, and the signal for expressing that message, that's an optimal trade off between the interpreter's and her own preferences and beliefs on what's achievable. Indeed, Grice [1975] claimed, but never

---

[3]Such other constraints include: no other quantifier that binds x intervenes between the quantifier $\exists x$ and the free variable x, and if $\exists x$ is within the scope of a negation ($\neg$), then so is the free variable x. For details, consult Groenendijk and Stokhof 1991 and Gamut 1991b.

[4]Note that $\exists x$ can be treated as a formula in dynamic semantics!

[5]See also (175), discussed in #67, for another example where the antecedent to an anaphor is a proposition.

showed, that the Gricean Maxims of conversation that he proposed (see #89) are derivable from an assumption that people are rational (in game theoretic terms: they aim for an optimal trade off between preferences and beliefs) and cooperative (in game theoretic terms: their preferences are aligned, i.e., it's a game of coordination).

Several researchers have now provided supporting evidence for Grice's claim by modeling the rational behaviors of speakers and hearers in *signaling games* [see Benz et al., 2005]. A signaling game is a game of two players—a speaker and a recipient. Only the speaker can observe the true state of the world. On observing it, she issues a signal, and the recipient reacts by inferring what the speaker believes about the world. Both the speaker and recipient receive a reward, dependent on the speaker's signal and the recipient's reaction to (or interpretation of) that signal. There are several definitions of equilibria in signaling games; researchers typically use one that's known as *iterated best response* (IBR) [Franke, 2009] to predict what speakers and interpreters do. IBR has been used to explain several intuitively compelling implicatures; for instance, that the signal *some dogs barked* carries the scalar implicature that not all dogs barked.

Game theory also forms the basis for the generation component of many current dialogue systems, the component often called the *dialogue manager*. The current state of the art is to represent decisions on what to say and how to say it as a Partially Observable Markov Decision Process (POMDP)—a particular kind of stochastic game. The parameters of the POMDP are acquired via machine learning (in particular, reinforcement learning [Sutton and Barto, 1998]), using a training corpus consisting of dialogues where each dialogue is labeled with a numeric score of how successful it was [see Georgila et al., 2006, Rieser and Lemon, 2011, Williams and Young, 2007]. This training material can be a corpus of human-generated dialogues, or dialogue simulations using a range of implemented dialogue agents that differ in the policies they adopt, or even a mixture of both.

This research represents significant progress. However, there is a fundamental problem with basing decisions about language interpretation and production on formal game theory alone. This is because learning and inference in formal game theory places very high demands on what the players must know in advance of any reasoning they do and any decisions they make about action. For example, to compute a best response in a signaling game, the recipient must know not only what the speaker said, but she must also be aware of all the signals that the speaker deliberated about saying, but chose not to say. But how do interlocutors isolate a relevant set of signals to consider as part of the game, given that there are an unbounded number of possible signals that the grammars of natural languages allow, and there are even an unbounded number of coherent signals in context? In reasoning about how to interpret a speaker's signal, interlocutors in general have the problem of identifying a set of signals (and their attendant possible messages) that is small enough to effectively perform inference over, but large enough to provide reliable estimates about optimal interpretations. Addressing this problem—i.e., identifying what the set of possible signals is, given what a speaker has just said—is currently an open research question.

Whatever the solution ends up being, we know that the method for isolating a game of an appropriate size (measured in terms of the set of possible signals the speaker might say) must be inherently defeasible. Interlocutors need to be able to adapt the game "on the fly" if they observe a speaker saying something that wasn't a part of their representation of the signaling game prior to the speaker saying it. In short, speakers can say things that their interlocutors had not foreseen, and since they must now respond to it, they must extend their representation of the game to include it. To illustrate this, consider the following negotiation over trades in the board game *Monopoly*, from the BBC radio 4 comedy program *Cabin Pressure*:

(193)   So, the deal is that I pay you three hundred and sixty-two pounds now plus you don't pay any rent next time you land on any of my greens, my yellows—excluding Leicester Square—or on Park Lane, unless I've built a hotel on it, unless you mortgage something.

It's highly unlikely that prior to hearing (193), the recipient of this trade offer (a man called Hercules) had included (193) in his set of signals that the speaker might say: this particular offer was unforeseen prior to the negotiation process. But Hercules must now adapt his model of the signaling game to include it, and respond. This takes us beyond the theory of signaling games, and even of formal game theory itself. In formal game theory, two games that have a distinct set of possible states and/or possible actions are considered to be completely unrelated. Accordingly, POMDPs represent a sequential decision process in a way that doesn't allow the set of possible dialogue states to change over time, or the set of dialogue actions: only the *actual* states and actions change, but not the set of possibilities. Thus, POMDPs as they apply to modeling dialogue do not offer a logic of change to the set of possible states or actions when unforeseen options are observed. But intuitively, there is a logic of change to one's signaling game when one observes an unforeseen contribution to the dialogue, such as (193) [Asher and Lascarides, 2013].

The above is an example of an unforeseen signal (and the attendant offer that it expresses), which must somehow be added to the game "on the fly," if one is to use the notion of game equilibria to compute a response. Participants in a conversation can also discover unforeseen states of the world—or to put this another way, they can discover an unforeseen property or concept, which is an integral part of how the person they're conversing with perceives and interprets the state of the world. On discovering an unforeseen domain-level concept, one may be compelled to revise one's preferences about what to do and what to say. For example, suppose two speakers are discussing which restaurant to go to for dinner, and one expresses a preference for *meze*, a kind of food unknown to the other speaker. Now that the second speaker is aware that this type of food is an option, she must extend her model of the possible states accordingly. Further discussion might make *meze* sound so appealing that this speaker updates her preferences to make it her preferred option. Traditional game theory doesn't offer any logic for transitioning from the (old) version of the game (without *meze* as a possible option) to the new (and larger) game that the second speaker now uses to react to the *meze* option, as revealed by the first speaker's utterance.

Intuitively, when this happens people adapt their model of the domain (and of the conversation they're having) in predictable ways [Cadilhac et al., 2013, Hansson, 1995]. Formal game theory as it stands doesn't provide a model of how to adapt, because it treats two games with distinct possibilities as unrelated. Some steps in this direction include Wang et al.'s [2016] work, in which the agent learns to map neologisms (e.g., *meze* in the above example) to domain level concepts, so that it can exploit an expert's utterances to guide its search for an optimal domain plan. But this work assumes that the agent is aware of the domain concept that *meze* denotes (but not aware of the word *meze*), and so it doesn't handle the scenario we described above. Formal models of games where players are unaware of options that are critical to optimal decisions exist [e.g., Feinberg, 2004, Halpern and Rêgo, 2005, Rong, 2016], and furthermore there are models which enable an agent to adapt their conceptualization of the domain, and the decision problem they face in that revised representation, through interaction with a domain expert [Innes and Lascarides, 2019a,b]. But the general problem of extending game theoretic approaches to dialogue modeling to handle the perfectly ordinary case of unforeseen possibilities arising in conversation remains to be solved.

CHAPTER 10

Reference Resolution

#71 Discourse processing requires reference resolution.

Reference resolution is the general problem of determining what is referred to by linguistic expressions for which identifying the referent is dependent on the expression's context of use. In this chapter, we will focus on natural language expressions whose referents depend on identifying an antecedent in the linguistic context. We therefore ignore deixis here, since deictic reference depends on the non-verbal context rather than the linguistic one (see #12).

One obvious example of a natural language expression whose denotation depends on identifying an antecedent in the linguistic context is pronouns—the referent of a pronoun is identical to the referent of its antecedent. Another example is reflexives (e.g., *Kim and Sandy love each other*). The MUC shared tasks [Chinchor, 2001, Chinchor and Sundheim, 2003, Hirschman and Chinchor, 1997] looked at NP coreference chains in English, as in (194), where *The sleepy boys and girls* and *their* are marked as coreferential. The CoNLL 2011 and 2012 shared tasks [Pradhan et al., 2011, 2012] broaden this to include events (expressed by both verbal and nominal constituents as in (195)) with CoNLL 2012 also including data from Mandarin and Arabic (196).

(194)   **The sleepy boys and girls** enjoyed **their** breakfast.

(195)   Sales of passenger cars **grew** 22%. **The strong growth** followed year-to-year increases.

(196)   لقد (نما)الإقتصاد الأوروبي بسرعة خلال السنوات الماضية ، (هذا النمو)ساهم في رفع

  ləqəd   nima æl-ɪqtɪsad   ʊl-ʔʊrʊbi-jʊn   bɪsʊrʕa xɪlæ
  AUX.PST.PF grow DEF-economy.MASC DEF-Europe-ADJ.MASC quickly through
  as-sæw-æːt   ʊl-mædi-jətu,   hæðæ æl-nʊmʊw   saːham-a   fi rafaʕ-a
  DEF-year-PL.FEM DEF-past-ADJ.FEM, this   DEF-growth.MASC contribute-PST to raise-PST

  "The European economy **grew** rapidly over the past years, **this growth** helped raising..."
  [arb]

These are all examples of *co*-reference resolution: the referents of the expression and its antecedent are identical. But as we'll see in the course of this chapter, identity of the referents of an expression and its antecedent is just one of many possible relations. This is why we will refer to this phenomenon as reference resolution, rather than co-reference resolution.

Tense markers also require reference resolution in order to find their reference time (see #60): all three of Reichenbach's [1947] reference, speech, and event times refer to specific times that must be resolved for full interpretation [Aqvist, 1976, Johnson, 1977, Nerbonne, 1986]. In (197), the speech time is resolved to the time of utterance (not necessarily the same as the time a hearer encounters the utterance), the reference time for *eat* (the point in time from which the action is "viewed") is interpreted as the event time of *say*, and the event time for *eat* as before that reference time:

(197)   After they had eaten everything, they said goodbye.

Sometimes what needs its reference resolved is not a particular expression, but an element that's missing, such as the unexpressed (optional) arguments to predicate symbols, discussed in #36. This is illustrated for Japanese in (198), where the unexpressed subject of the verb 食べる *taberu* "eat" in B's utterance is resolved to the speaker and the unexpressed object to the cake, mentioned in the previous utterance.

(198)   A: ケーキ は   どう なった？
             keeki ha   dou nat-ta?
             cake   TOP how become-PST

        "What happened to the cake?" [jpn]

        B: 食べた。
             tabe-ta
             eat-PST

        "(I) ate (it)." [jpn]

This is also true for larger constituents that "go missing" in elided constructions as in (199).

(199)   Sara saw her friend and Sally did too.

What's particularly interesting about English ellipsis is that the antecedent must be found in the linguistic context, but the interpretation can be either strict (here: Sally saw Sara's friend) or sloppy (Sally saw Sally's friend) [Dalrymple et al., 1991, Hobbs and Kehler, 1997]. Note, however, that in naturally occurring text, this type of ambiguity rarely occurs, and when it does the sloppy reading is usually the intended one [Bos and Spenader, 2011].

We've been carefully using the term *reference resolution* and not the more common *coreference resolution* because in the general case, the relationship between the expression whose referent needs resolving and the prior expression in the discourse is not actually coreference. For example, we find *bridging relations* as in (200) where *the engine* is interpreted as the engine of the car mentioned in the first sentence. Sometimes, the antecedent in a bridging relation is an implicit argument, as in (201), where the *the salmon* is interpreted as referring to part of the meal, which is introduced into the semantics by *ate*, but not expressed overtly (see #31).

(200)   My car broke down. The engine blew up.

(201)   I ate well last night. The salmon was perfect.

Reference resolution is critical for a wide variety of NLP tasks. For example: in machine translation into a language which marks gender on pronouns, the referent of the pronoun determines its gender;[1] dialogue systems must allow for users to refer to the same entity multiple times without requiring long-winded fully descriptive NPs in order to be natural and usable; information extraction depends on reference resolution for the arguments of all predicates of interest. Indeed, the performance of an information extraction system can depend on reference among events: e.g., in the following document from the EventCorefBank (ECB) corpus [Bejan and Harabagiu, 2010], one needs to recognize that *came to the rescue* is *elaborated* by the subsequent *boarding* and *seizing* events, and recognizing this supports the inference that the 23 raiders were 12 Somalis and 11 Yemeni nationals:

(202)   Indian naval forces **came to the rescue** of a merchant vessel under attack by pirates in the Gulf of Ade on Saturday, capturing 23 of the raiders, India said…
Indian commandos **boarded** the larger pirate boat, **seizing** 12 Somali and 11 Yemeni nationals as well as arms and equipment, the statement said.

Reference resolution is a very complex problem which requires taking account of the type of referent (#72), grammatical features of the expression whose reference is being resolved and those of candidate antecedents (#73), the logical form of the sentence containing the antecedent (#74), modal subordination and similar phenomena (#75), and discourse structure (#76).

#72 An antecedent to a pronoun can be abstract content expressed by a whole sentence.

The canonical case of reference resolution [e.g., Soon et al., 2001] involves antecedents that are expressed by nominal constituents. However, we also find pronouns that take events as their antecedent (like *It* in (203)) as well as those that take propositions (like *it* in (204)).

(203)   Kim kicked Sandy. It hurt.

(204)   John said that Kim kicked Sandy. But Bill didn't believe it.

Furthermore, non-pronominal expressions denoting events can be coreferential with each other, or more generally can have reference that is dependent on that of another event-denoting expression.

Recent NLP work has begun to address these kinds of coreference, thanks in part to the TAC KBP 2016 Event Nugget Detection and Coreference task [Mitamura et al., 2016], with data in English, Chinese, and Spanish.[2] The goal of this task is to identify events in a corpus and estimate when they corefer. Discourse (205) is an example from the labeled training corpus that they provide, and it labels *left* and *departed* as triggers for the same event:

---

[1]It won't do to transfer the gender of the pronoun from the source language, because the source language might not mark gender or pronouns, or might have a different grammaticized gender system than the target language. See note 3 on page 127.
[2]https://tac.nist.gov/2016/KBP/Event/

(205)   Georges Cipriani left the prison in Ensisheim in northern France on parole on Wednesday.

He departed Ensisheim in a police vehicle bound for an open prison near Strasbourg.

Accordingly, the denotations of the NPs in the various semantic roles in these two sentences are in coreference and other bridging relationships to one another [see, e.g., Lu and Ng, 2017]. But the defining criteria for labeling two events as coreferent in TAC KBP 2016 corpus are unclear. If the events in discourse (205) are assumed to be coreferent, then the defining criteria cannot correspond to spatio-temporal equivalence: according to the lexical semantics of the verbs, the spatial extent of the *depart* event is larger than that of *left* [Asher and Sablayrolles, 1995].

Reference resolution involving events requires a solution for detecting events in text, and that remains a challenging task [Kumaran and Allan, 2004], partly because an event and its participants are introduced by a wide variety of syntactic constructions: active sentences (*Kim kicked Sandy*), passive sentences (*Sandy was kicked by Kim*), gerunds (*the kicking of Sandy by Kim* or *Kim's kicking of Sandy*), and so on. Recognizing semantic relationships among events is likewise extremely challenging: coreference, as discussed above, is just one possible relationship. Others include part-whole relations (e.g., *eating a meal* and *devouring cheese*), a causal relation (e.g., *Kim flipped the switch and the light went out*) or some other contingent relationship (e.g., *Pat entered the room and Pat sat down*). To some extent this is analogous to the bridging relations that hold among reference to entities: just as entity referents can stand in a range of relations other than identity, so can event referents, but the range of possible connections between events (e.g., cause-effect) is different from those between entities. Furthermore, inferring these relationships is dependent on rich and diverse information, such as real-world knowledge. Nonetheless, it is a crucial component of text understanding.

Via the TimeML initiative [Pustejovsky et al., 2003], there has been a major effort to provide a taxonomy of temporal relations among eventualities (that is, events and states) introduced in text, which in turn has been used to annotate open domain text with its temporal structure. The annotation methods have deployed automated labeling when feasible, but even so it is a very labor intensive and error-prone task. This labeled data has enabled researchers to explore supervised learning approaches to inferring temporal structure [e.g., Boguraev and Ando, 2005]. But supervised learning, especially when the task is to tackle open domain text or social media posts such as Twitter, will always be hampered by the size of available training sets. This makes unsupervised methods for learning event structures particularly attractive [e.g., Chambers and Jurafsky, 2008].

In #67, we described the claim made by Asher [1993] and others that the way an extended discourse context is coherently structured constrains subsequent reference to its *abstract concepts*, as well as to its individuals. For example, in (175), repeated here, *this* can refer to the proposition expressed by (175c) or to all three claims (expressed by the extended segment (175a–c)), but not to the proposition expressed by (175a) on its own, or (175b) on its own:

(175)   a. One plaintiff was passed over for promotion three times.

b. Another didn't get a raise for five years.

c. A third plaintiff was given a lower wage compared to males who were doing the same work.

d. But the jury didn't believe this.

As things stand, existing statistical models encode constraints on reference to prior individuals via shallow parsing techniques that induce lexical or topic chains [e.g., Lee et al., 2011]. These techniques would need to be refined to extend such models to reflect constraints on reference to prior abstract concepts.

#73 Reference resolution depends on grammatical factors.

Reference resolution is constrained by many different grammatical factors. On the one hand, pronouns can be marked for features such as person (206a), number (206b), or gender (206c), which restricts the range of antecedents they can take.[3]

(206)   a. You have a Rover. He is lucky. (He≠you)

b. John has a Rover. It is red/*They are red.

c. John has a Rover. He is attractive. (He≠the Rover)

There are also constraints on possible configurations of pronouns and their antecedents when both are found within the same sentence. These constraints are known as "Binding Theory" constraints after Chomsky 1981. The exact nature of the constraints shows some crosslinguistic variation [e.g., Hickmann and Hendriks, 1999], but for English they include effects like the following:

(207)   John bought him a Rover. (He≠John)

(208)   He claims that he sold John a Rover. (He≠John)

In addition, there are many further features of linguistic form that impose softer constraints on pronoun interpretation, yielding preferences for one antecedent over another. These include *recency*, such that more recent antecedents are preferred (209); *repeated mention*, such

---

[3]Languages vary in how much information gender distinctions in pronouns provide. Some languages don't employ gender distinctions at all. For example, in spoken Mandarin, there is only one third-person singular animate pronoun, pronounced *tā*, although the written form differentiates masculine (他) and feminine (她). In languages with grammatical gender systems, such as the Romance languages, all nouns are assigned to a grammatical gender. For example, in French *voiture* "car" is feminine and thus can only be coreferent with the feminine third-person pronoun:

(i) Jean a   une   voiture. Elle/*Il   est   rouge.
     Jean have.3SG.PRS INDEF.SG.FEM voiture. 3SG.FEM/3SG.MASC be.3SG.PRS red.

     "John has a car. It is red." [fra]

Bantu languages such as Swahili and Zulu famously have elaborate noun class system which function in similar ways, dividing the nominal lexicon into up to 21 different classes with associated pronominal forms (and agreement markers) [Katamba et al., 2003].

that entities that are the focus of prior discourse are more likely to continue to be in focus (210); and *parallelism*, such that we prefer anaphoric bindings that induce parallelism effects in the discourse (211) [Stevenson et al., 1995].

(209)   John has a Rover. Bill has a Ford. Mary likes to drive it. (it=Ford)

(210)   Cara needed a new car.
        She decided she wanted something sporty.
        Holly went to the car dealers with her.
        She bought an MG. (She=Cara)

(211)   John went to Paris with Bill. Sue also went to Toulouse with him. (him=Bill)

We also see effects of the lexical semantics of particular verbs, which set up expectations as to which of their arguments is most likely to be in focus in the following discourse [Kehler, 2002, Rohde, 2008]:

(212)   a. John asked Bill for help. He forgot to lock the house. (He=John)

        b. John criticized Bill. He forgot to lock the house. (He=Bill)

Finally, there is also an effect of *grammatical role*: According to Centering Theory [Grosz et al., 1995], the degree to which an NP is the preferred antecedent to a subsequent pronoun is (normally) dependent on that NP's grammatical function according to the ranking in (213):[4] They illustrate this with example (214a), where there is a preference for interpreting *she* as co-referent with Susan rather than Betsy, while that preference is eliminated in (214b).

(213)   subject ≻ object ≻ *oblique-position*

(214)   a. Susan gave Betsy a pet hamster. She reminded her that hamsters are quite shy. (She=Susan)

        b. Susan and Betsy looked at a pet hamster. She reminded her that hamsters are quite shy. (She=??)

The illustrative examples we've used above show that: (a) the various principles that influence coreference can yield conflicting clues about which antecedent to prefer; and (b) when they do conflict, the preferred interpretation usually follows one of those clues and overrides the other (in other words, the ambiguity is resolved). For instance, the preferred antecedent in (211) is a case where parallelism overrides the preferences afforded by grammatical function; similarly in (210), we see a case where considerations of repeated mention override parallelism (at least with respect to the immediately preceding sentence) and grammatical function. As we'll see in #76 below, discourse structure and in particular discourse coherence also plays a critical role in reference resolution. Indeed, Asher and Lascarides [2003] claim that when the various linguistic

---

[4]Roughly, an NP is in an oblique position if it is a part of a PP complement or an adjunct to the VP or S.

factors that influence preferred pronoun interpretations conflict with each other the conflict is always resolved in favor of an interpretation that maximizes discourse coherence.

There are many systems that estimate coreference based on supervised learning (see Ng, 2010 for a recent survey); many of these systems use the MUC6[5] or MUC7[6] corpora for training.[7] These models draw on many features, as proposed in both theoretical and computational linguistics [Grosz et al., 1995, Lappin and Leass, 1994], including the features that we mentioned above. More recently, as with many other NLP tasks, there are coreference models which aim to select appropriate features automatically via deep learning [Lee et al., 2017] as well as unsupervised approaches [Bergsma and Lin, 2006, Kehler et al., 2004, Ng and Cardie, 2002].

#74 Reference resolution depends on logical form.

In developing Montague Grammar, Montague [1974] aimed to show that while constructing a formal semantic representation of sentences off of syntax trees is highly convenient, it isn't necessary for analyzing meaning—one can, in principle at least, not construct semantic representations at all, and instead construct models directly, which would be satisfied by such representations (if those representations had been built from the syntax trees).

This early work in formal semantics was highly inspirational, but controversial. Several researchers later argued that the formal semantic representation of sentences, constructed via their linguistic syntax, is in fact not an eliminable part of modeling meaning [Heim, 1982, Kamp, 1981, Kamp and Reyle, 1993, Partee, 1984] (see also #69). For example, contrast (215a), which we discussed in #69, with (215b):

(215)   a.   Kim bought a table. It was expensive.

        b.   It's not the case that every table isn't bought by Kim. #It was expensive.

The syntax of the first sentence of (215b) yields a distinct semantic representation to that of (215a), as shown in (216):

(216)   a. $\exists x (buy(k, x) \land table(x))$

        b. $\neg \forall y (table(y) \rightarrow \neg buy(k, y))$

But crucially, these two formulae are logically equivalent with respect to the classical logic of Frege and Russell [Gamut, 1991a]. And yet, they have distinct effects on the interpretation of subsequent anaphoric expressions. So at some level, the first sentences of these discourses mean the same thing; but at another level, they don't, because what they make salient and available as antecedents to subsequent pronouns is different.

Discourse Representation Theory (DRT) [Kamp, 1981, Kamp and Reyle, 1993] addresses this puzzle by making the semantic representation that's derived from linguistic syntax an irreducible part of interpreting the discourse. In DRT, one cannot replace one logical form for

---

[5]https://catalog.ldc.upenn.edu/LDC2003T13

[6]https://catalog.ldc.upenn.edu/LDC2001T02

[7]These corpora both contain English data only.

a sentence with a logically equivalent one (according to classical logic) when constructing the meaning representation of multi-sentence discourse: in effect, while constructing the representation of the discourse (215b), one cannot replace (216b) with (216a). This is because which antecedents are available for pronouns in subsequent sentences is dependent on the logical structure of the semantic representation of the prior discourse, given how that discourse was expressed. Note how (216a) and (216b) have a distinct logical structure (in the former an existential quantifier binding x outscopes all other predications; in the latter this is not the case).

Dynamic semantics [Groenendijk and Stokhof, 1991] effectively combines insights from Montague Grammar and from DRT to make semantic representations eliminable again. It assigns formulae a dynamic interpretation (as we described informally in #69), and these dynamic interpretations yield a quite different notion of logical equivalence from classical logic. In dynamic logic, the formulae (216) are not logically equivalent. Indeed, they can predict the difference in felicity of (215a) vs. (215b) thanks to these different interpretations of the formulae (216a) vs. (216b), and so semantic representations can be made eliminable, like they are for Montague Grammar, when the model theoretic interpretation of the formulae are those for dynamic predicate logic.

#75 Reference resolution interacts with modals in interesting ways.

As we explained in #74, taking a dynamic semantic approach to discourse interpretation is motivated by cases where an (indefinite) noun phrase serves as an antecedent to a pronoun that's (syntactically) outside its scope [Groenendijk and Stokhof, 1991, Heim, 1982, Kamp and Reyle, 1993]. In other words, it's as if the semantic scope of the existential quantifier that's introduced by the indefinite NP transcends its syntactic boundary, as set by the discourse's sentence boundaries. The fact that indefinite NPs behave like this at all is a challenge. But to complicate matters, the contexts in which such coreference is successful are quite subtle. Although we forego formal details here, dynamic semantics predicts that an indefinite that's introduced within the scope of a semantic operator like a negation or a modal is generally not accessible for coreference with anaphoric expressions in subsequent utterances:

(217)   A wolf might come in. #It is hungry.

But when that subsequent sentence also features a semantic operator that is in some way compatible with the first (e.g., with respect to its mood), then coreference can occur:

(218)   A wolf might come in. It would eat you.

The cover term for this phenomenon is *modal subordination* [Roberts, 1989]. It's so-called because intuitively, the second sentence is interpreted in a context that's subordinate to the modal in the first sentence—(218) can be paraphrased as "A wolf might come in, and *if it does then* it would eat you".

Roberts [1989], among others, offers a formal analysis of modal subordination and its interaction with coreference. Her analysis builds on both dynamic semantics and an analysis of presupposition (see Chapter 11). Informally, Roberts treats the modal *would* as denoting a relation between the proposition it operates over and a presupposed proposition. Thus, the second sentence in (218) is represented by a formula of the form $would(q, p)$, where p is the logical form of the clause that *would* modifies in syntax, and q is a presupposed (and hence contextually determined) proposition. Further, $would(q, p)$ is true only if in all worlds where q is true, p is true too. As usual with presuppositions, the presupposed proposition q can be accommodated into the context in which the modal sentence is interpreted (Lewis, 1979; see also #77). Here, the only available proposition one can accommodate is that a wolf comes in. In other words, the discourse (218) ends up with a logical form that's (roughly) as follows, where $\Diamond$ is the modal operator that represents "it's possible that" in modal logic [Chellas, 1980, p. 4]:

(218′) $\Diamond(\exists x(wolf(x) \wedge come(x))) \wedge$
$$would(\exists x(wolf(x) \wedge come(x)), eat(x, u))$$

The dynamic semantic interpretation of $would(\exists x\phi, \psi)$ ensures that the variable x, introduced by the formula in the first argument to *would*, has a defined referent in the input context for interpreting ψ.

Dynamic semantics uses a similar solution to handle so-called *donkey anaphora*,[8] like *it* in (219), even though such examples don't obviously involve modals.

(219)   If John buys a book he reads it.

The dynamic interpretation of the formula $(\exists x\phi) \rightarrow \psi$ is one where the variable assignment functions in the input context for interpreting ψ define a referent for the variable x; not only that, but for the conditional formula to be true, every way of defining a referent for x that makes ϕ true must also make ψ true. Thus, dynamic semantics not only (correctly) predicts that coreference between the indefinite NP and the pronoun in (219) is possible, but it also captures its intuitive truth conditions: i.e., that John must read every book he buys (and not just some of them) for (219) to be true.

Overall, any model of coreference must reflect the fact that it interacts in complex ways with semantic operators like negation, conditionals and modals. It is not simply the presence or absence of such operators in the discourse that constrains coreference, but also their semantic relation to each other. The process of accommodating content that is linguistically implicit into the context in which a sentence is interpreted, which is a part of the analysis of modal subordination of Roberts [1989] and others, is clearly a very powerful mechanism. We'll examine constraints on accommodation in more detail in Chapter 11.

---

[8]This term comes from the original example sentences that were used to illustrate the phenomenon in Geach 1962, which involved donkeys. See also Groenendijk and Stokhof 1991, Kamp and Reyle 1993 and Roberts 1989 among many others.

#76 Reference resolution depends on discourse structure.

In addition to being sensitive to the actual logical form of utterances (see #74), anaphora are affected by the discourse structure that's induced by the coherence relations, such as *elaboration* and *narration*, that connect the segments in the discourse.

First, discourse coherence is not a yes/no matter, but can vary in quality. Hobbs [1979] argues that the choice of coherence relation and of pronoun resolution are logically co-dependent. Asher and Lascarides [2003] refine this to the claim that speakers prefer pronominal reference to be resolved in a way that maximizes the coherence of the discourse. For example, consider the following examples from Hobbs [1979], which we also discussed in #3:

(3)   a. John can open Bill's safe. He knows the combination.

     b. John can open Bill's safe. He should change the combination.

Suppose we replace *He* in (3a) with *Bill*; i.e., its dispreferred interpretation. The result is coherent—the second sentence elaborates the same topic as the first. But the interpretation where *he* denotes John does this and more. In (3b), on the other hand, the more coherent interpretation is one where *he* denotes Bill: either referent would yield a (coherent) connection between the sentences, but the connection is much more tenuous if *he* denotes John.[9] In (3b), the principle that a discourse interpretation should maximize its coherence overrides the preferences afforded by grammatical function (which favors antecedents to be subjects rather than oblique, see #73).

Further evidence for a complex interaction between coherence and pronominal reference comes from Kehler and Rohde's [2017] psycholinguistic experiments. They use self-paced reading and completion tasks to investigate the impact that different coherence relations have on preferences among antecedents to pronouns. Specifically, they show different preferences for two different coherence relations: *explanation* (which they call the *Why?* condition) and *narration* (the *What-next?* condition). In the *Why?* condition, comprehenders take less time to read the text when the pronoun is coreferential with the Source (i.e., the subject NP) while in the *What-next?* condition reading times are quicker when the pronoun is coreferential with the Goal (the oblique NP):

(220)   (*Source referring pronoun*): Jessica served chili to Emily. She explained to Emily

     a. (*Why?*) …in the kitchen that morning that everyone needs to try chili once.

     b. (*What-next?*) …in the kitchen that night that the secret to chili is real jalapeños.

(221)   (*Goal referring pronoun*): Jessica served chili to Emily. She explained to Jessica

     a. (*Why?*) …in the kitchen that morning that she can only eat soft foods.

     b. (*What-next?*) …in the kitchen that night that the chili was a bit too spicy

---

[9]This interpretation of (3b) with *he* denoting John is is coherent via an inference that the first sentence causes a situation where John should now block Bill from opening his own safe.

Finally, the sequence of coherence relations in an extended prior discourse, and in particular how those coherence relations organize the prior discourse segments into a hierarchy, constrains anaphoric reference. For illustration, consider the discourse (222), from Asher and Lascarides, 2003, p. 8:

(222)   a. John had a lovely evening last night.

     b. He had a great meal.

     c. He ate salmon.

     d. He devoured lots of cheese.

     e. He won a dancing competition.

     f. #It was a beautiful pink.

All the individuals that are introduced in (222a–e) are introduced either with a definite or an indefinite determiner, and none of these are within the scope of negation, a conditional structure (e.g., introduced by *if*) or within the scope of a modal. Consequently, traditional dynamic semantics [Groenendijk and Stokhof, 1991, Kamp and Reyle, 1993] predicts that they are all available as antecedents for interpreting the pronoun in (222f). But this isn't the case: in particular (222f) cannot mean that the salmon John ate was a beautiful pink.

Intuitively, pronominal reference to the salmon after (222d) is anomalous because the narrative has "moved on" from talking about the meal (and the salmon that was a part of that meal) to talking about what happened after it. To put this another way, pronouns are constrained by the current topic of the discourse and the salmon is no longer a part of that topic. Coherence-based theories of discourse interpretation claim that the right frontier of the discourse structure encapsulates the appropriate notion of topic for constraining anaphoric reference (see #67). *Elaboration* induces subordination in the discourse structure, whereas *narration*, induces coordination, to reflect the different effects these relations have on the "granularity" or level of detail being given in the discourse. So the discourse structure for (222), given in Figure 10.1, is one where the salmon is not introduced in a unit that's on the right frontier, and so it's not available as an antecedent to subsequent anaphoric expressions.

Discourse (222) is an example where traditional dynamic semantics overgenerates the antecedents. Discourse (223) is an example where it undergenerates antecedents.

(223)   a. Kim said that Sandy cried.

     b. But Sam did.

Interpreting (223b) requires finding an antecedent for the elided VP in the linguistic context. There are two events in the preceding sentence (a saying event and a crying event). However, the verb *say* is a non-truth preserving operator (i.e., *Kim said X* doesn't entail *X* occurred, see #79), and dynamic semantics models the event in its complement as inaccessible as an antecedent for later expressions. Thus, traditional dynamic semantics incorrectly predicts that (223b) can't

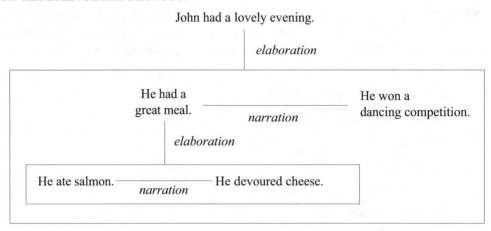

Figure 10.1: A diagram representing the discourse structure of discourse (222).

mean "But Sam cried." In fact this is the preferred interpretation here, compared to the alternative where the second sentence means "But Sam said that Sandy cried." In a coherence-based theory, the definition of which antecedents are accessible is different. In particular, when the units are related with the coherence relations *contrast* or *parallel*, what's available as an antecedent depends on the similarities in the logical structures of the two units so related, and this can result in antecedents being available that, according to dynamic semantics, are inaccessible. In particular here, the coherence-based prediction is that proposition that Sam cried is available as an antecedent for resolving the ellipsis.

Furthermore, the preferences change with a change in the rhetorical connection between the clauses. Compare (223) with (224):

(224)   Kim said that Sandy cried. Sam did too.

The ways in which *contrast* (as introduced by *but*) and *parallel* or *resemblance* (as introduced by *too*) constrain anaphora introduce complexities that we ignore here (but see Asher 1993 for details). The main point we want to make here is that these examples show that coherence relations play an irreducible role in interpreting anaphoric expressions.

Statistical models of coreference [e.g., Ng and Cardie, 2002] use features stemming from predicate-argument structure, distributional lexical semantics and the so-called lexical chains they induce, and grammatical roles, as inspired by Centering Theory [Grosz et al., 1995]. Most statistical models of coreference ignore the discourse structure that's induced by coherence relations like *elaboration*, *narration*, and *contrast*, instead exploiting a slightly different notion of local coherence that's captured in an entity grid [Barzilay et al., 2008]. How to make reasoning about coherence and degrees of coherence a computationally tractable component of discourse interpretation, so that it contributes to a computational model of reference resolution, remains an open research question. While there are data-intensive approaches to predicting coherence relations [e.g., Soricut and Marcu, 2003], state-of-the-art results aren't sufficiently accurate to be informative for a complex task like reference resolution.

CHAPTER 11

Presupposition

#77 Utterances can have both entailments and presuppositions.

Sentence (225) implies that someone took an aspirin; it also implies that Kim has a cousin, and that there is someone called Kim:

(225)   Kim's cousin took an aspirin.

But these implications exhibit differing behaviors. Intuitively, if Kim's cousin didn't take an aspirin, or if no one took an aspirin, then (225) is false; on the other hand, if Kim doesn't have a cousin, or there's no one called Kim, then arguably sentence (225) would be meaningless rather than false, on the grounds that one of its referring expressions fails to refer. The linguistics literature has different terms for these two kinds of implied contents. (225) *entails* that someone took aspirin, but it *presupposes* that Kim has a cousin, and *Kim has a cousin* presupposes that there is someone called Kim.

   The test for whether something is entailed vs. presupposed rests on the fact that presuppositions tend to semantically outscope non-truth preserving operators (e.g., negation, the predicate *believe* or the conditional structure *if...then*), even if in the syntax the phrase that "triggers" the presupposed content is embedded below the phrase corresponding to the non-truth preserving operator. For example, observe how the sentences in (226) imply that Kim has a cousin (and that there is someone called Kim) but they do not imply that someone took aspirin:

(226)   a. It's not the case that Kim's cousin took an aspirin.

   b. I believe that Kim's cousin took an aspirin.

   c. It's possible that Kim's cousin took an aspirin.

   d. If the medicine cabinet door is open, then Kim's cousin took an aspirin.

   This pattern is not specific to English, but indeed attested in other languages as well, as illustrated in (227) with examples from Korean, Russian, Danish, and Italian, which all share the presupposition that there's someone named Kim and that Kim has a cousin.

(227)   a. 김의   사촌이   아스피린을   먹은것은   사실이   아니다
            Kim-uy   sachon-i   asuphilin-ul   mek-un-kes-un   sasil-i   ani-ta
            Kim-GEN cousin-NOM aspirin-ACC eat-ADN-thing-TOP fact-NOM COP.NEG-DECL

       "That Kim's cousin ate an aspirin is not true." [kor]

b. Я   думаю,   что кузина   Ким   приняла
  Ya   dumayu,   chto kuzina   Kim   prinyala
  1SG.NOM think.PRS.1SG that cousin.FEM.SG.NOM Kim.GEN take.PST.SG.FEM
  аспирин.
  aspirin.
  aspirin.SG.ACC

  "I think that Kim's cousin took an aspirin." [rus]

c. Det er   muligt at Kim-s   kusine tog   en   hovedpinepille.
  It   be.3SG.PRS possible that Kim-POSS cousin take.PST INDEF.COM.SG aspirin

  "It's possible that Kim's cousin took an aspirin." [dan]

d. Se la   porta del   mobiletto del   bagno è
  If DEF.SG.FEM door of.DEF.DET.MASC cabinet   of.DEF.DET.MASC bath be.3SG.PRS
  aperta, vuol   dire   che il   cugino di Kim ha   preso
  open,   want.3SG.PRS say.INF that DEF.DET.MASC cousin of Kim have.3SG.PRS take.PTCP
  un'-aspirina.
  one-aspirin.

  "If the medicine cabinet door is open, then Kim's cousin took an aspirin." [ita]

This test must be applied with care, however. One can construct (complex) sentences or discourses like those in (226) where the presupposition is *canceled*, which means that the discourse implies that the presupposition is false. One can also construct (complex) sentences or discourses where the presupposition is *filtered out*, which means that the discourse doesn't imply the presupposition or its negation [Gazdar, 1979]. The discourse (228a) is a case where the presupposition that Kim has a cousin is canceled; discourses (228b–d) are cases where it is filtered:

(228)   a. It's not the case that Kim's cousin took an aspirin. Kim hasn't got a cousin.

    b. Either Kim's cousin took an aspirin or Kim hasn't got a cousin and the cat swallowed it by mistake.

    c. It's possible that Kim's cousin took an aspirin, but it's also possible that Kim has no cousin and the cat took it.

    d. If Kim has a cousin, then Kim's cousin took an aspirin.

These examples show that to test whether something is presupposed or not, one must make sure that the other clauses in the constructed discourse have contents that are logically independent of the content whose presupposed status is being tested. Because presuppositions can be canceled or filtered, we say that the appropriate word or phrase, which is known as a *presupposition trigger* (see #78 for several examples), *potentially presupposes* certain content. Examples like (228) show that whether a presupposition trigger actually does presuppose the relevant content (meaning that the discourse implies it) is highly context sensitive (see #79).

Another characteristic of presuppositions is that they don't have to be already a part of the common ground for the sentence with the presupposition to be felicitous. Hearers have the capacity, subject to certain constraints, to adjust the context quietly and without fuss so that the speaker's utterance is felicitous. In other words, hearers have the capacity to add the presupposition to the context in which the utterance is interpreted. You may not know prior to a speaker saying (229) that Sandy has an officemate, but the utterance is felicitous because you can add this fact to the common ground.

(229)   Sandy's officemate is a ballroom dancing champion.

This process of context adjustment is known as *presupposition accommodation* [Karttunen, 1974, Stalnaker, 1974]. For a range of theoretical proposals of how to model this process, including a variety of takes on the types of constraints that influence how a presupposition gets accommodated into the context, see Asher and Lascarides 1998, Beaver 1992, Gazdar 1979, Geurts 1996, Karttunen 1974, van der Sandt 1992; and von Fintel 2008. For an implementation of van der Sandt's [1992] theory of presupposition, see Bos 2003.

#78 Presupposition triggers are a wide and varied set.

Presuppositions are usually introduced by particular linguistic words or phrases; these are known as *presupposition triggers*. For example, in (225) above, the trigger for the presupposition that there's someone called Kim is the proper name *Kim*, and the trigger for the presupposition that Kim has a cousin is the possessive construction *X's Y*. The same test described in #77 (projection from certain embedded contexts) can be used to identify a wide and heterogeneous set of presupposition triggers [Levinson, 1993]. We give a brief rundown here:

Factive predicates   Verbs like *know* and *regret* and nouns like *fact* and *knowledge* presuppose the truth of their complement:

(230)   a. Kim knows that a parrot talked.

  b. Kim regretted that the game was rigged.

  c. The fact that the parrot talked surprised Kim.

  d. The knowledge that the game was rigged troubled Sandy.

Implicative verbs   Other verbs introduce presuppositions of a more lexically contentful nature. For example, (231a) presupposes that Kim intended to lock the door, (231b) presupposes that Kim said something to Sandy, and (231c) presupposes that Kim tried to sing.

(231)   a. Kim forgot to lock the door.

  b. Kim lied to Sandy.

  c. Kim managed to sing.

Proper names   Proper names presuppose that there is someone (or something) that is denoted by that proper name [van der Sandt, 1992]; for instance, *Kim slept* presupposes there is someone called Kim.

Relational nouns   Nouns that describe an entity in terms of its relationship to another entity presuppose the existence of the relationship. Accordingly, (232) presupposes that the speaker is married. (This example also involves presuppositions provided by the possessive construction; see below.)

(232)   My spouse is tall.

Expressions of repetition   (233a) and (233b) presuppose that someone other than Kim lives in NYC, (233c) presupposes that Kim made at least one previous trip to Antarctica, (233d) presupposes that Kim also has a first book, and (233e) presupposes that Kim has been in NYC before.

(233)   a. Kim also lives in NYC.

      b. Kim lives in NYC too.

      c. Kim went to Antarctica again.

      d. Kim's second book is about pragmatics.

      e. Kim returned to NYC.

Syntactically, these presupposition triggers vary: they include verbs, and modifiers of verbs and nouns.

Determinatives   Various expressions that fill the determiner slot in English noun phrases introduce presuppositions: The definite determiner *the* presupposes the existence of a uniquely identifiable referent for the noun phrase (a boat, in (234a)). Possessives, also a kind of definite description in English, presuppose that there is a referent that stands in a possessive relationship to the possessor (e.g., that Kim has a child, in (234b)). Finally, quantifiers all presuppose their domains of quantification. For example, (234c) presupposes a set of cats that *most* quantifies over, and entails the content that most cats within that set are cute.

(234)   a. The boat sank.

      b. Kim's child goes to school.

      c. Most cats are cute.

Information structure   Information structure (see Chapter 12) is also associated with presuppositions. For example, in English, focus can be marked with the *it*-cleft construction (235a) or prosody (235b), inter alia (see #85). Similarly, *wh-* questions focus the questioned constituent (235c) [Ginzburg, 1995a,b]. In these constructions, the non-focused part of the sentence is presupposed: (235a) presupposes that someone ate the beans, (235b) presupposes that someone talked, and (235c) presupposes that someone ran.[1]

(235)   a. It was Kim who ate the beans.

       b. KIM talked.

       c. Who ran?

Relatedly, the focus-sensitive operator *only* introduces a presupposition of a salient set of alternatives. In (236a), where prosody shows that the focus is on *Kim*, the set of alternatives is other people who might have eaten the beans; in (236b), where prosody shows the focus is on the beans, the set of alternatives is other things Kim might have eaten.

(236)   a. KIM only ate the beans.

       b. Kim only at the BEANS.

There are several things we should note about this list of presupposition triggers. First, the set of triggers is very heterogeneous: they involve constructions, lexical items of various syntactic categories, individual lexical items (e.g., *forget*) or a whole semantic class of lexical items (e.g., proper names), and so on. Second, this list is not exhaustive—there are many more presupposition triggers in English. Nor is the heterogeneity of presupposition triggers unique to English. Tonhauser et al. [2013] present a methodology for eliciting judgments about presuppositions and other projective content with non-linguistically trained speakers, with a case study of Paraguayan Guaraní. The triggers they identify include (among others), *aimete* "almost" (237) and *n(d)(a)-…-vé-i-ma*, morphological marking which expresses "not anymore" (238):

(237)   [Context: As children, Maria and her brother once had to cross a field with two bulls in it.]

      Ha kyhyje-pó-pe ro-hasa   ha che-kyvy   aimete ho'a   mbokaja ratĩ-'ári.
      and scared-hand-in A1PL.EXCL-pass and B1SG-brother almost A3.fall coco   thorn-on

      "And we passed fearfully and my brother almost fell into the spines of a coconut plant." Implication: The brother came close to falling into the spines, but did not. [gug] [Tonhauser et al., 2013, p. 73]

(238)   Juan nd-o-pita-vé-i-ma.
      Juan NEG-A3-smoke-more-NEG-PF

      "Juan does not smoke anymore." Implication: Juan did smoke previously. [gug] [Tonhauser et al., 2013, p. 72]

Third, the potential presupposition sometimes introduces semantic concepts that are additional to those that are expressed in the sentence of which the presupposition trigger is a part—for instance, the presupposition for *lie* is expressed in terms of the concept *say*, the presupposition

---

[1]This last one might be somewhat subtle. Consider it in an embedded context, e.g., *Kim doesn't know who ran.*

for *forget* is expressed in terms of the concept of *intend*; and that for *manage* is expressed in terms of *try*. In these cases, the presupposition seems to stem from real-world knowledge about the kind of referent that is denoted by the presupposition trigger (e.g., intending something and not doing it is what it means to forget something). As such, it's not necessarily the case that a representation of the presupposition should be composed directly from the syntax tree within the grammar. Rather, it can be computed in a post-processing step.

Finally, the presupposition triggers vary in whether or not their presuppositions can be accommodated (see #77). For example, even though it is common knowledge that lots of people live in NYC, *Kim lives in NYC too* is felicitous only if the discourse context has explicitly introduced (either linguistically or non-linguistically) a prior individual that lives in NYC [Kripke, 2009].

#79 Some linguistic expressions pass embedded presuppositions up, some don't, and with others it depends.

As mentioned in #77, a characteristic property of presuppositions is that they *project*: that is, certain types of complex sentences will share the presuppositions of their component parts, but not necessarily their entailments.[2] This is illustrated in (226), repeated here (see #77 for discussion):

(226)   a. It's not the case that Kim's cousin took an aspirin.

     b. I believe that Kim's cousin took an aspirin.

     c. It's possible that Kim's cousin took an aspirin.

     d. If the medicine cabinet door is open, then Kim's cousin took an aspirin.

In #77 we noted that the projectivity test for distinguishing presupposition from entailment has to be applied carefully, because not all types of embedding contexts behave the same way. Here, we elaborate on those differences.

Karttunen [1973] classifies embedding predicates into three types: *holes*, *plugs*, and *filters*. Holes are the simplest case. These are the predicates that pass up or "let through" all presuppositions of embedded content:

(239)   a. Kim stopped smoking.

     b. Kim didn't stop smoking.

     c. Kim hesitated to stop smoking.

     d. It surprised Sandy that Kim hesitated to stop smoking.

     e. Pat knew that it surprised Sandy that Kim hesitated to stop smoking.

---

[2]Tonhauser et al. [2013] argue that projectivity is not restricted to the classical set of presuppositions, but applies to various other content as well, including expressives (see #8 and Potts, 2007) and offer a preliminary taxonomy of projective content.

The verb *stop* in (239a) triggers the presupposition that Kim has smoked previously. Sentences (239b–e) all share this presupposition, because all of the embedding predicates (in (239e) all of *know*, *surprise*, and *hesitate*) are of the hole type.

The other straightforward case is the plugs. These are predicates that block (fail to let through) presuppositions of their complements, and they are typically verbs describing speech acts:

(240)   a.   Kim promised the kids to introduce them to the present king of France.

       b.   Kim accused the kids of hiding their candy.

       c.   Kim asked Sandy to read the book again.

(240a) does not carry the presupposition that there is a present king of France (compare *Kim introduced the kids to the present king of France*). Similarly, (240b) and (240c) don't presuppose that the kids have candy or that Sandy has already read the book, although simplex clauses with the possessive construction or the iterative adverb *again* would introduce such a presupposition.

The complicated cases involve what Karttunen calls filters. These are embedding contexts where presuppositions are passed up, except if part of the sentence entails either the presupposition or its negation (depending on the filter), in which case the presupposition is not passed up. The filters Karttunen identifies are conditionals, conjunction, and disjunction, as illustrated in (241)–(243) below. In the (a) sentences, the presupposition is passed through; in the (b) sentences, it is blocked:

(241)   a.   Sandy believes that if the medicine cabinet door is open, then Kim's cousin took an apsirin.

       b.   Sandy believes that if Kim has a cousin, then Kim's cousin took an aspirin.

(242)   a.   Sandy believes that Kim's cousin had a headache and Kim's cousin took an aspirin.

       b.   Sandy believes that Kim has a cousin and Kim's cousin took an aspirin.

(243)   a.   Sandy believes that either the medicine cabinet door is closed, or Kim's cousin took an aspirin.

       b.   Sandy believes that either Kim doesn't have a cousin, or Kim's cousin took an aspirin.

We have embedded the complex sentences with the filters under a predicate which is a hole (*believe*) to illustrate how the (potential) presupposition that Kim has a cousin projects in the (a) sentences but not the (b) sentences.

Karttunen also observes that the entailment relation which influences the effects of filters on projection is not just logical entailment, but rather involves entailments stemming from real-world knowledge, as illustrated in (244) [see also Kalouli and Crouch, 2018].

(244)   If Sara sells a beer to a 15-year-old, then she will regret breaking the law regarding the minimum drinking age.

The verb *regret* triggers a presupposition that Sara has broken the law regarding the minimum drinking age, but this presupposition gets filtered: we can paraphrase (244) as *If Sara sells a beer to a 15-year-old, then she is breaking the law regarding the minimum drinking age and she will regret it*. Thus, the presupposition about breaking the law doesn't project from its embedded context to be entailed by the whole sentence. The claim is that this resolution of the presupposition depends on world knowledge that 15 is below the minimum drinking age.[3] The compositional semantics of these complex sentences provides the backbone for calculating the projection (or not) of presupposed content, because it is the compositional semantics that tells us what content is in the scope of a hole, plug, or filter.

Whether such processing should be done in the grammar or as a post-processing step is a matter of debate. The strategy taken by the developers of the English Resource Grammar (ERG) [Flickinger, 2000, 2011] is to assume that the grammar does not construct a semantic representation in which the potentially presupposed content of a sentence is (a) identified and (b) separated from the sentence's non-presupposed content: i.e., the grammar doesn't need to know the relationship between the verb *forget* and its (potential) presupposition involving the concept *intend*, let alone decide on the relative semantic scope of *intend* to other scope-bearing expressions. Rather, both of these tasks are left to a post-processing step outside of the grammar, which would use the semantic representation that's composed within the grammar, in combination with a lexicon of presupposition triggers and what they potentially presuppose (e.g., *forget to X* potentially presupposes *intend to X*), a classification of embedding predicates as plugs, holes, and filters, and finally the relevant notion of (commonsense) entailment and real-world knowledge that determines the scopal position of (potential) presuppositions in the discourse as a whole.

To the extent that world knowledge is required to determine whether a presupposition is filtered or not, and also given that some potential presuppositions invoke concepts that aren't explicitly a part of the compositional semantics of the trigger (as with *forget* and *intend*), this post-processing approach makes sense. On the other hand, if a parser can give even partial information about presupposition as an integrated part of the semantic representations it returns, that is also useful. This is the approach taken by the wide-coverage semantic construction system Boxer [Bos, 2008, Bos et al., 2004] that accompanies output from the C&C Parser [Clark and Curran, 2004] for English: this semantics separates potential presuppositions from the rest of the content directly via the CCG derivation.

---

[3]If we replace *15-year-old* with *70-year-old* in (244), then arguably the presupposition isn't filtered, but the whole sentence becomes quite anomalous because one can't construct any coherent connection between the antecedent of the condition (selling beers to 70-year-olds) and the consequent (regret on breaking the law, of which the antecedent is now not an instance).

#80 Presupposition accommodation depends on the absence of accessible antecedents in the discourse.

Van der Sandt [1992] observed a tight connection between presupposition and anaphora. Specifically, there are many cases where the presupposition introduced by some trigger finds an antecedent in the preceding discourse in a way that is parallel to how pronouns find their antecedents:

(245)   a. Kim bought a table. The table was expensive.

     b. If a farmer owns a donkey she houses the donkey in a stable.

     c. Either there is no bathroom or the bathroom is in a funny place.

     d. Kim bought a table. It was expensive.

     e. If a farmer owns a donkey she houses it in a stable.

     f. Either there is no bathroom or it's in a funny place.

In (245a–c), the definite description in the second clause (*the table*, *the donkey*, *the bathroom*) triggers a presupposition of the existence of a salient uniquely identifiable entity of that description. And in all of these cases, that entity is introduced into the discourse by an indefinite NP in the first clause, the same indefinite NP that serves as the antecedent for a pronoun in the versions in (245d–f).

    We find similar parallels to other kinds of anaphora beyond NP-anaphora (see #72). The *it*-cleft in (246a) triggers the presupposition that someone solved the problem. This presupposition binds to the content of the VP in the antecedent of the conditional the same way that anaphoric VP *did* does. The verb *regret* in (246b) triggers the presupposition that the proposition expressed by its complement is true. This presupposition binds to the proposition in the antecedent of the conditional the same way that the pronoun *it* takes that proposition as its antecedent. Finally, the adverb *still* in (246c) introduces the presupposition that Sara loved Pat in the past, which binds to the first conjunct the same way that the VP anaphor *does* does.

(246)   a. *VP anaphora and* it-*clefts:*
        If someone solved the problem it was Leigh who solved it.
        If someone solved the problem it was Leigh who did.

     b. *Propositional anaphora and* regrets:
        If Kim loves Sandy then Pat regrets that Kim loves Sandy.
        If Kim loves Sandy then Pat regrets it.

     c. *VP anaphora and* still:
        Perhaps Sara loved Pat and perhaps she still loves Pat.
        Perhaps Sara loved Pat and perhaps Sara still does.

Note that in most of these cases (the exception being (245a)) the presuppositions are filtered (see #79) once they are bound, thanks to the structures that the triggers are embedded under.

Regardless of whether there is a filter construction around, a presupposition that cannot be linked or "bound" directly to prior content is a candidate for accommodation; that is, the process by which the context is quietly adjusted to fulfill the presupposition (see #77). This stands in contrast to pronouns and other anaphoric phenomena which can't be accommodated. In (247), the utterances that feature the presupposition triggers are felicitous even without the preceding clauses that introduced the antecedents in the versions given in (245) and (246) above;[4] the utterances that feature the pronouns or other anaphoric expressions are not.

(247)   a. The table was expensive.
          #It was expensive.

        b. If a farmer is prudent, she houses her donkey in a stable.
          #If a farmer is prudent, she houses it in a stable.

        c. Either I'm turned around or the bathroom is in a funny place.
          #Either I'm turned around or it's in a funny place.

        d. It was Leigh who solved the problem.
          #It was Leigh who did.

        e. Pat regrets that Kim loves Sandy.
          #Pat regrets it.

Van der Sandt concludes from data like these that presuppositions are anaphoric expressions, but with richer semantic content. They are anaphoric expressions because whenever possible, a presupposition *binds* to an antecedent in the discourse context. It's possible when: (a) the content of the antecedent entails the content of the (potential) presupposition; and (b) that antecedent content is *available*—in other words, it is sufficiently salient that one could refer back to it with an anaphoric expression. However, unlike the antecedents for pronouns, presuppositions can get accommodated when there is no such antecedent available. Intuitively, that's because the compositional semantic content of a presupposition is much richer than that of a pronoun like *it* or a VP anaphora like *did*—the lexical semantics of *he* entails that the referent is male, but that of *the man in the hat* is much more specific. So when no suitable antecedent for the presupposition exists, one can accommodate it.

Van der Sandt proposed two constraints on accommodation, which determine the relative semantic scope of the presupposition to other content in the discourse: (a) global accommodation is preferred to local accommodation,[5] but (b) accommodation is successful only if the result is

---

[4]As described in #78, the presuppositions triggered by *too*, *also* and *again* are an exception: it is much harder to accommodate them (though it's not impossible in face to face situations where certain content is made non-linguistically, rather than linguistically, salient).

[5]To illustrate what we mean by a presupposition projecting from its embedding to take wide semantic scope, consider the sentence *Kim believes that Sandy regrets smoking*. The phrase *Sandy regrets smoking* has the following two properties: (a) it's

consistent and does not render any part of the proffered content redundant. This means that one prefers an interpretation where the presupposition projects from its embedding to take wide semantic scope, but if the constraint in (b) isn't met by global accommodation, then one tries to accommodate the presupposition in a position where it has narrower semantic scope.

To illustrate the theory, consider (248):

(248)   If John is married, then his spouse is bald.

The proper name *John* is a presupposition trigger, presupposing that there is someone called John. This cannot bind to any prior antecedent (there isn't one), and so this individual named John must get accommodated. The preference for global accommodation succeeds, because the result is consistent and doesn't render any part of the proffered content redundant: There is someone called John and if he is married then his spouse is bald. Now consider the possessive NP *his spouse*, which potentially presupposes that John has a spouse (we'll assume that the pronoun *his* is already interpreted as bound to John). There is no available antecedent referent—while *John is married* entails that John has a spouse this individual is not salient to act as an antecedent to subsequent pronouns (cf. *#If John is married, she is bald*). So John's spouse must be accommodated. The three options for accommodation—global, intermediate, and local—are as in (249):

(249)   a.   John has a spouse and if he is married then she is bald.
             (global accommodation)

        b.   If John is married and has a spouse, then she is bald.
             (intermediate accommodation)

        c.   If John is married, then he has a spouse and she is bald.
             (local accommodation)

Of these, (249c) is most natural, because of the entailment between being married and having a spouse. Global accommodation is ruled out on the grounds that it makes the antecedent to the conditional redundant (*he is married* is entailed by *John has a spouse*).[6] Both intermediate and local accommodation in this example satisfy this criterion, and so the principle that one prefers accommodation in as wide a scopal position as possible, subject to consistency and no redundancy, predicts intermediate accommodation. However, if one takes into account the commonsense relationship between being married and having a spouse, then the intermediate accommodation case can be paraphrased as *If John is married and (hence) has a spouse, then she is bald* which is logically equivalent to (249c), the local accommodation version anyway! We'll

syntactically embedded within *believe*, which in turn introduces a scope bearing element into semantics (since the predicate symbol *believe* takes a proposition as its argument); and (b) it presupposes that Sandy smoked (because of the factive verb *regret*). But the logical form of this sentence should ensure that the content that Sandy smoked takes wide semantic scope over the predicate symbol *believe* (with the propositional argument to this predicate also denoting the content that Sandy smoked); in other words, the sentence can be paraphrased as *Sandy smoked and Kim believes that Sandy regrets this.*

[6]In other words, where p is the (globally) accommodated presupposition and $q \rightarrow r$ is the conditional utterance, we have that $p \wedge (q \rightarrow r))$ entails $p \wedge r$, because p entails q—thus global accommodation is ruled out because it renders the conditional redundant.

return to this issue in #81, when we examine constraints over and above consistency and non-redundancy that others have used to predict the part of the context in which a presuppositions get accommodated (and hence whether or not they project from their embeddings).

Discourse (250) is an example where both binding and accommodation are predicted to fail, making the discourse anomalous:

(250)   John hasn't got a spouse. #His spouse is bald.

The possessive NP *his spouse* presupposes that John has a spouse. It can't bind to *a spouse* in the first sentence (assuming the commonsense interpretation, where negation takes wide scope over the existential *a spouse*), because the negation makes it unavailable as an antecedent.[7] So the presupposition must be accommodated. It cannot be accommodated globally, because the result creates a contradiction: John has a spouse and John hasn't got a spouse. There is no alternative scopal position into which it can be accommodated, however, because the presupposition trigger *his spouse* is not embedded within any logical operators (e.g., conditional, negation, or a propositional attitude verb). Thus, the presupposition cannot be bound or accommodated, and so the sentence is predicted to be anomalous.

Bos [2003] provides an implementation of the interpretation of presuppositions that's proposed by van der Sandt [1992], using off the shelf theorem provers to predict when the constraints on accommodation, defined in terms of consistency and redundancy, are satisfied.

#81 Presuppositions interact with discourse coherence.

In #79 and #80 we have discussed various factors that influence the relative semantic scope of presupposed content to proffered content in a discourse. In van der Sandt's [1992] foundational paper, his approach was to assume that presuppositions take as wide scope as possible, subject to the result being consistent and no proffered content being rendered uninformative. But these factors on their own don't always make the right predictions: this analysis tends to over-generate the cases where the presupposition takes wide semantic scope. Consider (251), modified from Beaver 1997:

(251)   Either Kim didn't solve the problem or else Sandy realizes that the problem has been solved.

---

[7]The prediction is quite different if the indefinite noun phrase *a spouse* in the first sentence is replaced with a noun phrase that triggers a presupposition (or that is definite and so makes a reading where it semantically outscopes the negation more acceptable). In contrast to (250), (i) is acceptable.

    (i) John hasn't got his homework. His homework is at school.

Here, the possessive NP in the first sentence triggers a presupposition, which by van der Sandt's principles is globally accommodated and so outscopes the negation, making it available for the presupposition triggered by *his homework* in the second sentence to bind to. The result can be paraphrased as: John has homework, (but) he hasn't got it (because) it's at school. We've signaled the implicated relations between the propositions expressed by the presuppositions and proffered content with cue phrases in parentheses; see #81 and #67 for further discussion.

The factive verb *realizes* in the second disjunct generates the potential presupposition that the problem has been solved. There is no suitable available antecedent (the problem solving in the first disjunct is unavailable because it's embedded under the negation and disjunction). So it must be accommodated. The result of global accommodation is both consistent and informative. It corresponds to: The problem's been solved, and either Kim didn't solve it or Sandy realizes it's been solved. Note how the first disjunct remains informative (i.e., one cannot reduce the disjunction to just the second disjunct while preserving the truth conditions). But global accommodation doesn't match the intuitive interpretation of (251), which is: either Kim didn't solve the problem, or it's solved and Sandy realizes it.

Beaver [1992, 1997] argues that accommodation is affected by what interlocutors find most plausible and because of this they may entertain various alternatives as the discourse proceeds, revising what they think is most plausible as subsequent content gets expressed. But he doesn't spell out the details of the role of plausibility in general (and doesn't apply it to (251)).

Asher and Lascarides [1998] argue that it's not plausibility *per se* that influences where a presupposition gets accommodated, but rather the principle that people interpret discourse so as to maximize its coherence (see also #76). In other words, presuppositions default to having wide semantic scope in the discourse, but that default is overridden if accommodation in a narrow scope position yields a more coherent interpretation of the discourse. Real-world knowledge, and hence plausibility, is therefore a factor when interpreting presuppositions, in as much as it influences which coherence relations interlocutors infer among the content of the discourse's segments.

This idea of maximizing discourse coherence helps to explain local accommodation in (251). The quality of a disjunction depends on the extent to which the alternatives expressed by the disjuncts address a common theme and the extent to which they also offer contrasting cases [Asher and Lascarides, 2003, Txurruka, 1997, 2001]. If the presupposition in (251) is locally accommodated, then the result expresses a contrast between someone (namely Kim) not solving the problem and someone (not specified) solving it. But with global accommodation, the presupposition *The problem's been solved (by someone)* is outside the scope of the coherence relation (here, the disjunction relation) expressed by *or*, and this reduces the extent to which the alternative cases contrast with one another, and so the disjunction is coherent but of an inferior quality to the disjunction one gets via local accommodation. Thus, an account in terms coherence predicts that speakers prefer local accommodation in this type of example.

CHAPTER 12

Information Status and Information Structure

#82 Information status is a property of linguistic descriptions of referents, describing their relationship to the common ground.

Languages have a variety of means that speakers can use to signal to their interlocutors whether to look for the referent of a particular linguistic description among the referents already being discussed, or whether to add a new entry to that set. See, for example, the sentences in (252), and consider what the speaker's expectations are about how central the dog in question is to the hearer's awareness.

(252) a. I saw a dog.

  b. I saw this dog.

  c. I saw the dog.

  d. I saw that dog.

  e. I saw that.

  f. I saw it.

These contrasts are usually referred to in syntax as *definiteness* (with a particular focus on *the* vs. *a*), and are sometimes simplified in semantic discussions to *given* vs. *new*. But in fact, the distinctions are more fine-grained than that. Gundel et al. [1993], building on the work of Prince [1981a], defines an implicational hierarchy of givenness, as shown in (253):[1]

(253) In focus > Activated > Familiar > Uniquely identifiable

> Referential > Type identifiable

At the far extreme are referents that are *type identifiable*. That is, all the hearer is expected to be able to do is to understand the type of referent being described by the referring expression. The next category, *referential* involves cases where the speaker intends to refer to a particular instance of an identifiable type. Referring expressions that signal that their referents are *uniquely identifiable* indicate that the hearer should be able to identify the referent in question on the basis of the referring expression alone. The next steps are referents which are already *familiar*

---

[1]The examples in (252) are arranged going from the right edge of this hierarchy to the left.

to the hearer, then already *activated* in the current discourse context (through linguistic or non-linguistic means), and finally the referents which are currently *in focus* in the discussion.

This set of categories is called an implicational hierarchy, because anything that is referential is necessarily also type identifiable, anything that is uniquely identifiable is necessarily also referential and type identifiable, and so on. Individual linguistic forms signal that their referents are at some position or some range in the hierarchy, though not all languages have distinct forms for each of the positions, as discussed further in #83 below. By relating all of these categories in one hierarchy, Gundel et al. [1993] illuminate how referring expressions from unstressed pronouns (and even dropped arguments) to indefinite noun phrases operate as a single system for signaling information status. Modeling this information is beneficial for reference resolution [Denis and Baldridge, 2008].

Finally, it is important to note that the notion of "givenness" in information status is distinct from the notion of "givenness" in information structure, discussed in #84 below. Information status has to do with the identifiability of particular discourse referents; information structure relates to propositional content and what is presented as new vs. given information.

#83 Information status is reflected in the morphology and syntax in different ways across languages.

A key locus for the marking of information status is in the form of noun phrases. Gundel et al. [1993] present a corpus-based study of English [eng], Japanese [jpn], Mandarin [cmn], Russian [rus], and Spanish [spa] and identify which forms are associated with which of the positions in the givenness hierarchy in (253) in #82 above. Their results are summarized in Table 12.1. Across these languages, the most minimal expressions possible, which is unstressed personal pronouns (all languages except Japanese) or dropped arguments (all languages except English), can only be used to refer to referents which are in focus. Stressed pronouns (and in fact all pronouns in Japanese), all demonstrative pronouns, and certain demonstrative determiners, can only be used to refer to arguments which are at least activated. Mandarin doesn't have any expressions which are specific to the familiar category, but the rest of the languages locate some of their demonstrative determiners there. In the rest of the hierarchy, there is more crosslinguistic variation: Japanese and Russian use bare NPs for all the categories from uniquely identifiable to type identifiable. Mandarin has a specific form for uniquely identifiable (NPs with the demonstrative determiner 那 *nèi* "that") and associates both bare NPs and those marked with the determiner 一 *yī* "a" for type identifiable referents, but has no forms associated specifically for the referential category. Spanish uses definite determiners (e.g., *el*) for uniquely identifiable referents and associates unmarked NPs and those with the indefinite determiners (e.g., *un*) with both type identifiable and referential referents. Finally, English is the only language that Gundel et al. find distinguishes all five categories. This suggests that a study of more languages might turn up finer-grained distinctions not marked in English.

Table 12.1: Linguistic forms associated with different information status categories, adapted from Gundel et al. 1993, p. 284

	In Focus	Activated	Familiar	Unique ID	Reference	Type ID
Mandarin	ϕ *tā* '3sg'	*tā* '3sg' *zhè* 'this' *nèi* 'that' *zhè* N 'this N'		*nèi* N 'that N'		*yī* N 'a N' ϕ N
English	it	*HE, this, that* *this N*	*that N*	*the* N	indefinite *this* N	*a* N
Japanese	ϕ	*kare* 'he' *kore, sore, are* 'demonstrative' *kono* N 'this N' *sono* N 'that N' (medial)	*ano* N 'that N' (distal)		ϕ N	
Russian	ϕ *on* 'he'	*ON* 'he' *èto* 'this' *to* 'that'	*èto* N 'this N' *to* N 'that N'		ϕ N	
Spanish	ϕ *él* 'he'	*ÉL* 'he' *éste* 'this' *ése* 'that (medial) *aquél* 'that' (distal) *este* N 'this' N	*ese* N 'that N' (medial) *aquel* N 'that N' (distal)	*el* N 'the N'	ϕ N *un* N 'a N'	

As can be seen in Table 12.1, the languages treat their demonstrative determiners differently. First, where Mandarin, English, and Russian have only a two-way distinction among demonstratives (*this* vs. *that*), Spanish and Japanese differentiate medial (*ese*, そ の *sono*) from distal (*aquel*, あ の *ano*) forms. Furthermore, English is the only language to have an indefinite use of a demonstrative determiner, as illustrated in (254).

(254)   I couldn't sleep last night. This dog next door kept me awake.

Finally, Mandarin differs from the other languages in using the demonstrative determiner 那 *nèi* "that" with uniquely identifiable referents, rather than those that are at least familiar. This is illustrated in (255a), which, unlike (255b), is appropriate even if the addressee doesn't already know the neighbor has a dog:

(255) a. 昨天　　晚上　　　我 睡不着.　　　　　隔壁的　　　　那条　　　狗 叫　得
Zuótiān wǎnshàng wǒ shuì-bù-zháo.　Gébì-de　　　nèi-tiáo　gǒu jiào de
yesterday evening　I　sleep-NEG-achieve next.door-POSS that-NUMCL dog bark DEG
厉害.
lìhài.
extremely.

"I couldn't sleep last night. The dog next door was barking." [cmn] [Gundel et al., 1993, p. 285]

b. I couldn't sleep last night. That dog next door was barking.

All of the forms considered in Table 12.1 involve only the internal structure of a noun phrase. There are also syntactic contexts which mark information status. Many if not all languages have presentational constructions, i.e., specialized constructions for introducing a new referent into the discourse. (256) gives examples for English, French, Japanese, and Mandarin:

(256) a. Once upon a time there was a bear.

b. Il était　　une　　　fois un　　　　ours.
it be.3SG.IMP INDEF.FEM.SG time INDEF.MASC.SG bear.

"Once upon a time there was a bear." [fra]

c. 昔昔　　　　　熊　が　いました。
Mukashimukashi kuma ga　ima-shi-ta.
long.ago　　　　bear　NOM exist.ANIM-AHON:+PST

"Once upon a time there was a bear." [jpn]

d. 从前　　有 一只　　　熊.
Cóngqián yǒu yìzhī　　xióng
long.ago　exist one-NUMCL bear

"Once upon a time there was a bear." [cmn]

In these examples, both English and French use the *be* verb (*was, était*) with an existential subject and the new discourse entity as a complement. Japanese has an intransitive existential verb (いました *imashita*) which takes the new entity as its subject. Mandarin has an existential verb (有 *yǒu*) which appears only with a complement.[2]

In addition, some languages use case marking to indicate information status. For example, in both Turkish and Persian[3] type identifiable direct objects appear without case marking, whereas all other direct objects take accusative case [Hedberg et al., 2009, pp. 4–5]:

---

[2]The same word form can be used as a possessive verb (a verb meaning "have") with two arguments.
[3]These languages are not related to each other; Turkish is classified as Turkic, within Altaic, and Persian and Indo-Iranian, within Indo-European.

(257)   a. Bugün bir avukat-ı   gör-üyor-um.
            today   one lawyer-ACC see-PROG-ISG

        "I am seeing a (particular) lawyer today." [tur]

        b. Bugün bir avukat gör-üyor-um.
            today   one lawyer see-PROG-ISG

        "I am seeing a lawyer today (some lawyer or other)." [tur]

(258)   a. وکیلو   یه   امروز   می‌بینم
            Emruz ye   vakil-o   mi-bin-am.
            today   a/one lawyer-ACC DUR-see-ISG

        "I am seeing a (particular) lawyer today." [fas]

        b. وکیل   یه   امروز   می‌بینم
            Emruz ye   vakil mi-bin-am.
            today   a/one lawyer DUR-see-ISG

        "I am seeing a lawyer today (some lawyer or other)." [fas]

#84 The information structure of a sentence distinguishes what the speaker expresses as given vs. new.

Information status, discussed in #82 and #83 above, concerns the relationship of referents of linguistic descriptions to the common ground. Information structure, in contrast, concerns the relationship of propositional content of utterances to the common ground. In the simplest case, the entire utterance might be new information, such as B's utterance in (259):

(259)   A: What happened next?

        B: A student who likes to bake brought cupcakes.

The other possibility is that some of the information is new and some is given, as in (260):

(260)   A: Who brought cupcakes?

        B: A student who likes to bake brought cupcakes.

In (259) and (260), the very same utterance is used in different discourse contexts. Unlike (259), B's response in (260) is in a context where the proposition that someone brought cupcakes is given or shared information (because *wh*-questions presuppose non-empty answers [Ginzburg, 1995a,b], see #78) and what's new in B's utterance is that the bringer of the cupcakes is a student who likes to bake.[4]

---

[4]The third logical possibility, that nothing in the sentence is new, is predicted to be anomalous on the grounds that it violates Gricean Maxims of conversation [Grice, 1975]; see #90.

The examples in (259) and (260) are carefully constructed so that one and the same string has a different division into given/new in different discourse contexts. This is possible because English primarily uses prosody (stress and intonation) to mark information structure and doesn't represent that intonation in the writing system. Where prosody is important for some of the examples in this chapter, we will indicate stress by using CAPITAL LETTERS on the word or syllable that's stressed and we will attempt to indicate the tune by placing characters lower for low pitch and higher for high pitch. Using those conventions, the B examples in (259) and (260) can be rendered like this:

(259′)   B: A STU_{DENT} who likes to _bake brought ^CUPCAKES.

(260′)   B: A ^STUDENT who likes to bake brought cupcakes.

As discussed in #86 below, languages can also use morphology and syntax to mark information structure.

Just because something is expressed as given doesn't mean it's already mutually known. It might indeed be novel information, but it can be accommodated into the common ground, given that certain constraints are met [Steedman, 2014]:

(261)   A: What did the kids want?
        B: They wanted some ^TOYS they saw.

The deaccented modifier to the NP *toys* is not given in this discourse context, but it can be accommodated as a part of the common ground (after all, it's not surprising that kids should see toys!).

In contrast, what's expressed as new had better not already be in the common ground [e.g., Büring, 2003, Halliday, 1967]. If it is, then the utterance is infelicitous, as B's utterance is in (262).

(262)   A: Who voted for Sandy?
        B: #Kim voted for SANDY.

In describing and researching information structure, it is important to keep the information structure meaning (the division into given and new, and related concepts) and the information structure marking (how these are expressed in linguistic form) distinct. Doing so is often difficult because the literature tends to name the contrasts in form after the meanings they express (e.g., calling the stress used to indicate focus "focus"). We will discuss information structure meaning first in #85 and then turn to marking in #86 and #87.

#85 Given v. new content in sentences can be understood in terms of topic, background, focus, and contrast.

Information structure is a critical component connecting the compositional semantics of sentences to their contributions to on-going discourse and thus has attracted much study. At the same time, there is considerable variation across languages in the grammatical (including prosodic) means used to signal information structure (see #86), so scholarly traditions studying different languages approach the problem from different initial vantage points. In this text, we adopt the terms *topic, focus, background,* and *contrast*. Following Song [2017], we define topic as that which a sentence is about, focus as the new or important information expressed by a sentence, and background is the rest. Contrast cross-cuts topic and focus (see below). All sentences have foci (possibly including the entire sentence, e.g., (259B) above), but not all sentences have topics. In (263), *ice cream* is a topic; in (264) it is a focus.

(263)   As for ice cream, Kim prefers chocolate.

(264)   It's ice cream that Kim prefers chocolate-flavored.

We choose our terms out of a larger set provided by the long and diverse linguistic literature on information structure, which presents many different conceptualizations and corresponding terminologies for the distinctions at play. Mathesius [1915], Hockett [1958], and others look at sentences as divided into *topic* (what the speaker is saying something about) and *comment* (what they say about it). The Prague school conceptualizes the division of sentences into *theme* (the part with lower "communicative dynamism" or "informational value") and *rheme* (the part with higher communicative dynamism) (Firbas, 1992, p. 105; see also Halliday, 1967). Vallduví [1992] divides sentences into *focus*, defined as "the only information of the sentence" (p. v) and *ground*, with *ground* further subdivided into *link* (the connection to previous discourse) and *tail* (the rest). Lambrecht [1996] and others highlight the roles of *focus* (new information) and *topic* (link to preceding discourse). For overviews, see Vallduví 1992 and Song 2017.

One property of information structure that has made it particularly difficult to model is that the category of *contrast* cross-cuts topic and focus: both topic (the old information, link to the previous discourse) and the focus (what is presented as new) can be either contrastive or non-contrastive. Contrast evokes an alternative set and conveys that of that set only the topic (respectively, focus) has the property expressed. For example, *Kim* in B's response in the English example in (265) is contrastively focused, and *la frutta* and *la verdura* in the Italian example in (266) are contrastive topics.

(265)   A: Did Sandy tell Pat or did Kim?

        B: Kim told Pat.

(266)   Context: a farm producing a set of goods that are known to the people involved in the conversation.

La   frutt-a   la   regal-iamo,   la   verdur-a   la   vend-iamo.
DEF.FEM.SG fruit-SG 3SG.FEM give-PRS.1PL, DEF.FEM.SG vegetable-SG 3SG.FEM sell-PRS.1PL

"We give the fruit for free, while we sell the vegetables." [ita] [Gryllia, 2009, p. 33]

Gryllia [2009] proposes tests to identify contrast, including the following:

(i) The *wh* question test: The answer to a *wh* question is non-contrastive focus.

(ii) The choice test: The answer to an alternative question is contrastive focus.

(iii) Substitution test: If two items can be substituted with *the former* and *the latter*, they are contrastive topics.

Thus, for example, *Kim* in B's response in (265) is contrastive, even though the same response would have non-contrastive focus in the context provided by A's different question in (267).

(267)   A: Who told Pat?

      B: Kim told Pat.

Furthermore, we can establish that (266) involves contrastive topics because the phrases in question can be replaced by *la prima* "the first" and *la seconda* "the second":

(268)   Context: a farm producing a set of goods that are known to the people involved in the conversation.

    La   prima   la   regal-iamo,   la   seconda   la   vend-iamo.
    DEF.FEM.SG first.FEM 3SG.FEM give-PRS.1PL, DEF.FEM.SG second.FEM 3SG.FEM sell-PRS.1PL

    "We give the former, while we sell the latter." [ita] [Gryllia, 2009, p. 33]

    We thus expect that when languages have specific marking for contrast in general, contrastive focus, or contrastive topic (see #86), such marking should be incompatible with environments that set up non-contrastive focus/topic, and vice versa.

#86 Different languages mark information structure differently.

Song [2017] provides a survey of the different strategies used for marking information structure in the world's languages. He finds three major categories: prosody, lexical markers (including both affixes and separate words), and syntactic positioning. We illustrate each in turn:

Prosodic marking   This strategy is well illustrated in English, where two different accent types are typically associated with topic and focus, respectively [Bolinger, 1958]:

(269)   A: What about Chris? What did Chris eat?

      B: Chris ate the QUICHE.

    These accents tend to fall on just one word, but topic and focus can include more than that. This leads to *focus projection*, where the actual focus is a larger phrase containing the constituent prosodically marked for focus. For example, (270), with stress on *POSSUMS* can be the answer to any of the questions in (271a–e), but how much of the content is focused varies because the focus depends on the question [Selkirk, 1995]:

(270)   Kim wrote a book about POSSUMS.

(271)   a. What did Kim write a book about?

      b. What kind of book did Kim write?

      c. What did Kim write?

      d. What did Kim do?

      e. What's been happening?

As discussed further in #87, prosodic marking involves more than just the placement of stress/accent and in fact can only be fully modeled by taking into account both stress and tune.

Lexical marking   Many languages have dedicated lexical items for marking topic, focus, or contrast, taking the form of separate words or affixes. To take a few examples, Rendile uses the clitics *é* and *á* to mark focus on arguments and predicates respectively (Oomen 1978, cited in Lecarme 1999, p. 277):

(272)   a. ínam=é yimi.
        boy=FOC come.PST

        "THE BOY came." [rel]

      b. ínam á=yimi.
        boy FOC=come.PST

        "The boy CAME." [rel]

Similarly, Cantonese uses lexical items including *aa4* and *aa3* to mark topic and focus [Man, 2007, p. 16].

(273)   a. 呢 本   書 啊, 我 睇過   好多   次。
        nei1 bun2 syu1 aa4, ngo5 tai2-gwo3 hou2do1 ci3
        This NUMCL book TOP 1.SG read-EXP many   times

        "As for this book, I have read it for many times." [yue]

      b. 佢 啊, 本   書 我 俾咗。
        keoi5 aa3, bun2   syu1 ngo5 bei2-zo2
        3SG FOC NUMCL book 1SG give.-PF

        "It is him/her who I have given the book to." [yue]

Vietnamese has a similar lexical marker which specifically marks contrastive topics [Nguyen, 2006, p. 1]:

(274)   Nam thì   đi Hà Nội.
        Nam CONTRAST.TOP go Ha Noi

        "Nam goes to Hanoi(, but nobody else)." [vie]

Marking via syntactic position   Finally, there is marking via syntactic position. This can take the form of specific constructions, such as the English *it*-cleft in (275), where the NP in the *it*-cleft marks focus, and English left-dislocation in (276), which marks the sentence-initial constituent as topic or focus (but not background):[5]

(275)   It's bagels that Kim likes.

(276)   Bagels, Bill likes; crackers, he hates.

In other languages, especially those with freer word order, specific positions can be associated with particular information structural roles. Song [2017] notes four such positions: clause-initial, clause-final, preverbal, and postverbal. For example, Basque uses the preverbal position for focus. (277a) illustrates the information-structurally neutral word order, whereas in both (277b) and (277c), the subject is the focus [de Urbina, 1999, p. 312]:

(277)   a. Jon-ek   eskutitz-a   irakur-ri d-u.
             Jon-ERG.SG letter-ABS.SG read-PF have.PRS.3SG.3SG

             "Jon has read the letter." [eus]

         b. Jon-ek   irakur-ri d-u   eskutitz-a.
             Jon-ERG.SG read-PF have.PRS.3SG.3SG letter-ABS.SG

             "JON has read the letter." [eus]

         c. Eskutitz-a, Jon-ek   irakur-ri d-u.
             letter-ABS.SG Jon-ERG.SG read-PF have.PRS.3SG.3SG

             "JON has read the letter." [eus]

Regardless of the form that information structure marking takes, it is always incomplete with respect to the actual information structure of a situated utterance. That is, grammatical processing (including prosody) provides some information about what is marked as topic, focus, contrast or background in the linguistic signal, but a complete analysis of the information structure also requires further processing that takes further information into account, such as the current state of the discourse, world knowledge, and models of speaker intent.

#87 Languages that mark information structure with intonation require joint semantic models of stress and tune.

Prosody includes both *stress* and *tune*, but most research on the prosodic marking of focus considers only stress and furthermore only indicates stress in the data that is given. For instance, Kratzer [1989] claims that (278) presupposes that someone who is not Sandy lives in Paris (and this contrasts with the proffered content, that Sandy doesn't live in Paris).

---

[5]Confusingly, this construction is referred to in the syntactic literature as *topicalization*, but its information structural import is not specific to topic [Prince, 1981b].

(278)   SANDY does not live in Paris.
     ↝ *someone else lives in Paris*

But in fact, depending on the tune with which (278) is produced, it gets very different interpretations. This is illustrated in (279)–(280), where A's utterances establish the context, the placement of the letters indicates the tune and the material after ↝ gives what's implicated (we also highlight what's not implicated with ↬, so as to contrast the interpretations of the same sentence in the same context, but uttered with different intonation):

(279)   a. A: Does Sandy live in Paris?

     b. B: $_{SAN}{}^{DY}$ do$_{es}$ not live in Par^{is}.
        ↝ *someone (else) does live in Paris*

     b′ B:# ^{SAN}D$_Y$ does not live in Par$_{is}$.

     b″ B: Sandy does $^{NO}{}^{T}$ l$_{ive}$ in Par$_{is}$.
        ↬ *someone (else) does live in Paris*

(280)   a. A: Who does not live in Paris?

     b. B: $_{SAN}{}^{DY}$ do$_{es}$ not live in Par^{is}.
        ↝ *I thought you knew this already* or
        ↝ *But is this what you wanted to know?*

     b′ B: ^{SAN}D$_Y$ does not live in Par$_{is}$.
        ↬ *someone (else) does live in Paris*

The difference in the information structural meaning between the different prosodies (i.e., tune—stress combinations) is apparent both in the differing felicity of (279b′) and (280b′) and in the differing implied contents of (279b) and (279b′). The contrast between the infelicitous (279b′) and the felicitous (279b″) furthermore shows that the issue isn't the combination of the falling tune and the discourse context (for they both have a falling tune), but the full constellation of tune, context, and also where the stress is placed. In other words, successful modeling of prosodic marking of information structure requires a joint model of both stress and tune [Beaver and Clark, 2009, p. 47; Roberts, 2012, p. 29].

Intonation patterns are subject to significant variability across different varieties of English. For example, for mainstream American English speakers, (281a) is only appropriate as an echo question [Ladd, 2008, pp. 113–4] (i.e., in a context where someone has just asserted that they have bought a Mercedes), and if the question were being asked "out of the blue" (or to shift topic) then it would be uttered as (281b).

(281)   a. You ^{BOUGHT} a MER^{CE}DES?

b. You BOUGHT a MERCEDES?

However in contrast to this, British speakers use the contour in (281a) much more widely for "out of the blue" yes/no questions, and this sounds condescending to Americans!

#88 Information structure can interact with truth conditions.

It is tempting to think of information structure as a separate representation layer that does not interact with truth conditions. However, as noted by Halliday [1970] and Partee [1991], there are examples which show that these aspects of meaning interact. For instance, in the absence of prosody and any discourse context there are several alternative readings to (282), as shown in the paraphrases given, although world knowledge makes the interpretation (282b) more plausible than the others:

(282)   Dogs must be carried on this escalator.

    a. You can ride this escalator only if you are carrying a dog.

    b. If you are riding this escalator with a dog, then carry it.

    c. You can't carry your dog on any escalator other than this one.

These readings stem from an ambiguity in the relative semantic scope of the quantified NPs *dogs* and *this escalator* and the modality *must*.

    The information structure that's derived from prosody can help to resolve the ambiguity, even if it conflicts with the reading that's made plausible by world knowledge. The prosody in (283a–c) yields the readings (282a–c), respectively:

(283)   a.   DOGS must be carried on this escalator.

    b.   DOGS must be CARRIED on this escalator.

    c.   DOGS must be carried on THIS escalator.

These prosodic tunes indicate focus, i.e., new information. Depending on which information is new, the utterance answers different implied questions (see Roberts, 2012, and more generally the Questions Under Discussion (QUD) framework for representing the semantics of discourse; Ginzburg, 2012). For (283a), the question is: What must be carried on this escalator? (Note that this question presupposes that something must be carried.) The answer (283a) supplies is "dogs." Where there are multiple points of stress, the question typically corresponds to replacing the most recent stressed word with a *wh*-element. So for (283b), the question is: What must you do with dogs on this escalator? And for (283c) it is: On which escalator must you carry dogs?

CHAPTER 13

Implicature and Dialogue

#89 Implicature is an implied meaning that goes beyond what the speaker explicitly expressed.

Speakers often convey content that goes beyond the lexical and compositional semantics of their utterances—recall the distinction we made in #4 between sentence meaning and speaker meaning. Any aspect of the speaker's meaning that is not a part of sentence meaning (i.e., the meaning that is derivable just from linguistic form, independently of its context of use) is called an *implicature* [Grice, 1975].[1] For example, B's response in (284) implicates that either B doesn't know whether the kids picked up all their toys or that B knows that they picked up some but not all of them (this is an example of a *scalar implicature*); in (285), B implicates that A can get gas at the gas station around the corner; in (286), B implicates a negative answer to the question; and in (287), the speaker implicates that Kim and Sandy adopted a baby and then got married:

(284)   A: Did the kids pick up their toys from the floor?
        B: They picked up some of them.

(285)   A: I'm out of gas.
        B: There's a gas station around the corner

(286)   A: Are you coming out tonight?
        B: I have to work.

(287)   Kim and Sandy adopted a baby and got married.

A characteristic feature of implicatures is that, unlike logical entailments, they can be overridden by adding further content to the discourse:

(288)   A: Did the kid pick up their toys from the floor?
        B: They picked up some of them; in fact, remarkably, they picked up all of them.

(289)   A: I'm out of gas.
        B: There's a gas station around the corner, but it's shut.

(290)   A: Are you coming out tonight?
        B: I have to work, but I'll come out anyway.

(291)   Kim and Sandy adopted a baby and got married, but not in that order.

[1]We'll return to where presuppositions, discussed in Chapter 11, fit into this picture in #90.

#90 Implicatures can be conversational or conventional.

Grice [1975] distinguishes *conversational* implicatures from *conventional* ones. Conversational implicatures follow from premises consisting of the compositional and lexical semantics of the sentence, plus an assumption that the speaker is behaving rationally and cooperatively and is thereby adhering to certain maxims of language use (more on the maxims shortly). As such, conversational implicatures depend on the linguistic meaning of the whole sentence rather than the fact that a particular lexical item or phrase was used, and they are also *cancelable* because predictions about which action is rational and cooperative are highly context-dependent. Indeed, cancellability is a test for whether a implicature is conversational; so, e.g., (288)–(290) show that the implicatures we described in #89 for the sentences (284)–(286) are all examples of conversational implicatures.

Conventional implicatures, on the other hand, are a part of a lexical expression's agreed meaning, and are not derivable from general principles of rational and cooperative behavior [Potts, 2012]. Rather, Potts argues, conventional implicatures are (a) commitments made by speakers by virtue of the meaning of the words they choose and (b) logically independent of the so-called "at issue" content they convey.[2] Grice used the word *but* to illustrate his definition of conventional implicatures: (292a) implicates that honesty is unexpected in rich people. This is linked to the connective *but* because replacing it with another connective (see (292b)) removes the implicature:

(292)   a. Kim is rich but honest.

       b. Kim is rich and honest.

(292b) conveys no contrast between Kim being rich and Kim being honest, and hence no implicature that rich people are normally dishonest. Further, the *contrast* relation is always a part of the meaning of *but*, whatever the contents of the phrases it connects. But the grounds for satisfying the *contrast* relation are context-dependent and hence implicated. (Here, the interlocutor chooses to ensure that the contrast relation that *but* demands is satisfied by assuming that the proposition that rich people are normally dishonest is true.) Accordingly, one can create anomalies when no contrast can be inferred, as in (293):

(293)   #Kim is rich but a billionaire.

There is some controversy, however, over whether *but* is a good example of conventional implicature (see Potts, 2012 for an extensive discussion), because the contrast relation conveyed by *but* should be a part of its truth conditions [see also Asher and Lascarides, 2003], making it a semantic entailment. However, although the existence of a *contrast* relation is semantic, the

---

[2]Roughly speaking, "at-issue" content, also known as proffered content [Roberts, 2012], is the central part of the speaker's message, and distinguished from its presuppositions—the content that must be a part of the context in order for one to be able to evaluate the truth of the at-issue content (see Chapter 11).

assumptions one makes about the contrasted referents in order to ensure that the contrast between them is satisfiable are highly context dependent (and hence implicated), and in particular are influenced by real-world knowledge.

At any rate, there are many other examples of linguistic constructions that satisfy the above definition—for instance, English appositives as illustrated in (294), adapted from Potts 2012:

(294)   a. Sandy, a confirmed psychopath, is fit to watch the kids.

     b. Kim says that Sandy, a confirmed psychopath, is fit to watch the kids.

     c. Kim says that Sandy is a confirmed psychopath and fit to watch the kids.

Utterance (294a) can be paraphrased with the following conjunction: Sandy is a confirmed psychopath and is fit to watch the kids. But replacing (294a) with this paraphrase in the embedded (indirect speech) construction in (294b) gives (294c), which does not preserve (294b)'s meaning. That's because Sandy being a confirmed psychopath is a part of the speaker's commitment in (294b), not Kim's. Conversely, the speaker does not commit to Sandy's being fit to watch the kids; rather, she commits to Kim saying (and therefore committing) to this proposition. Thus, the appositive construction, which attributes the property expressed by the appositive phrase to the head noun that it modifies, is a conventional implicature: this aspect of the content of (294a) is a part of the speaker's commitment even when the sentence is embedded in a non-truth preserving context (like indirect speech); and it is logically independent of the at-issue entailment (in (294a), that Sandy is fit to watch the kids, or in (294b) that Kim said Sandy is fit to watch the kids).[3]

Conversational implicatures are *calculable* while conventional implicatures are not. Being calculable means that conversational implicatures are predictable from the compositional and lexical semantics of the discourse on the basis of an assumption that speakers and hearers are rational and cooperative: in other words, the implicature is detached from the particular words and linguistic constructions that were used to express the content but rather depends only on the semantics that you can construct from the utterance's linguistic form. Grice [1975, p. 276] proposed that the following *four maxims of conversation* are all derivable from general principles of rational and cooperative behavior (though he never demonstrated this):

Maxim of Quality: Do not say what you believe to be false; do not say that for which you lack adequate evidence.

Maxim of Quantity: Make your contribution as informative as is required (for the current purposes of the conversation); do not make it *more* informative than is required.

Maxim of Relation: Be relevant.

Maxim of Manner: Avoid obscurity of expression; avoid ambiguity; be brief; be orderly.

---

[3]Conventional implicatures, under Potts's definition, are in fact very closely related to presuppositions (see Chapter 11), but we gloss over this here.

By and large, conversational implicatures are derived from these four maxims via the following pattern of inference: (i) what appears to be a violation of a maxim is not a violation so long as some proposition p is true (typically, the proposition p that stops a maxim being violated is identified by comparing what the speaker chose to say with what she chose not to say); and (ii) therefore, assuming that people are rational and cooperative (and so following the maxims), p must be true.

Consider the (scalar) implicature of (284), that either B does know whether the kids picked up all of the toys, or B believes that the kids picked up some but not all of them:

(284)   A: Did the kids pick up their toys from the floor?
        B: They picked up some of them.

Inferring this conversational implicature goes like this: B's response appears to violate the Maxim of Quantity (say what is required for the current purposes), for in this case what's required for the current purposes is an answer to A's yes/no question such as (284B′):

(284)   B′: They picked up the toys from the floor.

So assuming B is following the maxims means that this alternative response must violate them (otherwise, the maxim of Quantity would have compelled B to say this instead). (284B′) clearly satisfies the maxims of Relation and Manner; so it must violate the maxim of Quality. Thus, either B believes (284B′) to be false (in which case given what she explicitly said, she believes that the kids picked up some but not all the toys), or she lacks adequate evidence that it's true.

There are three important things to note about this line of reasoning. First, it involves reasoning about B's cognitive state, including her beliefs and intentions. Second, this makes the reasoning inherently defeasible, because we cannot directly observe what's going on inside B's head. Finally, the maxims of Quantity and Quality place conflicting demands in this example on what B should say (the former demands a response that entails either that the kids picked up the toys or that they didn't, while the latter demands a response that B believes to be true, and she believes neither of those things), and the maxim of Quality "wins." This apparent conflict among the maxims is very common, and Grice doesn't provide a sufficiently precise model of inference to predict how such conflicts get resolved when computing implicatures in context.

As mentioned above, Grice did not establish how his four maxims follow (as claimed) from a model of rational and cooperative behavior. Benz et al. [2005], Franke et al. [2012], van Rooij [2004], and others have modeled this link using signaling games of various kinds and an accompanying solution concept in game theory (where a solution concept is a formal rule that predicts how a game will be played) called *iterated best response*. They show that the maxims correspond to optimal policies within these signaling games. In doing so, they also provide a sufficiently precise model of optimal policies in conversation to predict how conflict among the maxims gets resolved in context. But the signaling games they propose assume that both the speaker and interlocutor have complete and accurate knowledge of every signal that the speaker deliberated about when making their choice of which signal to utter; similarly, both the speaker and interlocutor have complete and accurate knowledge of every possible interpretation the interlocutor considers in reaction to those signals. One major gap in this work is that they don't provide general principles by which one can bound the size of the signaling game to the "right" set of possible signals and possible interpretations. This is a drawback: since natural language admits an unbounded number of signals (and interpretations), one needs to justify the (bounded) size of the signaling game that's used to model implicatures, if one is to be confident that the predictions about optimal moves in the signaling game reflects the real dilemmas that speakers and interlocutors seek to solve. For instance, the signaling game they use to demonstrated that iterated best response predicts that *some* implicates *not all* asssumes that the set possible signals from which the speaker chooses one consists of: *some*, *all* and *no*. It does not include the signal *some but not all*. But why wouldn't the speaker consider saying *some but not all* in a context where that is the message she wants to convey? If this signal is added to the set of possibilities, then predictions about implicatures change as well.

In #4, we emphasized the importance of distinguishing three different levels of meaning: (1) the content that's derivable from just the sentence's linguistic form; (2) the content that a speaker of that sentence publicly commits to [Hamblin, 1970]; and (3) further content that is derivable from (2). Where do implicatures fall within this classification? Conventional implicatures are always a part of the speaker's public commitment, but conversational implicatures cut across (2) and (3): some of them are public commitments; others are perlocutionary effects that are defeasibly derivable from the public commitment (on a default assumption that the speaker is rational, for instance).

For instance, the "and then" reading implicated by speaker A's move in (295) is calculated on the basis of recognizing *narrative* as the coherence relation between the conjoined clauses. This implicature is available as an antecedent for *no* (which requires an antecedent that is being disagreed with).[4]

(295)   A: Kim and Sandy adopted a baby and got married.
        B: No. They got married before they adopted the baby.

This availability to serve as an antecedent for *no* shows that the "and then" implicature is part of (2), i.e., A's public commitments.

In contrast, (296) shows a dialogue where A attempts to deny the implicature that A should be able to get gas at that station now, which is calculable from B's response to A's question via the same axioms of rationality and cooperativity that Grice talks about:

(296)   A: I need gas.
        B: There's a gas station around the corner.
        A: #But I can't. It's shut.

---

[4]We can tell it's just the coherence relation that's being denied because the rest of B's utterance expresses agreement with the rest of A's.

But the elided clause in this denial is infelicitous, even if A augments this response with the reason why she cannot get gas at the gas station; namely it's shut. This shows that the implicature falls into (3), i.e., that B is not publicly committed to A being able to get gas at the gas station now. The coherence relation at play here is *elaboration*, such that B's move is interpreted as elaborating a plan to help A get gas (which in turn is the purpose behind A's utterance). But it doesn't necessarily follow from this coherence relation that the gas station is open now—e.g., a valid plan for getting gas involving the gas station is to wait until morning (when the gas station opens) and then buy gas at the gas station. Thus, B's move does not publicly commit her to the claim that A can get gas at the gas station now, because the coherence relation (that she commits to) does not strictly entail this.

Fully modeling implicature (and its contributions to communication) requires recognizing both conventional and conversational implicature, and among the latter, differentiating between public commitments and further perlocutionary effects.

#91 Implicatures can often (but not always) be recognized without appealing to cognitive states.

In #90 we briefly described the Gricean approach to deriving implicatures: reasoning about the cognitive state of the speaker is an inherent feature of it, because the inference is derived from an assumption that speakers act cooperatively and rationally—in other words, they act according to an optimal trade-off between what they prefer and what they believe they can achieve [Savage, 1954].

Accordingly, one popular method for formalising Gricean reasoning is to develop a model that makes valid (defeasible) inferences about the speaker's beliefs, desires, and intentions given the (observed) premises of what they do and say (see also #90): early models of such inferences adopted a symbolic approach [e.g., Lochbaum, 1998], while more recently, stochastic approaches train on simulations where agents participate in signaling games [e.g., Benz et al., 2005]. A stochastic model of rationality also underpins recent approaches to learning dialogue policies—i.e., learning what to say, given observations of the current dialogue state. In particular, researchers use reinforcement learning to estimate the parameters of a Partially Observable Markov Decision Process (POMDP), using evidence from a human corpus and/or agent simulations [Georgila et al., 2006, Rieser and Lemon, 2011, Williams and Young, 2007] (see #70).

Relevance Theory [Sperber and Wilson, 1995] replaces all the (potentially conflicting) Gricean maxims with a single principle—the Principle of Relevance: this stipulates that the interpretation of an utterance is an optimal trade off between the informativeness or "usefulness" of what one can infer from an utterance (in its context of use) and the effort involved in making such an inference. This contrasts with the definition of rational action—i.e., an optimal trade off between beliefs and preferences—which underlies signaling games and the Gricean Maxims.

All these approaches assume that it is necessary to reason about the speaker's and hearer's cognitive states—their preferences and beliefs, and the link between those and intentions—

in order to compute implicatures. The manner in which preferences and beliefs are formally represented varies widely in these accounts: from modal operators in symbolic approaches [e.g., Asher and Lascarides, 2013, Litman and Allen, 1990, Lochbaum, 1998] to numeric reward functions (for preferences) and Bayesian models (for beliefs) in game theoretic approaches [e.g., Benz et al., 2005, Williams and Young, 2007]. But however cognitive states are represented, they are an inherent part of the derivation of implicatures.

In contrast, coherence-based theories of discourse (see #67) take the view that reasoning about cognitive states isn't always necessary for inferring implicatures. In (5), for instance, it is the lexical semantics of *fall* and *push*, combined with an assumption that the discourse is coherent—which means that the two sentences in (5) must be connected with a coherence relation—that leads to the (defeasible) inference that the content of the second sentence *explains* that of the first (and so the pushing caused the falling):

(5)   Max fell. Kim pushed him.

One doesn't need to reason about the speaker's beliefs or intentions to infer this relation: it stems from the meanings of *fall* and *push* and the predicate-argument structures of these sentences as derived from their linguistic form. Of course, the assumption that speakers make their utterances coherent might be derivable from a general model of rationality (i.e., derivable from an optimal trade-off between beliefs and preferences), but one needn't derive that rational behavior online to infer a particular coherent interpretation.

In essence, the assumption that contributions to a discourse are coherent can be treated as a convention. Or to put this another way, it is a question of information flow: Griceans assume that information always flows from cognitive states to implicatures; but coherence-based theories of discourse allow it to flow the other way too—from linguistic features plus coherence, to implicatures, some of which are propositions concerning cognitive states.

#92 Constructing a representation of what was said is distinct from evaluating whether what was said is true.

Many models of semantic interpretation assume that the logic speakers use to construct a formal semantic representation of a sentence or discourse is the same as the logic in which they interpret that semantic representation [e.g., Hobbs et al., 1993, Lochbaum, 1998, Montague, 1974]. But semantic representations must be at least first-order to handle the expressive power of natural language, and the validity problem of first-order languages that contain equality and predicate symbols that take at least two arguments—that is the problem of deciding whether a formula ϕ is entailed by a set of premises Γ—is not decidable [Monk, 1976, p. 279]. In other words, no algorithm guarantees a true answer to the question: is ϕ entailed by Γ? We've seen in prior chapters and this one, however, that constructing a semantic representation of an utterance is defeasible. All forms of defeasible inference demand a *consistency test*: to defeasibly infer ϕ from Γ one must test whether ϕ is consistent with Γ. But for first-order logic, that consistency test isn't decidable. Therefore, constructing a semantic representation of an utterance isn't decidable either, if it's modeled in the same logic as the one used to interpret those semantic representations.

Worst-case complexity is not always a good predictor for the performance of an implementation in practical NLP systems [Carroll, 1994]. However, even if implementing an undecidable approach to constructing representations is achievable, there is a philosophical objection to modeling language this way. Specifically, competent language users tend to agree on the speaker's message, if not on why the speaker conveyed it, or whether to believe it. One can explain that agreement if constructing logical form is decidable: this guarantees that interlocutors with sufficient resources will infer logical forms that accurately capture the speaker's message and discard those that don't. But making logical form construction decidable entails it must be done within a different logic from the one used for evaluating whether a logical form inferred as a representation of the speaker's message is true (or to be believed).

To illustrate the point, consider (297):

(297)   A: There are some unsolvable problems in number theory.
        B: The conjecture that every even number greater than two is expressible as the sum of two primes is unsolvable.

In (297), B *elaborates* A's claim by providing a specific example of an unsolvable problem in number theory (specifically, Goldbach's conjecture). Resolving the coherence relation between the two utterance in this way is tantamount to understanding the discourse. But inferring coherence relations is defeasible [Hobbs, 1979]. Thus, constructing the semantic representation of this discourse, including the elaboration relation between the content of its clauses, necessarily involves a consistency test. In particular, given that *elaboration* is a *veridical* relation—in other words elaboration(a, b) is true only if the contents a and b are true too—it is consistent to assume that B's utterance elaborates A's only if A's and B's utterances are satisfiable. In other words, we would need to test whether Goldbach's conjecture is unsolvable, or not, something we have no idea how to do! But even the most mathematically inept interpreter can easily understand the discourse (297) and construct its logical form: one has a clear picture of what is being said without having any idea how to evaluate whether what is said is true.

The logic one needs for constructing logical form can be much simpler than the one needed for evaluating the logical form. In Segmented Discourse Representation Theory (SDRT) [Asher and Lascarides, 2003], for instance, the logic for constructing logical form doesn't have access to every valid inference from first-order logical forms. For instance, their logic for constructing logical form has access to the information that $\exists x (man(x) \land walk(e, x))$ ("a man walked") entails $\exists x (walk(e, x))$ ("something walked"), but it is denied access to the entailment that $\neg \forall x (man(x) \rightarrow \neg walk(e, x))$ ("it's not the case that every man didn't walk"). This strategy helps make the construction of logical form decidable, even though it requires consistency checks because of the defeasible inference of coherence relations.

#93 In strategic conversation, implicatures can be safe or unsafe.

Solan and Tiersma [2005] discuss in detail dialogue (298), an extract of the cross examination of the defendant Bronston by the prosecutor, which took place in a landmark trial in the U.S. (Bronston v. United States, 409 U.S. 352 (1973)):

(298)   a. P(rosecutor): Do you have any bank accounts in Swiss banks, Mr Bronston?

   b. B(ronston): No, sir.

   c. P: Have you ever?

   d. B: My company had an account there for about six months, in Zurich.

The locutionary content of both (298b) and (298d) are true: i.e., Bronston did not have a Swiss bank account at the time, and in the past his company had a bank account in Zurich for six months. But Bronston *implicates* with (298d) a negative answer to the prosecutor's question (298c), that he has never had a Swiss bank account. This is false. Bronston was convicted for perjury, but the U.S. Supreme Court overruled this conviction: they acknowledged that (298d) was misleading, but ruled that it is dangerous to base perjury on content that is not clearly a matter of public record.

Solan and Tiersma [2005] and Pinker et al. [2008] point out that what is a matter of public record is open to debate and speakers can exploit this. They can choose an utterance from which an interlocutor computes implicatures that are in fact false, while leaving open the option of subsequently plausibly denying that the implicature was ever a part of their message. In other words, it is not always *safe* to treat implicatures as a matter of public record. Bronston's answer (298d) is an example of this, and that's why the Supreme Court overturned the conviction for perjury.

But it is not the case that all implicatures are unsafe [Asher and Lascarides, 2013]. First, no one would dispute that (298b) is sufficient for a perjury conviction if Bronston did have a Swiss bank account at the time of utterance: in other words the context-sensitive (and hence defeasibly) resolved meaning of *no* would be enough for Bronston to perjure himself. Second, Asher and Lascarides [2013] suggest that the Supreme Court ruling would have been different if Bronston had said (298d′) instead of (298d):

(298)   d′ Only my company had an account, for about six months, in Zurich.

Interpreting (298d′) as a negative answer to (298c) is the product of defeasible inference too, and so it's implicated. It's defeasible because the meaning of *only* is context sensitive [Rooth, 1992]: it presupposes a set of alternatives, and asserts that the property that (298d′) attributes to *my company* is not attributed to the other members of this set. But work on presupposition has shown that binding a presupposition is preferable to accommodating it [Beaver, 1997, Geurts, 1996, van der Sandt, 1992] (see also #80); further, binding it, like binding anaphora generally, depends on which antecedents are available in the discourse context. Here, binding the presupposed alternatives set to an available antecedent makes Bronston a member of that set: so this (defeasible) way of interpreting the presupposition yields an interpretation that Bronston didn't have a Swiss bank account. It's an implicature in that it is content that is inferred defeasibly via context-sensitive information, but here the implicature is intuitively safe: that is, in contrast to (298d), Bronston could not plausibly deny that saying (298d′) committed him to never having had a Swiss bank account.

Asher and Lascarides [2013] argue that coherence is critical to analyzing what's going on with (298d). Specifically, speakers are obliged to publicly commit to a coherent interpretation of their utterances, but they can misdirect their interlocutors as to which coherence relation connects the utterance to its context. A highly salient coherence relation for connecting (298d) to its context is that it's an answer to the question (298c). If one interprets (298d) this way, then an inference that the answer is negative is supported via a scalar implicature. But there are alternative, albeit less salient, coherence relation for connecting (298d) to its context: e.g., it could be interpreted as a commentary on Bronston's prior answer—in other words, it's not coherently related to the question (298c) at all! If it is interpreted this way, it does not follow that Bronston never had a Swiss bank account. This contrasts with (298d′): both of these alternative ways in which (298d′) can coherently contribute to the dialogue require identifying the set of alternatives that's introduced by the word *only*; and in both cases, it binds to an available antecedent, namely Bronston. So unlike (298d), all the possible ways in which (298d′) might make a coherent contribution to the dialogue so far entail that Bronston never had a Swiss bank account.

There are some general lessons to draw from this example. Most formal analyses of deception that deploy signaling games [e.g., Crawford and Sobel, 1982] assume that the speaker's message is observable, and what's hidden is whether the speaker believes her message. But examples like (298) show that the message—or, equivalently, the speaker's public commitment—is hidden rather than observable, even if the utterance exhibits no syntactic, lexical or anaphoric ambiguity! The fact that plausible deniability is possible arises directly from the fact that messages are hidden.

This suggests that signaling games are not only useful for predicting whether a speaker believes her message, but also for predicting what her message is in the first place, given her signal. To put this another way, predicting whether the implicatures are safe—i.e., a matter of public record, rather than plausibly deniable—is a game. This idea is formalized in Asher and Paul 2018, in a way that (unlike traditional signaling games) takes into account the fact that the speaker and interlocutor have to estimate in a state of uncertainty the actions that the other considers to be a part of the game.

#94 Agreement and denial can be implicated, and implicatures can be agreed upon or denied.

Speakers can reject or deny prior utterances by directly saying so (299b), by using a linguistic form dedicated for this purpose (299b′), or by producing an utterance that is inconsistent with the prior one (299b″):

(299)   a.   A: It's a lovely day out.

    b.   B: I disagree.

    b.′   B: No.

    b.″   B: It's too hot.

All of these forms involve linguistically explicit denial. However, we also find that denial may also be expressed through implication, specifically implicated inconsistency. For example, in (300) (extracted from the BNC by Schlöder and Fernandez [2015]), the inconsistency between A's and B's utterance is sourced in a scalar implicature, of the kind we discussed in #89:

(300)   A: We're all mad, aren't we? $\forall x.M(x)$
        B: Well, some of us. $\exists x.M(x)$
           $\rightsquigarrow$ *Not all of us* $\rightsquigarrow \neg\forall x.M(x)$

Walker [1996] cites similar examples to (300), observing that these kinds of rejections often demand a particular prosodic production (i.e., a fall-rise tune [Ladd, 1980, Liberman and Sag, 1974]), a tune we discussed in #87, and return to in #96:

(301)   A: He's brilliant and imaginative.
        B: He's imaginative.

(302)   A: John is not a good speaker because he's hard to understand.
        B: I agree he's hard to understand.

In these examples, B implicates a denial of the prior contribution by agreeing with only a strict sub-part of it, i.e., scalar implicatures are at work here, too.

In addition to denial itself being expressible through implication, we also find that implicatures can be denied. For instance, in dialogue (10), discussed in #4 and #66, B agrees with everything A says but denies the implicated *explanation* relation between the contents of the two sentences A utters:[5]

(10)   A: John went to jail. He embezzled the company funds.
      B: No. He embezzled the funds but he went to jail because he was convicted of tax evasion.

---

[5]For the sake of simplicity we have illustrated this phenomenon with a constructed example, but Lascarides and Asher [2009] provide (more complex) naturally occurring examples.

So far we've seen that rejection can be implicated, and implicatures rejected. The same is true of agreement. Consider (303), a naturally occurring dialogue that's discussed by Sacks et al. [1974, p. 717]:

(303)   Mark (to Karen and Sharon): Karen 'n' I're having a fight,
                              after she went out with Keith and not me.
        Karen (to Mark and Sharon): Wul Mark, you never asked me out.

Intuitively, Mark and Karen agree that they had a fight, and that this was caused by Karen going out with Keith and not Mark. So an implicature gets agreed upon—that the contents of the sentences Mark utters are related by *explanation* goes beyond compositional and lexical semantics. Furthermore, agreement here is implicated: Karen's utterance is intuitively sufficient in this context to implicate her agreement with Mark that they had a fight, caused by her going out with Keith and not him, but her utterance doesn't make that agreement linguistically explicit—she does not repeat Mark's utterance, or utter *OK* or *I agree* to indicate agreement.

#95 Silence can be a meaningful act.

In #90, we described how implicatures are inferred as a byproduct of making what appears to be a violation of general principles that govern how language is used in conversation not a real violation at all. But actually violating such principles (rather than simply appearing to violate them) can also be meaningful. Grice called this *flouting* the maxims [Grice, 1975]. For example, B's response to A's question in (304) is not just an apparent violation of Grice's Maxim of Relation ("make your utterance relevant") but a real violation of it:

(304)   A: Is Smith having an affair?
        B: How about them Giants?

By flouting the maxim of Relation, B is implicating to A her refusal to answer the question.

Similarly, because questions and requests place a social obligation on the interlocutor to respond, by violating such obligations and remaining silent, the interlocutor can implicate her refusal to adopt the speaker's intentions. In this way, silence can be a meaningful act. The STAC Corpus from Afantenos et al. [2012b], in which players negotiate trades over restricted resources, has several examples like that in (305), where the recipient of the trade offer doesn't provide a response at all and so implicates that she refuses the offer and also, through her silence, refuses to answer the literal question (and so doesn't reveal whether or not she has wheat).

(305)   A: B, do you have any wheat?
        B: [no response]

These kinds of moves are currently under-researched. They take place in scenarios where the dialogue participants have conflicting interests, so it makes sense to model them as a game. But how one does this is an open question: for instance, modeling B's choice of action in (305) requires one to make the action of not saying anything a possible choice in the game, and so one must model the possible outcomes of this, and they are highly context sensitive: e.g., remaining silent carries nothing like the meaning we ascribed to it in (305) if the speaker choosing to be silent is a part of a multi-party conversation and not the addressee of the latest utterance. Modeling the meaning expressed by silence thus requires also first detecting which silence is meaningful.

#96 The prosody of an utterance affects what the speaker publicly commits to.

Ladd [1980] observes that if B says (306b), which features a falling tune (i.e., stress on *fool* with a high tone and a falling boundary tone) then this implies that B agrees that Harry is the biggest liar in town (by offering a further property of Harry), and so B commits to Harry being both a liar and a fool:[6]

(306) a. A: Harry is the biggest liar in town.

   b. B: The biggest ^{FOOL} m$_{aybe}$.

   b′. The biggest $_{FO}$^{OL} m$_{a}$^{ybe}.

However, if B says (306b′)—i.e., the same utterance with a fall—rise tune, again with stress on *fool* but now with a low and then high tone, and a rising boundary tone—then B is denying A's utterance, conveying that Harry is (maybe) the biggest fool but not the biggest liar in town. This shows how prosody can affect what content a speaker publicly commits to.

Steedman [2000] also observes how prosody affects updates to the common ground, or in our terms the public commitments. If B responds to A's question in (307) with a falling tune, then it simply implicates a positive answer ("Yes, I'm rich"); if it is uttered with a rising tune then it conveys a qualified positive answer ("Yes, I'm rich, if being a millionaire counts?"); and if it's said with a fall—rise tune then it implies not only a positive answer but also that A should have already known this answer ("I thought you knew this already"):

(307) A: Are you rich?
       B: I'm a MILLionaire.

Incorporating this kind of subtlety into spoken dialogue systems may seem like a far-off goal. But understanding the ways in which people use prosody to express content is useful even in building simpler automated systems, for at least two reasons: first, it can help us understand which parts of human-human interaction we are and aren't trying to mimic; and second, it can help us understand and manage the expectations users have of the systems we build.

---

[6]Recordings of B's two alternative responses are available at `jjsch.github.io/audio/fool.html`.

CHAPTER 14

Resources

#97 Lexical resources systematize useful information about word sense and semantic roles.

Chapter 4 describes word senses and their importance to understanding natural language meaning—as well as the fact that word senses aren't cleanly delineated, discrete units. Nonetheless, and even with the advent of pre-trained word vectors, broad-coverage resources which attempt to catalogue word senses can be very useful components of a wide range of NLP applications.

The most prominent example of such a resource is the Princeton WordNet of English[1] (WordNet) [Fellbaum, 1998, Miller, 1995], which is organized around *synsets*, groups containing words which share a particular sense (see #18). WordNet also includes definitions for each synset as well as relations between synsets, including hypernymy/hyponymy, meronymy (part-whole), antonymy, and others. The Princeton WordNet of English has inspired the creation of wordnets for many other languages, a large number of which have been collected and made interoperable through the Open Multilingual Wordnet project[2] [Bond and Paik, 2012]. The Global WordNet Association maintains a list of wordnets at http://globalwordnet.org/wordnets-in-the-world/.

In addition to the sense inventories, WordNet projects have produced sense-tagged corpora. These include English SemCor [Landes et al., 1998], Italian SemCor [Bentivogli and Pianta, 2005], and Japanese SemCor [Bond et al., 2012], plus sense-tagged corpora for several other languages. The Parallel Meaning Bank (PMB; see #98) is also sense-tagged with WordNet senses [Abzianidze et al., 2017]. The Global WordNet Association maintains a list of WordNet annotated corpora at http://globalwordnet.org/wordnet-annotated-corpora/. Several of these, including the resource for Italian and English presented by Bentivogli and Pianta [2005] are multilingual resources, with annotations over parallel corpora.

There are also large-scale lexical resources focused on describing the semantic roles that arguments bear with respect to their predicates (see Chapter 5). The most prominent such project is English FrameNet [Baker et al., 1998, Baker, 2017] (see also #34), which presents an inventory of frames, each associated with a collection of *frame elements* (named semantic roles) and lexical units associated with the frame. The frame elements themselves are specific to the frame, but organized into a hierarchy such that frame elements that share properties inherit those from

[1]https://wordnet.princeton.edu/
[2]http://compling.hss.ntu.edu.sg/omw/

the same, more abstract, frame elements. FrameNet also provides text annotated with both the frame evoked by particular words and information about how their semantic roles are filled (by other parts of the sentence or not).[3] As with WordNet, the English FrameNet has inspired work on other languages too, including French [Candito et al., 2014a], Chinese [You and Liu, 2005], and others.[4]

Another prominent lexicographic resource that includes information about semantic roles is English VerbNet [Palmer et al., 2017]. English VerbNet provides entries for verbs with semantic rolesets for each which are mapped to both the very general roles of PropBank[5] (see Palmer et al., 2005 and #98) and the very specific ones of FrameNet. The PMB is also VerbNet role-tagged [Abzianidze et al., 2017].

There are also several resources annotated with rich information about multi-word expressions (MWEs), see Chapter 6. STREUSLE[6] [Schneider and Smith, 2015] and DiMSUM[7] [Schneider et al., 2016] consist of English data, while multi-lingual corpus MWE data was collected for the PARSEME shared tasks [Ramisch et al., 2018]. Finally, Wiki50 [Vincze et al., 2011] is annotated with named entities and several kinds of MWEs in English Wikipedia articles.

#98 There are also resources annotated with sentence-level semantic information.

Sembanks are collections of running text with semantic annotations. The computational linguistics community has produced a wide variety of sembanks, not only for different natural languages but also with different semantic representations, targeting different aspects of meaning. Here we give a brief overview of some of these resources.

Proposition banks, starting with English PropBank [Palmer et al., 2005], focus on predicate-argument structure (#47), where annotations are grounded in the words and constituents of the sentence, per the Penn Treebank syntactic annotations [Marcus et al., 1993]. In addition to English, there are PropBanks for at least Chinese [Xue and Palmer, 2009], Arabic [Zaghouani et al., 2010], Hindi [Vaidya et al., 2011], Portuguese [Branco et al., 2012], Basque [Aldezabal Roteta et al., 2013], Finnish [Haverinen et al., 2015], and Turkish [Şahin and Adalı, 2018]. Similarly, the annotated corpora that accompany some FrameNet projects contain annotations about which words and phrases serve as which frame elements for the predicates of interest. These include at least the annotated texts provided along with the English FrameNet [Baker et al., 2003] and the French texts annotated in the ASFALDA project [Djemaa et al., 2016]. The OntoNotes project combines the PropBank annotations with additional

---

[3]In this respect, the FrameNet annotated resources are similar to the resources discussed in #98 below.
[4]See https://framenet.icsi.berkeley.edu/fndrupal/framenets_in_other_languages
[5]Note that even though PropBank uses very general role names, their interpretation is still lexical-item specific.
[6]https://github.com/nert-nlp/streusle/
[7]https://github.com/dimsum16/dimsum-data

information about word sense and coreference, and includes data for English, Chinese, and Arabic [Pradhan and Ramshaw, 2017].

The Prague Dependency Treebank (PDT) [Böhmová et al., 2003, Hajič et al., 2017] includes a level of annotation called the *tectogrammatical* layer, based on Functional Generative Description [Sgall et al., 1986]. Like PropBank, PDT includes information about predicate-argument structure. But in contrast to PropBank, it also includes information about topic-focus articulation (#85), coreference information (Chapter 10), and discourse relations (#67). The PDT project has produced annotated corpora for Czech and English. Semantic role annotations in the same style are also available for Croatian [Ljubešić et al., 2018].

Another approach to sembanking takes a precision implemented grammar which produces semantic representations alongside the syntactic ones as its starting point and has annotators choose among the candidate analyses proposed by the grammar. This is the approach taken by the Redwoods treebank for English [Oepen et al., 2002], using the English Resource Grammar [Flickinger, 2000, 2011]. On this approach, the grammar is hand constructed and the analyses are hand selected, but the semantic representations themselves are automatically produced, making it feasible to account for the semantic contribution of every word and construction in even very long sentences (provided these are known to the grammar). The Redwoods annotations include predicate-argument structure (#47), partial constraints on the scope of quantifiers, and other scopal operators (including negation and modality) (#53, #54), as well as morphosemantic attributes such as number or tense/aspect (#58). These representations are in the formalism of Minimal Recursion Semantics [Copestake et al., 2005], which is formal language for representing underspecified logical forms (see #53). The SDP 2016 sembank [Oepen et al., 2016] provides two derived versions of the semantic annotations in Redwoods: (a) Elementary Dependency Structures (EDS) [Oepen and Lønning, 2006]) which are semantic dependency graphs, preserving most of the information in the original MRSs; and (b) DELPH-IN MRS bi-lexical dependencies (DM) [Ivanova et al., 2012]) which distill the information further into labeled dependencies holding exclusively between lexical items. Semantic banks in the Redwoods style are also available for at least Japanese [Bond et al., 2004] and Spanish [Marimon, 2015].

The English Groningen Meaning Bank (GMB) [Bos et al., 2017] also takes a compositional approach to producing annotations and then enriches them with both expert and crowd-sourced additions. The underlying grammatical processing is done with the C&C syntactic parser [Clark and Curran, 2007] trained on CCGBank [Hockenmaier and Steedman, 2007], combined with the Boxer system [Curran et al., 2007] for producing Discourse Representation Structures [Kamp and Reyle, 1993] on the basis of CCG derivations. The annotations in the GMB include word sense (#18), predicate-argument structure (drawing on VerbNet for semantic role labeling), scope, and tense, as well as discourse-based phenomena such as coreference (#71), coherence relations (#67), and presuppositions (Chapter 11).

Similar annotations are provided over parallel text for English, German, Dutch, and Italian in the Parallel Meaning Bank (PMB) [Abzianidze et al., 2017]. There are essentially two differences in the meaning representations in the GMB vs. the PMB. First, the former annotates logical forms for multi-sentence discourse, drawing on the coherence relations from SDRT [Asher and Lascarides, 2003], while the PMB assigns logical forms to individual sentences only. Second, the representations in the PMB are langauge neutral, and all symbols are grounded; this is not the case in the GMB or other sembanks, that have a lot of English words such as prepositions in their representations. Both of these meaning banks share the important property, however, that their semantic representations are logically interpretable, making (automated) logical inference possible without further ado.

In Abstract Meaning Representation (AMR) [Banarescu et al., 2013], the representations are also semantic graphs representing predicate-argument structure enhanced with word sense information (but for verbs only) and coreference relations, but they are produced completely manually, in a specifically non-compositional fashion.[8] A consequence of this is that the nodes in the graphs are semantic predicates (rather than word tokens) and there is no alignment between the words or phrases that are a part of the sentence and the AMR annotation. AMR annotated corpora exist for at least English [Knight and et al., 2017] and Chinese [Li et al., 2016].

Further examples of corpora annotated with sentence-spanning semantic representations include the TLGbank, which provides type-logical annotations for French [Moot, 2015],[9] and the Treebank Semantics Parsed Corpus,[10] which is annotated with DRT [Kamp and Reyle, 1993] and provides data for English, Modern Japanese, and Old Japanese. There are also corpora annotated with the enhanced dependencies being developed by the Universal Dependencies initiative, which include information that is closer to semantic than to predicate-argument structures. An example of a corpus annotated in this way is the French sembank DEEP-SEQUOIA [Candito et al., 2014b]. The Universal Cognitive Conceptual Annotation (UCCA)[11] has semantic resources for English, German, and French, with annotations for argument structure and lexical senses [Abend and Rappoport, 2013].

Moving away from predicate-argument structure, we find annotations for varying aspects of meaning: The MPQA Opinion Corpus provides detailed information about opinions, sentiments and other private states expressed in language over English news articles [Wilson et al., 2017] and the JDPA Sentiment Corpus provides annotations for sentiment over English blog posts about automobiles [Kessler et al., 2010]. The TempEval2 corpus [Verhagen et al., 2010] provides TimeML [Pustejovsky et al., 2003, Pustejovsky, 2017] annotations of temporal and event information over data from Chinese, English, French, Italian, Korean, and Spanish. Similarly, the NewsReader MEANTIME corpus provides TimeML annotations for Wikinews data in English, Spanish, Italian, and Dutch [Minard et al., 2016]. The VU Amsterdam Metaphor-Corpus provides annotations of metaphors in English text [Krennmayer and Steen, 2017].

---

[8]For an extended discussion of why a compositional approach is preferable, see Bender et al. 2015.

[9]http://richardmoot.github.io/TLGbank/

[10]http://www.compling.jp/ajb129/ts.html

[11]http://www.cs.huji.ac.il/~oabend/ucca.html

There are also projects built around creating semantic annotations out of questions that non-expert speakers can answer. These include the crowd-sourced annotations done via gamification in GMB [Bos et al., 2017], using games to annotate coreference (`phrasedetectiv es.org`; Chamberlain et al. 2008), the English semantic role labels produced by the QASRL Bank [FitzGerald et al., 2018], and the English semantic role, factuality, genericity, and other annotations provided by the Decompositional Semantics Initiative [e.g., White et al., 2016].[12]

Finally, there are data sets consisting of a set of images (or videos), where each image (or video) is accompanied with a set of natural language descriptions, usually collected via crowd-sourcing.[13] In each of these cases, one could conceive of the image as a model or denotation for its natural language description, but most of these datasets don't exploit this idea to its full potential. One notable exception is the Visual Genome dataset[14] [Krishna et al., 2016], which consists of 108K images, associated with one or more descriptions in English. In this corpus, it's not only the whole sentence that is associated with an image, but also parts of the sentence get associated with parts of the image. Specifically, the noun phrases (and their parts, such as adjectives like *yellow*), the verbs and the prepositions are mapped to (sub-)regions (or bounding boxes) of the accompanying image, corresponding to the location of the relevant denotation of the English phrase. (In the case of verbs and prepositions, whose denotations are typically relations among objects, the location of the relation includes the location of the related objects.) These objects and their attributes also form nodes in so-called *region graphs*, where each region graph is an abstract, structured representation of the relevant sub-region of the image, with the arcs corresponding to dependencies (e.g., a relation node gets linked to the objects it relates).

#99 Some sentence parsing systems produce semantic representations.

The existence of the sembanks listed in #98 enables the development of sembank-trained parsers which reproduce the annotations in the sembank and can therefore be used to provide similar annotations for additional text. The AllenNLP suite [Gardner et al., 2017] includes a semantic role labeler (providing annotations like PropBank) and coreference resolver, among other tools. These include pre-trained models for English, but the open source software could be trained on data from other languages with compatible annotations. Stanford CoreNLP also provides a suite of coreference resolvers for English and Chinese, which use deterministic [Lee et al., 2013], statistical [Clark and Manning, 2015], and neural [Clark and Manning, 2016] methods.

There are also grammar-based methods of producing semantic annotations on new text. The DELPH-IN suite of resources produce Minimal Recursion Semantics [Copestake et al., 2005] representations for text on the basis of a grammar and a treebank-trained parse selection

---

[12]`http://decomp.io`

[13]Such datasets for English include Flickr 8K [Rashtchian et al., 2010], COCO [Lin et al., 2014], NLVR [Suhr et al., 2017], and NLVR[2] [Suhr et al., 2018], and SCONE [Long et al., 2016]. In the case of SCONE, the description is an instruction as opposed to a statement, which is associated with an (artificial) image of the "before" and "after" states of the action that's described by the instruction [Long et al., 2016].

[14]`https://visualgenome.org/`

model. The largest (and therefore broadest coverage) such grammar is the English Resource Grammar [Flickinger, 2000, 2011], but grammars (and associated treebanks) are also being developed for Japanese [Siegel et al., 2016], German [Crysmann, 2003, Müller and Kasper, 2000], Indonesian [Moeljadi et al., 2015], and other languages.[15]

Finally, midway between sembank-trained and grammar-based parsers, we find systems for turning treebank-trained syntactic representations into semantic representations. These include Boxer [Bos, 2015, Curran et al., 2007], which produces Discourse Representation Structures [Kamp and Reyle, 1993] on the basis of CCG parses. Boxer is used in the construction of the English GMB [Bos et al., 2017], and its successor the PMB [Abzianidze et al., 2017], which annotates sentences from English, German, Dutch, and Italian with DRSs.[16] Another example is Reddy et al.'s [2014] Graph Parser: like Boxer it produces logical forms for English on the basis of CCG derivations; but unlike Boxer those logical forms are expressed in λ-calculus formulae, which get converted into ungrounded semantic graphs that in turn get mapped to grounded semantic graphs in Freebase, a large-scale knowledge graph extracted semi-automatically from the web.[17]

Gawron et al. [1982] articulate the view that a grammar based on a linguistic theory, capturing detailed knowledge of syntactic and semantic structures in language, will be portable across domains. Zhang and Wang [2009] and Ivanova et al. [2016] find this to be the case for parsing to syntactic representations and Chen et al. [2018] show that the domain portability of the English Resource Grammar [Flickinger, 2000, 2011] can be leveraged by using it (and its associated parse selection model) to produce new training data on demand, improving a neural semantic dependency parser.

#100 Discourse information in available corpora comes in many guises.

There are a wide variety of corpora annotated with discourse-level information. They vary in the medium of the signal (text or spoken, embodied conversation, or disembodied), the genre (newspaper text, chit chat, negotiations, work meetings), and the type of information that's annotated.

The English Penn Discourse Treebank[18] [Miltsakaki et al., 2004, Prasad et al., 2008] consists of *Wall Street Journal* text that's annotated with discourse relations, akin to those posited by coherence-based theories of discourse such as Rhetorical Structure Theory (RST) [Mann and Thompson, 1986] and Segmented Discourse Representation Theory (SDRS) [Asher and Lascarides, 2003].[19] There are also Chinese [Zhou and Xue, 2015] and Arabic [Al-Saif and Markert, 2010] discourse treebanks with comparable annotations. The annotations don't include

---

[15]The DELPH-IN grammar catalogue is available at `http://moin.delph-in.net/GrammarCatalogue`.

[16]However, grammar-free semantic parsers that use neural networks typically outperform grammar-based parsers [e.g., Dozat and Manning, 2018, van Noord et al., 2018].

[17]`https://developers.google.com/freebase/`.

[18]`http://www.seas.upenn.edu/~pdtb/`

[19]See #67.

hierarchical discourse structure, however: a text segment that includes (annotated) discourse relations among smaller text segments cannot itself be an argument to a discourse relation in their resources.

Corpora that are annotated with hierarchical discourse structure also exist: for instance, the English RST Treebank[20] [Carlson et al., 2002]; the English Groningen Meaning Bank [Bos et al., 2017]; and the French ANNODIS corpus[21] [Afantenos et al., 2012a]. The latter two corpora are annotated with SDRSs, and in contrast to Rhetorical Structure Theory (RST), [Mann and Thompson, 1986], this allows discourse structures to be rooted acyclic graphs as opposed to trees [Asher and Lascarides, 2003]. The English STAC Corpus[22] [Afantenos et al., 2012b] is also annotated with SDRSs, but in contrast to all other corpora annotated with discourse relations, the conversations are embodied—specifically, they are trading negotiations in the board game the Settlers of Catan—and the non-linguistic events (e.g., dice rolls, building a road) are allowed to be arguments to discourse relations (as motivated and described in Hunter et al. 2018).

There are several other corpora that label embodied conversations with other sources of important syntactic and semantic information. Notably, the English AMI corpus[23] [Carletta, 2006] consists of videos, taken from several angles, of face-to-face conversations among four people who are tasked with designing a remote control. The speech is transcribed and temporally aligned to its audio signal. Those transcriptions are labeled (automatically) with information from POS taggers and chunk parsers, and in addition some of the communicative hand and head movements are labeled with their type (e.g., deictic gesture, head nod). These non-verbal signals are also temporally aligned to the appropriate portions of video, and they are linked where relevant with coreference relations to segments of the transcribed speech. The corpus is also labeled with dialogue acts from the DAMSL scheme [Core and Allen, 1997].

Like AMI, there are other annotated spoken dialogue corpora for English, where the annotations include dialogue acts as opposed to discourse relations: in other words, each sentence in the corpus is labeled with its illocutionary act (see #5) but sentences are not connected to each other with discourse relations. The dialogue acts include labels such as QUESTION and REQUEST, but they also include labels that, strictly speaking, should be conceived as relations: e.g., whether a sentence is YES-ANSWER (standing for a positive answer to a yes-no question), or not, depends on the content of a prior question, but corpora labeled with dialogue acts don't annotate which question the YES-ANSWER answers (see #7 for further discussion). English corpora with these kinds of annotations include the ICSI Meeting corpus of face to face meetings [Janin et al., 2003, Shriberg et al., 2004], the Santa Barbara Corpus[24] [Bois et al., 2005], and the HCRC

---

[20]https://catalog.ldc.upenn.edu/LDC2002T07
[21]http://redac.univ-tlse2.fr/corpus/annodis/
[22]http://www.irit.fr/STAC
[23]http://groups.inf.ed.ac.uk/ami/corpus/
[24]http://www.linguistics.ucsb.edu/research/santa-barbara-corpus

Map Task Corpus[25] [Anderson et al., 1991]. The Santa Barbara Corpus dialogue act annotations are based on those from Conversation Analysis [Sacks et al., 1974], and so the main focus is on interaction, including turn taking. The Santa Barbara Corpus is also annotated with prosodic information.

TimeBank[26] is annotated text with temporal information according to the TimeML annotation scheme [Pustejovsky et al., 2003]. Spans of text get tagged as denoting events or times, and these are then connected to each other via labels that capture temporal and causal relations. FactBank[27] [Saurí and Pustejovsky, 2009] and PragBank[28] [de Marneffe et al., 2012] also focus annotations on events in English text, which like those in the TimeML corpus get associated with particular spans in the text. However, the FactBank and PragBank are labeled with information about veridicality rather than only temporality: does the sentence entail that the event definitely happened or will happen? FactBank was concerned with veridicality information that is derivable from lexical meanings and local semantic interactions. But PragBank extends these to pragmatically informed information about veridicality: for instance, in PragBank the reliability of the source of information is taken into account.

Summary

There is of course much more to learn about the semantics and pragmatics of natural languages. The focus here has been largely on how linguistic form, word meaning, and the context of use all contribute to the interpretation of sentences in text or dialogue. The book has emphasized the ways in which on the one hand these three sources of information interact in ways that are extremely complex and on occasion idiosyncratic, but on the other there is much in this interaction that is predictable and systematic and so formalizable in a logically precise model of meaning. We have also emphasized the important role that inference plays, not only in the task of constructing a semantic representation of a linguistic utterance from its form and its context of use, but also in the task of evaluating the consequences of that semantic representation. Indeed, these tasks interact during discourse and dialogue interpretation, as discussed in Chapters 9–13. We have also attempted, where appropriate, to highlight examples of phenomena that vary across languages on the one hand, and also phenomena that appear to be language-independent on the other.

We focused on form, word meaning, context of use, and their interaction because this is deeply involved in working out who did what to whom. But for reasons of space, there are a wealth of phenomena that we have largely ignored in this book, even when they illustrate very effectively how their interaction jointly contributes to the meanings of utterances. One such example is the semantics and pragmatics of so-called negative polarity items [Ladusaw, 1980],

[25] http://groups.inf.ed.ac.uk/maptask
[26] https://catalog.ldc.upenn.edu/LDC2006T08
[27] https://catalog.ldc.upenn.edu/LDC2009T23
[28] http://compprag.christopherpotts.net/factbank.html

e.g., *any*, *either*, the idiom *lift a finger*. Another is the contribution to meaning in an embodied discourse of non-verbal moves such as hand gestures and eye gaze [e.g., McNeill, 1992]. In both these examples, the prior literature has established that they exemplify a complex, but systematic, interaction between linguistic form, word meaning, and context.

In general, there is broad scope for collaboration between linguists and NLP practitioners, and we hope that this book will provide a strong foundation from which NLP researchers can navigate their way through the myriad of work on semantics and pragmatics within the field linguistics. For the interested reader, there are many excellent introductory textbooks in linguistics for learning more about (formal) semantics and pragmatics. The two volumes Gamut 1991a,b, co-authored by Johan van Benthem, Jeroen Groenendijk, Dick de Jong, Martin Stokhof, and Henk Verkuyl are arguably the most comprehensive introduction, covering everything from the very beginnings (e.g., Frege's principle of compositionality) and an introduction to classical logic, through to Montague Grammar, and the more recent semantic frameworks such as Discourse Representation Theory which rest on a dynamic rather than a static concept of interpretation. Dowty et al. 1981 is also an excellent textbook that starts with an introduction to classical logic and ends with a very comprehensive exposition of Montague Grammar. Kamp and Reyle 1993 offers an excellent introduction to Discourse Representation Theory (DRT). Kadman 2001 offers an introduction to formal pragmatics; it is mainly focused on the dynamic semantic approach, and it covers DRT, presupposition and focus. Finally, while there is no introductory textbook on discourse structure and coherence relations, both Kehler 2002 and Chapter 21 (Computational Discourse) of Jurafsky and Martin 2000, which is authored by Andy Kehler, are easy to follow with no prior knowledge of the subject.

We believe that an understanding of how language works is fundamental to the ability to create successful language technology. We hope that this book will help readers working in NLP to begin to develop such an understanding and that it will serve to faciltiate interdisciplinary collaboration between linguists and NLP researchers.

APPENDIX A

Approaches to Discourse Structure

We provide a brief overview here of the broad range of work on formal models of discourse update (see #66). These models typically view a discourse $D_{1:n}$ as a sequence of minimal discourse units $u_1 \ldots u_n$, and computing the semantic representation $R(D_{1:n})$ of discourse $D_{1:n}$ is achieved by sequentially applying an *update function* to its minimal units $u_1 \ldots u_n$ [Asher and Lascarides, 2003, Kamp and Reyle, 1993, Poesio and Traum, 1997, 1998, Traum, 1994, Traum and Larsson, 2003]. This update function goes under the name of *discourse update* [e.g., Asher and Lascarides, 2003, Kamp and Reyle, 1993] or *information state update* [Poesio and Traum, 1997, and many others]. Here, we'll call it discourse update.

Discourse update functions can be monotonic [Kamp and Reyle, 1993] or non-monotonic [e.g., Asher and Lascarides, 2003, Ginzburg, 2012, Hobbs et al., 1993, Poesio and Traum, 1997]. The former places emphasis on the relevance of logical structure of the discourse context (e.g., the presence of scopal expressions like negation) for anaphora resolution; in contrast the latter is useful for modeling how interlocutors can and do revise their estimates of what a prior discourse meant, on hearing subsequent utterances.

Depending on the theory, the minimal units which are processed by the discourse update function can be complete sentences [e.g., Kamp and Reyle, 1993], complete sentences and also sentence fragments [e.g., Asher and Lascarides, 2003, Clark, 1992, Ginzburg, 2012, Poesio and Traum, 1998, Schlangen, 2003], or single words, to model incremental processing [e.g., Kempson et al., 2000]. We also find differences in what information is used as input to the discourse update function: prior discourse and all its entailments [e.g., Grosz and Sidner, 1986, Hobbs et al., 1993, Lochbaum, 1998, Poesio and Traum, 1998, Sperber and Wilson, 1986], limited access to its entailments [e.g., Asher and Lascarides, 2003][1] or no entailments at all [e.g., Kamp and Reyle, 1993]—discourse update in DRT has access to the syntactic form of the logical form of the prior discourse context but not any aspects of its interpretation. Some update functions have access to the natural language syntax of the sentences in the prior discourse and the current discourse unit (as well as to their semantic information) [e.g., Ginzburg, 2012, Kempson et al., 2000, Pickering and Garrod, 2004], while others access semantic representations only [e.g., Asher and Lascarides, 2003, Kamp and Reyle, 1993, Poesio and Traum, 1998]. Finally,

---

[1]For example, discourse update in Asher and Lascarides 2003 is informed by the fact that *A man talked* entails *Someone talked*, but not by the fact that *A man talked* entails that *It's not the case that every man didn't talk*.

the discourse update function may be defined via *symbolic default axioms* that capture common-sense knowledge and reasoning [Asher and Lascarides, 2003, Hobbs et al., 1993, Lochbaum, 1998, Poesio and Traum, 1998], or via predictions about equilibria in a signaling game [Benz et al., 2005, Franke et al., 2012, van Rooij, 2004, Wang et al., 2016, 2017].

While formal semantic models of discourse interpretation model a sequential approach to discourse update that we described above, there is a growing body of work that doesn't do this, but rather treats discourse interpretation as analogous to probabilistic sentential parsing. These models estimate the discourse structure of the discourse as a whole from its informative features (both syntactic and semantic), via a parsing algorithm that has been trained on a labeled corpus, where each training example is a discourse that's annotated with its discourse structure [Afantenos et al., 2015, Baldridge and Lascarides, 2005, Liu et al., 2018, Marcu, 1997] (see #100 for information about relevant corpora).

APPENDIX B

Grams Used in IGT

This appendix lists all the grams used in the interlinear glossed text (IGT) examples in the book. Each gram is given in the form it appears in the IGT, followed by a non-abbreviated form, and the larger class of grams it belongs to. For grams connected with semantic pheonema discussed in this text, pointers to relevant portions of this text are provided. For further explanation of the morphosyntactic concepts named by the others, see Bender 2013.

gram	long form	gram class	see also
1	first person	person	
2	second person	person	
3	third-person	person	
A	transitive subject	grammatical function	
A3	third person intransitive subject (specific to Paraguayan Guaraní)	person	
ABS	absolutive	case	
ACC	accusative	case	
ADN	adnominal	grammatical function	
AHON	addressee honorific	honorifics	#9, #36, #63, #65
ANIM	animate	animacy	
AUG	augmentative	evaluative	#8
AUX	auxiliary	part of speech	
CAUS	causative	valence alternations	
COM	common gender	gender/noun class	
COMP	completive	aspect	#42, #59, #61
COMP	complementizer	part of speech	
COMPASS	compassion	evaluative	#8
CONTRAST.TOP	contrastive topic	information structure	#84–#88
COP	copula	part of speech	
DAT	dative	case	
DECL	declarative	mood	

DEDUCTIVE.EV	deductive evidential	evidentiality	#59, #62
DEF	definite	information status	#82, #83
DEG	degree	comparatives	#49
DIM	diminuative	evaluative	#8
DUR	durative	aspect	#42, #59, #61
ERG	ergative	case	
EV	evidential	evidentiality	#59, #62
EXCL	exclusive	clusivity	
EXP	experiential	aspect	#42, #59, #61
FAM	familiar	honorifics	#9, #36, #63, #65
FEM	feminine	gender/noun class	
FOC	focus	information structure	#84–#88
GEN	genitive	case	
HAB	habitiual	aspect	#42, #59, #61
HON	honorific	honorifics	#9, #36, #63, #65
IMP	imperative	mood	
IMPF	imperfective	aspect	#42, #59, #61
INDEF	indefinite	information status	#82, #83
INDIC	indicative	mood	
INF	infinitive	verb form	
INSTR	instrumental	case	
MASC	masculine	gender/noun class	
NC	noun compound	grammatical function	
NEG	negation	polarity	#2, #10, #54 #55, #75, #76
NEUT	neuter	gender/noun class	
NOM	nomiantive	case	
NONVIS.EV	non-visual evidential	evidentiality	#59, #62
NPST	non-past	tense	#59–#62
NUMCL	numeral classifier	grammatical function	
O	object	grammatical function	
OM	object marker	agreement	
PART	partitive	case	
PARTICIPATORY.EV	participatory	evidentiality	#59, #62

	evidential		
PASS	passive	voice alternations	
PF	perfective	aspect	#42, #59, #61
PL	plural	number	
POSS	possessive	grammatical function	
PPL	participializer	verb forms	
PREP	prepositional	case	
PREVIOUS. EVIDENCE.EV	previous evidence evidential	evidentiality	#59, #62
PROG	progressive	aspect	#42, #59, #61
PRS	present	tense	#59–#62
PST	past	tense	#59–#62
PSTP	past participle	tense	#59–#62
PTCP	participle	verb forms	
REFL	reflexive	valence alternations	
SG	singular	number	
SHON	subject honorific	honorifics	#9, #36, #63, #65
SM	subject marker	agreement	
STAT	stative	aktionsart	#61
TOP	topic	information structure	#84–#88
TR	transitive	valence	
VIS.EV	visual evidential	evidentiality	#59, #62
VIS.EVIDENCE.EV	visual evidence evidential	evidentiality	#59, #62

Bibliography

O. Abend and A. Rappoport. Universal conceptual cognitive annotation (ucca). In *Proc. of the 51st Annual Meeting of the Association for Computational Linguistics (ACL)*, vol. 1, pages 228–238, 2013. 180

L. Abzianidze, J. Bjerva, K. Evang, H. Haagsma, R. van Noord, P. Ludmann, D. Nguyen, and J. Bos. The parallel meaning bank: Towards a multilingual corpus of translations annotated with compositional meaning representations. In *Proc. of the 15th Conference of the European Chapter of the Association for Computational Linguistics (EACL)*, pages 242–247, Valencia, Spain, 2017. 177, 178, 179, 182

S. Afantenos, N. Asher, F. Benamara, M. Bras, C. Fabre, M. Ho-Dac, A. Le Draoulec, P. Muller, M. Pery-Woodley, L. Prevot, J. Rebeyrolles, L. Tanguy, M. Vergez-Couret, and L. Vieu. An empirical resource for discovering cognitive principles of discourse organisation: The ANNODIS corpus. In *Proc. of the 8th International Conference on Language Resources and Evaluation (LREC'12)*, Istanbul, Turkey, 2012a. 183

S. Afantenos, N. Asher, F. Benamara, A. Cadilhac, C. Dégremont, P. Denis, M. Guhe, S. Keizer, A. Lascarides, O. Lemon, P. Muller, S. Paul, V. Popescu, V. Rieser, and L. Vieu. Modelling strategic conversation: Model, annotation design and corpus. In *Proc. of the 16th Workshop on the Semantics and Pragmatics of Dialogue (Seinedial)*, Paris, 2012b. 17, 26, 174, 183

S. Afantenos, E. Kow, N. Asher, and J. Perret. Discourse parsing for multi-party chat dialogues. In *Proc. of the Conference on Empirical Methods in Natural Language Processing, Association for Computational Linguistics*, pages 928–937, Lisbon, 2015. 188

A.Y. Aikhenvald. *Evidentiality*. Oxford University Press, 2004. 101

A. Al-Saif and K. Markert. The Leeds Arabic discourse treebank: Annotating discourse connectives for arabic. In *Proc. of the Conference on International Language Resources and Evaluation (LREC)*, pages 2046–2053, 2010. 182

I.A. Roteta, M.J.A. Urruzola, A.D. de I. Sánchez, and A.E. Ibarloza. A methodology for the semiautomatic annotation of EPEC-RolSem, a Basque corpus labeled at predicative level following the PropBank-VerbNet model. *Technical Report*, 2013. UPV/EHU/LSI/TR 01-2013. 178

194 BIBLIOGRAPHY

M. Alegre and P. Gordon. Frequency effects and the representational status of regular inflections. *Journal of Memory and Language*, 40:41–61, 1999. 43

H. Alshawi and R. Crouch. Monotonic semantic interpretation. In *Proc. of the 30th Annual Meeting of the Association for Computational Linguistics (ACL)*, pages 32–39, Delaware, 1992. 3

H. Alshawi, D. Carter, M. Rayner, and B. Gamback. Translation by quasi logical form transfer. In *29th Annual Meeting of the Association for National Linguistics*, 1991. http://www.aclweb .org/anthology/P91--1021 89

G. Altmann and M. Steedman. Interaction with context during human sentence processing. *Cognition*, 30(3):191–238, 1988. 24, 25

A. Anderson, M. Bader, E. Bard, E. Boyle, G.M. Doherty, S. Garrod, S. Isard, J. Kowtkow, J. McAllister, J. Miller, C. Sotillo, H.S. Thompson, and R. Weinert. The HCRC map task corpus. *Language and Speech*, 34:351–366, 1991. 184

J. Ang, R. Dhillon, A. Krupski, E. Shriberg, and A. Stolcke. Prosody-based automatic detection of annoyance and frustration in human-computer dialog. In *INTERSPEECH*, 2002. 20

L. Aqvist. Formal semantics for verb tenses as analyzed by reichenbach. *Pragmatics of Language and Literature*, pages 229–236, 1976. 124

Aristotle. *Prior Analytics*. Hackett, 1989. Translated by R. Smith. 5

P. Arndt. *Grammatik der Sika-Sprache*. 1931. Ende: Ende, Flores: Arnoldus. 78

M. Aronoff. *Word Formation in Generative Grammar*. MIT Press, 1976. 44

N. Asher. *Reference to Abstract Objects in Discourse*. Kluwer Academic Publishers, 1993. 109, 126, 134

N. Asher and A. Lascarides. Lexical disambiguation in a discourse context. *Journal of Semantics*, 12(1):69–108, 1995a. 51, 113

N. Asher and A. Lascarides. Metaphor in discourse. In *Proc. of the AAAI Spring Symposium Series: Representation and Acquisition of Lexical Knowledge: Polysemy, Ambiguity and Generativity*, pages 3–7, 1995b. 50

N. Asher and A. Lascarides. The semantics and pragmatics of presupposition. *Journal of Semantics*, 15(2):239–299, 1998. 139, 149

N. Asher and A. Lascarides. *Logics of Conversation*. Cambridge University Press, 2003. 2, 10, 13, 17, 18, 86, 107, 108, 109, 110, 111, 112, 113, 118, 128, 132, 133, 149, 164, 170, 180, 182, 183, 187, 188

N. Asher and A. Lascarides. Strategic conversation. *Semantics and Pragmatics*, 6(2):2:1–:62, 2013. 12, 120, 169, 171, 172

N. Asher and M. Morreau. Commonsense entailment. In J. Mylopoulos and R. Reiter, Eds., *Proc. of the 12th International Joint Conference on Artificial Intelligence*, pages 387–392, Morgan Kaufmann, Los Altos, CA, 1991. 11

N. Asher and S. Paul. Strategic conversation under imperfect information: Epistemic message exchange games. *Journal of Logic, Language and Information*, 2018. 172

N. Asher and L. Vieu. Subordinating and coordinating discourse relations. *Linga*, 115:590–610, 2005. 109

N. Asher, D. Hardt, and J. Busquets. Discourse parallelism, ellipsis and ambiguity. *Journal of Semantics*, 18(1), 2001. 40

N. Asher. *Lexical Meaning in Context: A web of words*. Cambridge University Press, 2011. 38, 41, 49, 64, 91, 113

N. Asher and P. Sablayrolles. A typology and discourse semantics for motion verbs and spatial PPS in French. *Journal of Semantics*, 12(2):163–209, 1995. 51, 126

R.E. Asher and T.C. Kumari. *Malayalam*. Routledge, London and New York, 1997. 59, 60

J.L. Austin. *How to Do Things With Words*. Oxford University Press, Oxford, 1962. 14, 16

S. Baccianella, A. Esuli, and F. Sebastiani. SentiWordNet 3.0: An enhanced lexical resource for sentiment analysis and opinion mining. In N. Calzolari (Conference Chair), K. Choukri, B. Maegaard, J. Mariani, J. Odijk, S. Piperidis, M. Rosner, and D. Tapias, Eds., *Proc. of the 7th Conference on International Language Resources and Evaluation (LREC'10)*, European Language Resources Association (ELRA), Valletta, Malta, May 2010. 20

C. Baker, C. Fillmore, and J. Lowe. The Berkeley FrameNet project. In *Proc. of the 17th International Conference on Computational Linguistics*, pages 86–90, Association for Computational Linguistics, 1998. 57, 60, 177

C. Baker, C. Fillmore, and B. Cronin. The structure of the framenet database. *International Journal of Lexicography*, 16(3):281–296, 2003. 178

C.F. Baker. Framenet: Frame semantic annotation in practice. In N. Ide and J. Pustejovsky, Eds., *Handbook of Linguistic Annotation*, pages 771–811, Springer, 2017. 177

J. Baldridge and A. Lascarides. Probabilistic head-driven parsing for discourse structure. In *Proc. of the 9th Conference on Computational Natural Language Learning (CoNLL)*, pages 96–103, 2005. 188

T. Baldwin and S.N. Kim. Multiword expressions. In N. Indurkhya and F.J. Damerau, Eds., *Handbook of Natural Language Processing*, 2nd ed., pages 267–292, CRC Press, Boca Raton, FL. 2010. 63

L. Banarescu, C. Bonial, S. Cai, M. Georgescu, K. Griffitt, U. Hermjakob, K. Knight, P. Koehn, M. Palmer, and N. Schneider. Abstract meaning representation for sembanking. In *Proc. of the 7th Linguistic Annotation Workshop and Interoperability with Discourse*, pages 178–186, Association for Computational Linguistics, Sofia, Bulgaria, August 2013. `http://www.ac lweb.org/anthology/W13--2322` 39, 180

C. Bannard. Acquiring phrasal lexicons from corpora. Ph.D. thesis, University of Edinburgh, 2006. 63, 70

E. Bard, A. Anderson, C. Sotillo, M. Aylett, G. Doherty-Sneddon, and A. Newlands. Controlling the intelligibility of referring expressions in dialogue. *Journal of Memory and Language*, 42(1):1–22, 2000. 24

M. Baroni, R. Bernardi, and R. Zamparelli. Frege in space: A program for compositional distributional semantics. *Linguistic Issues in Language Technology*, 9:241–346, 2014. 92

R. Barzilay and M. Elhadad. Using lexical chains for text summarization. *Advances in Automatic Text Summarization*, pages 111–121, 1999. 42

R. Barzilay and M. Lapata. Modeling local coherence: An entity-based approach. *Computational Linguistics*, 34(1):1–34, 2008. 134

L. Bauer. *English Word Formation*. Cambridge University Press, 1983. 45, 63

M. Beaney, Ed. *A Frege Reader*. Blackwell, Oxford, 1997. 7

D. Beaver. The kinematics of presupposition. In *Proc. of the 8th Amsterdam Colloquium*, pages 17–36, 1992. 139, 149

D. Beaver. Presupposition. In J. van Benthen and A. ter Meulen, Eds., *The Handbook of Logic and Language*. Elsevier, 1997. 148, 149, 171

D. Beaver and B. Clark. *Sense and Sensitivity: How Focus Determines Meaning*. Wiley–Blackwell, 2009. 161

C. Bejan and S. Harabagiu. Unsupervised event coreference resolution with rich linguistic features. In *Proc. of the 48th Annual Meeting of the Association for the Association for Computational Linguistics*, pages 1412–1422, 2010. 125

U. Bellugi and S. Fischer. A comparison of sign language and spoken language. *Cognition*, 1(2):173–200, 1972. `http://www.sciencedirect.com/science/article/pii/ 0010027772900182` 27

E. Bender, D. Flickinger, and S. Oepen. The grammar matrix: An open-source starter-kit for the rapid development of cross-linguistically consistent broad-coverage precision grammars. In *Proc. of the Workshop on Grammar Engineering and Evaluation*, vol. 15, pages 1–7, Association for Computational Linguistics, 2002. 3

E.M. Bender. *Linguistic Fundamentals for Natural Language Processing: 100 Essentials from Morphology and Syntax*. Morgan & Claypool Publishers, 2013. 43, 56, 57, 58, 60, 73, 189

E.M. Bender and B. Friedman. Data statements for NLP: Toward mitigating system bias and enabling better science. *Transactions of the Association for Computational Linguistics*, 2018. 48

E.M. Bender and A. Lascarides. On modeling scope of inflectional negation. In P. Hofmeister and E. Norcliffe, Eds., *The Core and the Periphery: Data Driven Perspectives on Syntax inspired by Ivan A. Sag*, pages 101–124, CSLI Publications, 2013. 88

E.M. Bender, D. Flickinger, S. Oepen, W. Packard, and A. Copestake. Layers of interpretation: On grammar and compositionality. In *Proc. of the 11th International Conference on Computational Semantics*, pages 239–249, Association for Computational Linguistics, London, UK, April 2015. http://www.aclweb.org/anthology/W15--0128 12, 13, 95, 180

L. Bentivogli, P.P. Clark, I. Dagan, and D. Giampiccolo. The fifth pascal recognizing textual entailment challenge. In *Proc. of the Text Analysis Conference (TAC)*, 2009. 8

L. Bentivogli and E. Pianta. Exploiting parallel texts in the creation of multilingual semantically annotated resources: The MultiSemCor corpus. *Natural Language Engineering*, 11(3):247–261, 2005. 177

A. Benz, G. Jäger, and R. van Rooij, Eds. *Game Theory and Pragmatics*. Palgrave Macmillan, 2005. 119, 166, 168, 169, 188

S. Bergsma and D. Lin. Bootstrapping path-based pronoun resolution. In *Proc. of the 21st International Conference on Computational Linguistics and the 44th Annual Meeting of the Association for Computational Linguistics*, pages 33–40, 2006. 129

A. Biletzki and A. Matar. Ludwig wittgenstein. In E.N. Zalta, Ed., *The Stanford Encyclopedia of Philosophy*. Metaphysics Research Lab, Stanford University, Summer 2018 edition, 2018. 46

P. Blackburn and J. Bos. *Representation and Inference for Natural Language: A First Course in Computational Semantics*. CSLI Publications, 2005. 6

B. Boguraev and R. Ando. TimeML-compliant text analysis for temporal reasoning. In *IJCAI*, vol. 5, pages 997–1003, 2005. 126

198 BIBLIOGRAPHY

A. Böhmová, J. Hajič, E. Hajičová, and B. Hladká. The Prague dependency treebank. In *Treebanks*, pages 103–127, Springer, 2003. 179

J. Du Bois, L. Wallace, C. Meyer, S. Thompson, R. Englebretson, and N. Martey. Santa Barbara corpus of spoken American English, parts 1–4. *Technical Report*, Linguistic Data Consortium, 2005. 183

D. Bolinger. *Aspects of Language*. Harcourt, Brace and Jovanovich, New York, 1975. 45

D. Bolinger. A theory of pitch accent in English. *Word*, 14:109–149, 1958. 158

T. Bolukbasi, K.-W. Chang, J.Y. Zou, V. Saligrama, and A.T. Kalai. Man is to computer programmer as woman is to homemaker? Debiasing word embeddings. In D.D. Lee, M. Sugiyama, U.V. Luxburg, I. Guyon, and R. Garnett, Eds., *Advances in Neural Information Processing Systems 29*, pages 4349–4357, Curran Associates, Inc., 2016. http://papers.nips.cc/paper/6228-man-is-to-computer-programmer-as-woman-is-to-homemaker-debiasing-word-embeddings.pdf 48

F. Bond and K. Paik. A survey of wordnets and their licenses. pages 64–71, 2012. 36, 42, 66, 177

F. Bond, S. Fujita, C. Hashimoto, K. Kasahara, S. Nariyama, E. Nichols, A. Ohtani, T. Tanaka, and S. Amano. The Hinoki treebank a treebank for text understanding. In *International Conference on Natural Language Processing*, pages 158–167, Springer, 2004. 179

F. Bond, T. Baldwin, R. Fothergill, and K. Uchimoto. Japanese SemCor: A sense-tagged corpus of Japanese. In *Proc. of the 6th Global WordNet Conference (GWC 2012)*, pages 56–63, 2012. 177

J. Bos. Predicate logic unplugged. In *Proc. of the 10th Amsterdam Colloquium*, pages 133–143, Amsterdam, 1995. 30, 76, 84, 90

J. Bos. Implementing the binding and accommodation theory for anaphora resolution and presupposition projection. *Computational Linguistics*, 29(2):179–210, 2003. 139, 148

J. Bos. Wide-coverage semantic analysis with boxer. In J. Bos and R. Delmonte, Eds., *Semantics in Text Processing. STEP 2008 Conference Proceedings*, Research in Computational Semantics, pages 277–286. College Publications, 2008. 144

J. Bos and K. Markert. Recognising textual entailment with logical inference. In *Proc. of Human Language Technology Conference and Conference on Empirical Methods in Natural Language Processing (HLT/EMNLP)*, pages 628–635, Vancouver, 2005. 42

J. Bos and T. Oka. Meaningful conversation with mobile robots. *Advanced Robotics*, 21(2):209–232, 2007. 28

J. Bos and J. Spenader. An annotated corpus for the analysis of VP ellipsis. *Language Resources and Evaluation*, 45(4):463–494, 2011. 124

J. Bos, S. Clark, M. Steedman, J. Curran, and J. Hockenmaier. Wide coverage semantic representations from a CCG parser. In *Proc. of the International Conference on Computational Linguistics (COLING 2004)*, Geneva, Switzerland, 2004. 76, 144

J. Bos. Open-domain semantic parsing with Boxer. In *Proc. of the 20th Nordic Conference of Computational Linguistics (NODALIDA 2015)*, pages 301–304, Vilnius, Lithuania, May 2015. Linköping University Electronic Press, Sweden. http://www.aclweb.org/anthology/W 15--1841 31, 182

J. Bos, V. Basile, K. Evang, N.J. Venhuizen, and J. Bjerva. The Groningen meaning bank. In N. Ide and J. Pustejovsky, Eds., *Handbook of Linguistic Annotation*, pages 463–496. Springer, 2017. 179, 181, 182, 183

A. Branco, C. Carvalheiro, S. Pereira, S. Silveira, J.R. Silva, S. Castro, and J. Graça. A PropBank for Portuguese: The CINTIL-PropBank. In *LREC*, pages 1516–1521, 2012. 178

M. Bréal. *Semantics: Studies in the Science of Meaning*. Dover, New York, 1964 [1900]. Transactions on by Mrs. Hentry Cust. 46

J. Breen and T. Baldwin. Corpus-based extraction of Japanese compound verbs. In *Proc. of the Australasian Language Technology Workshop (ALTW)*, pages 35–43, Sydney, Australia, 2009. 67

J. Bresnan and S.A. Mchombo. Topic, pronoun, and agreement in Chichewa. In M. Iida, S. Wechsler, and D. Zec, Eds., *Working Papers in Grammatical Theory and Discourse Structure: Interactions of Morphology, Syntax and Discourse*, pages 1–59, CSLI, Stanford, CA, 1987. 62

L.J. Brinton and E.C. Traugott. *Lexicalization and Language Change*. Cambridge University Press, Cambridge, 2005. 43, 68

E. J. Briscoe and A. Copestake. Lexical rules in constraint-based grammars. *Computational Linguistics*, 25(4):487–526, 1999. 44, 53

T. Briscoe, A. Copestake, and A. Lascarides. Blocking. In P. St Dizier and E. Viegas, Eds., *Computational Lexical Semantics*, pages 273–302, Cambridge University Press, 1995. 45

C. Brockmann and M. Lapata. Evaluating and combining approaches to selectional preference acquisition. In *Proc. of the 10th Conference on European Chapter of the Association for Computational Linguistics (EACL'03)*, vol. 1, pages 27–34, Association for Computational Linguistics, Stroudsburg, PA, 2003. https://doi.org/10.3115/1067807.1067813 59

P. Brown and S.C. Levinson. *Politeness: Some Universals and Language Usage*. Cambridge University Press, 1978. 102, 104

A. Budanitsky and G. Hirst. Evaluating wordnet-based measures of lexical semantic relatedness. *Computational Linguistics*, 32(1):13–47, 2006. 47

L. Bulat, S. Clark, and E. Shutova. Modelling metaphor with attribute-based semantics. In *Proc. of the European Chapter of the Association for Computational Linguistics (EACL)*, pages 523–531, 2017. 51

D. Büring. On d-trees, beans, and b-accents. *Linguistics and Philosophy*, 26(5):511–545, 2003. 156

L. Burnard. *Users Guide for the British National Corpus*. British National Corpus Consortium, Oxford University Computing Service, 1995. 44

A. Cadilhac, N. Asher, F. Benamara, and A. Lascarides. Grounding strategic conversation: Using negotiation dialogues to predict trades in a win-lose game. In *Proc. of EMNLP*, pages 357–368, Seattle, 2013. 121

K. Campbell-Kibler. The sociolinguistic variant as a carrier of social meaning. *Language Variation and Change*, 22(3):423–441, 2010. 21

M. Candito, P. Amsili, L. Barque, F. Benamara, G. De Chalendar, M. Djemaa, P. Haas, R. Huyghe, Y.Y. Mathieu, P. Muller, et al. Developing a French FrameNet: Methodology and first results. In *LREC—Language Resources and Evaluation Conference*, 9th ed., Reykjavik, Iceland, 2014a. 178

M. Candito, G. Perrier, B. Guillaume, C. Ribeyre, K. Fort, D. Seddah, and E. de la Clergerie. Deep syntax annotation of the sequoia French treebank. In *Proc. of the 9th International Conference on Language Resources and Evaluation (LREC)*. European Language Resources Association (ELRA), 2014b. http://www.lrec-conf.org/proceedings/lrec2014/pdf/494_Paper.pdf 180

J. Carletta. Unleashing the killer corpus: Experiences in creating the multi-everything AMI meeting corpus. In *Proc. of Language Resources and Evaluation (LREC)*, 2006. 183

L. Carlson, D. Marcu, and M.E. Okurowski. RST Discourse Treebank. Linguistic Data Consortium, 2002. 183

R. Carnap. Meaning postulates. *Philosophical Studies*, 3(5):65–73, 1952. 48

R. Carpenter. *The Logic of Typed Feature Structure*. Cambridge University Press, 1992. 7

J. Carroll. Relating complexity to practical performance in parsing with wide-coverage uni-fication grammars. In *Proc. of the 32nd Annual Meeting of the Association for Computational Linguistics (ACL)*, pages 287–294, Las Cruces, NM, 1994. 170

W.L. Chafe. Idiomaticity as an anomaly in the Chomskyan paradigm. *Foundations of Language*, 4:109–127, 1968. 63

J. Chamberlain, M. Poesio, and U. Kruschwitz. Phrase detectives: A web-based collaborative annotation game. In *Proc. of the International Conference on Semantic Systems (I-Semantics)*, pages 42–49, 2008. 181

N. Chambers and D. Jurafsky. Unsupervised learning of narrative event chains. In *ACL*, vol. 94305, pages 789–797, 2008. 126

C. Chang, M. Kayed, M. Girgis, and K. Shaalan. A survey of web information extraction systems. *IEEE Transactions on Knowledge and Data Engineering*, 18(10):1411–1428, 2006. 8, 11

R.P. Chaves. Coordinate structures: Constraint-based syntax-semantics processing. Ph.D. the-sis, Universidade de Lisboa, 2007. 79, 80

B. Chellas. *Modal Logic: An Introduction*. Cambridge University Press, 1980. 131

Y. Chen, S. Huang, F. Wang, J. Cao, W. Sun, and X. Wan. Neural maximum subgraph parsing for cross-domain semantic dependency analysis. In *Proc. of the 22nd Conference on Computa-tional Natural Language Learning*, pages 562–572. Association for Computational Linguistics, 2018. http://aclweb.org/anthology/K18--1054 182

J. Cheng, S. Reddy, V. Saraswat, and M. Lapata. Learning an executable neural semantic parser. *Computational Linguistics*, 45(1):59–94, 2019. https://www.aclweb.org/antholo gy/J19--1002 76

P. Cheng and K. Erk. Implicit argument prediction with event knowledge. In *Proc. of the 2018 Conference of the North American Chapter of the Association for Computational Linguistics: Human Language Technologies, Volume 1 (Long Papers)*, pages 831–840, Association for Computational Linguistics, New Orleans, LA, 2018. https://www.aclweb.org/anthology/N18--1076 62

N. Chinchor. Message understanding conference (MUC) 7. In *LDC2001T02*, 2001. 123

N. Chinchor and B. Sundheim. Message understanding conference (MUC) 6. In *LDC2003T13*, 2003. 123

N. Chomsky. *Lectures on Government and Binding*. Foris Publications, Dorrecht Holland, 1981. 127

N. Chomsky. *The Minimalist Program*. MIT Press, Boston, 1995. 84

H. Clark. *Arenas of Language Use*. University of Chicago Press, Chicago, 1992. 89, 187

K. Clark and C.D. Manning. Entity-centric coreference resolution with model stacking. In *Proc. of the 53rd Annual Meeting of the Association for Computational Linguistics and the 7th International Joint Conference on Natural Language Processing (Volume 1: Long Papers)*, pages 1405–1415, Association for Computational Linguistics, 2015. `http://aclweb.org/anthology/P15--1136` 181

K. Clark and C.D. Manning. Improving coreference resolution by learning entity-level distributed representations. In *Proc. of the 54th Annual Meeting of the Association for Computational Linguistics (Volume 1: Long Papers)*, pages 643–653, Association for Computational Linguistics, 2016. `http://aclweb.org/anthology/P16--1061` 181

S. Clark. Vector space models of lexical meaning. In S. Lappin and C. Fox, Eds., *Handbook of Contemporary Semantic Theory*, 2nd ed., pages 493–522, Wiley-Blackwell, 2015. 47

S. Clark and J. Curran. Parsing the WSJ with CCG and log-linear models. In *Proc. of the 42nd Annual Meeting of the Association for Computational Linguistics (ACL)*, pages 104–111, Barcelona, 2004. 76, 144

S. Clark and J.R. Curran. Wide-coverage efficient statistical parsing with CCG and log-linear mmodels. *Computational Linguistics*, 33(4):493–552, 2007. 179

J. Clarke and M. Lapata. Global inference for sentence compression: An integer linear programming approach. *Journal of Artificial Intelligence Research*, 31:399–429, 2008. 42

B. Coecke, M. Sadrzadeh, and S. Clark. Mathematical foundations for a compositional distributional model of meaning. In J. van Bentham, M. Moortgat, and W. Buszkowski, Eds., *Linguistic Analysis (Lambek Festschrift)*, pages 345–384, 2010. 93

M. Constant, G. Eryiğit, J. Monti, L. Van Der Plas, C. Ramisch, M. Rosner, and A. Todirascu. Multiword expression processing: A survey. *Computational Linguistics*, 43(4):837–892, 2017. 69

A. Copestake and E.J. Briscoe. Semi-productive polysemy and sense extension. *Journal of Semantics*, 12(1):15–67, 1995. 7, 38, 39, 43, 45, 48, 49

A. Copestake, D. Flickinger, I. Sag, and C. Pollard. Minimal recursion semantics: An introduction. *Research on Language and Computation*, 3(2–3):281–332, 2005. 30, 31, 76, 84, 85, 90, 179, 181

M. Core and J. Allen. Coding dialogs with the DAMSL annotation scheme. In *AAAI Fall Symposium on Communicative Action in Humans and Machines*, vol. 56, Boston, MA, 1997. 16, 183

S. Crain and M. Steedman. On not being led up the garden path: The use of context by the psychological parser. In D. Dowty L. Karttunen and A. Zwicky, Eds., *Natural Language Parsing*, pages 320–358, Cambridge University Press, 1985. 24

V. Crawford and J. Sobel. Strategic information transmission. *Econometrica*, 50(6):1431–1451, 1982. 172

A. Cruse. *Lexical Semantics*. Cambridge University Press, 1986. 63

B. Crysmann. On the efficient implementation of German verb placement in HPSG. In *Proc. of RANLP*, pages 112–116, 2003. 182

J.R. Curran, S. Clark, and J. Bos. Linguistically motivated large-scale NLP with C&C and Boxer. In *Proc. of the 45th Annual Meeting of the ACL on Interactive Poster and Demonstration Sessions*, pages 33–36, Association for Computational Linguistics, 2007. 179, 182

I. Dagan, O. Glickman, and B. Magnini. The pascal recognising textual entailment challenge. In *Machine Learning Challenges: Evaluating Predictive Uncertainty, Visual Object Classification, and Recognising Tectual Entailment*, pages 177–190, Springer, 2006. 8

O. Dahl and V. Velupillai. The past tense. In M.S. Dryer and M. Haspelmath, Eds., *The World Atlas of Language Structures Online*. Max Planck Institute for Evolutionary Anthropology, Leipzig, 2013a. https://wals.info/chapter/66 97

O. Dahl and V. Velupillai. Perfective/imperfective aspect. In M.S. Dryer and M. Haspelmath, Eds., *The World Atlas of Language Structures Online*. Max Planck Institute for Evolutionary Anthropology, Leipzig, 2013b. https://wals.info/chapter/65 97

M. Dalrymple, S. Shieber, and F. Pereira. Ellipsis and higher-order unification. *Linguistics and Philosophy*, 14(4):399–452, 1991. 124

D. Davidson. *Essays on Actions and Events*. Clarendon Press, 1980. 31, 55, 56, 74

J.P. Dayley. *Tzutujil Grammar*, vol. 107 of University of California Publications in Linguistics. University of California Press, Berkeley, 1985. 96

F. de Haan. Coding of evidentiality. In M.S. Dryer and M. Haspelmath, Eds., *The World Atlas of Language Structures Online*. Max Planck Institute for Evolutionary Anthropology, Leipzig, 2013. https://wals.info/chapter/78 97

M.C. de Marneffe, C. Manning, and C. Potts. Did it happen? the pragmatic complexity of veridicality assessment. *Computational Linguistics*, 38(2):301–333, 2012. 184

P. de Swart, M. Lamers, and S. Lestrade. Animacy, argument structure, and argument encoding. *Lingua*, 118(2):131–140, 2008. 59

J.O. de Urbina. Focus in basque. In *The Grammar of Focus*, pages 311–334, John Benjamins Amsterdam/Philadelphia, 1999. 160

J.M. Dedrick and E.H. Casad. *Sonora Yaqui Language Structures*. University of Arizona Press, 1999. 100

V. Demberg and F. Keller. Data from eye-tracking corpora as evidence for theories of syntactic processing complexity. *Cognition*, 109(2):193–210, 2008. 24

D. Deng and N. Xue. Translation divergences in Chinese–English machine translation: An empirical investigation. *American Journal of Computational Linguistics*, 43(3):521–565, 2017. https://www.aclweb.org/anthology/J17--3002 62

P. Denis and J. Baldridge. Specialized models and reranking for reference resolution. In *Proc. of Empirical Methods in Natural Language Processing (EMNLP)*, pages 660–669, Hawaii, 2008. 152

D.C. Derbyshire. *Hixkaryana and Linguistic Typology*. The Summer Institute of Linguistics and the University of Texas at Arlington, 1985. 78

D. DeVault and M. Stone. Scorekeeping in an uncertain language game. In *Proc. of the 10th Workshop on the Semantics and Pragmatics of Dialogue*, pages 139–146, 2006. 18

M. Djemaa, M. Candito, P. Muller, and L. Vieu. Corpus annotation within the French FrameNet: A domain-by-domain methodology. In N. Calzolari (Conference Chair), K. Choukri, T. Declerck, S. Goggi, M. Grobelnik, B. Maegaard, J. Mariani, H. Mazo, A. Moreno, J. Odijk, and S. Piperidis, Eds., *Proc. of the 10th International Conference on Language Resources and Evaluation (LREC)*, European Language Resources Association (ELRA), Paris, France, May 2016. 178

Q.N.T. Do, S. Bethard, and M.-F. Moens. Improving implicit semantic role labeling by predicting semantic frame arguments. In *Proc. of the 8th International Joint Conference on Natural Language Processing (Volume 1: Long Papers)*, Asian Federation of Natural Language Processing, pages 90–99, Taipei, Taiwan, 2017. https://www.aclweb.org/anthology/I17--1010 62

S. Dobnik, R. Cooper, and S. Larsson. Modelling language, action and perception in type theory with records. In D. Duchier and Y. Parmentier, Eds., *Constraint Solving and Language Processing*, pages 70–91, Springer, 2012. 27, 76

D. Downey, M. Broadhead, and O. Etzioni. Locating complex named entities in web text. In *IJCAI*, vol. 7, pages 2733–2739, 2007. 2

D. Dowty. *Word Meaning and Montague Grammar*. Reidel, Dordrecht, 1979. 99

D. Dowty. On the semantic content of the notion of thematic role. In B. Partee, G. Chierchia, and R. Turner, Eds., *Properties, Types and Meaning*. Kluwer Academic Publishers, 1989. 57

D. Dowty, R. Wall, and S. Peters. *Introduction to Montague Semantics*. Reidel, Dordrecht, 1981. 76, 185

D. Dowty. Thematic proto-roles and argument selection. *Language*, 67(3):547–619, 1991. 56, 57

T. Dozat and C. Manning. Simpler but more accurate semantic dependency parsing. In *Proc. of the 56th Annual Meeting of the Association for Computational Linguistics (ACL)*, pages 484–490, 2018. 182

M.S. Dryer and M. Haspelmath, Eds. *WALS Online*. Max Planck Institute for Evolutionary Anthropology, Leipzig, 2013. `https://wals.info/` 97

P. Eckert. The meaning of style. In *Texas Linguistic Forum*, vol. 47, pages 41–53, 2003. 21

P. Eckert and S. McConnell-Ginet. Think practically and look locally: Language and gender as community-based practice. *Annual Review of Anthropology*, pages 461–490, 1992. 46

M. Egg, A. Koller, and J. Niehren. The constraint language for lambda structures. *Journal of Logic, Language, and Information*, 10:457–485, 2001. 84, 86

G. Emerson. Functional distributional semantics: Learning linguistically informed representations from a precisely annotated corpus. Ph.D. thesis, University of Cambridge, 2018. 93

G. Emerson and A. Copestake. Functional distributional semantics. In *Proc. of the ACL Workshop on Representation Learning for NLP (RepL4NLP)*, 2016. 93

G. Evans. Pronouns, quantifiers and relative clauses II. *Canadian Journal of Philosophy*, 7(4):777–797, 1977. 115

R. Farkas, V. Vincze, G. Móra, J. Csirik, and G. Szarvas. The CoNLL-2010 shared task: Learning to detect hedges and their scope in natural language text. In *Proc. of the 14th Conference on Computational Natural Language Learning—Shared Task*, pages 1–12, Association for Computational Linguistics, 2010. 89

Y. Feinberg. Subjective reasoning—games with unawareness. *Technical Report 1875*, Graduate School of Business, Stanford University, 2004. 121

C. Fellbaum, Ed. *WordNet: An Electronic Lexical Database*. MIT Press, Cambridge, MA, 1998. 35, 42, 177

F. Ferreira and N. Patson. The "good enough" approach to language comprehension. *Language and Linguistics Compass*, 1(1–2):71–83, 2007. 24

C. Fillmore. Pragmatically controlled zero anaphora. *Berkely Linguistics Society*, 12:95–107, 1986. 53, 61

C. Fillmore. Frame semantics. In D. Geeraerts, Ed., *Cognitive Linguistics: Basic Readings*, pages 373–400, Berlin and New York, Mouton de Gruyter, 2006. 2

C.J. Fillmore and M.R.L. Petruck. Framenet glossary. *International Journal of Lexicography*, 16(3):359–361, 2003. http://dx.doi.org/10.1093/ijl/16.3.359 60

J. Firbas. *Functional Sentence Perspective in Written and Spoken Communication*. Cambridge University Press, 1992. 157

J.R. Firth. A synopsis of linguistic theory, 1930–1955. *Studies in Linguistic Analysis*, 1957. 46

N. FitzGerald, J. Michael, L. He, and L. Zettlemoyer. Large-scale QA-SRL parsing. In *Proc. of the 56th Annual Meeting of the Association for Computational Linguistics (Volume 1: Long Papers)*, pages 2051–2060, Association for Computational Linguistics, 2018. http://aclweb.org/anthology/P18--1191 181

D. Flickinger. On building a more efficient grammar by exploiting types. *Natural Language Engineering*, 6(1) (Special Issue on Efficient Processing with HPSG): 15–28, 2000. 57, 75, 144, 179, 182

D. Flickinger. Accuracy vs. robustness in grammar engineering. In E.M. Bender and J.E. Arnold, Eds., *Language from a Cognitive Perspective: Grammar, Usage and Processing*, pages 31–50, CSLI Publications, Stanford, CA, 2011. 57, 75, 144, 179, 182

M. Forbes, R. Rao, L. Zettlemoyer, and M. Cakmak. Robot programming by demonstration with situated spatial language understanding. In *Proc. of ICRA*, 2015. 27, 28

M. Franke. Signal to act: Game theory in pragmatics. Ph.D. thesis, ILLC, Universiteit van Amsterdam, 2009. 119

M. Franke, T. de Jager, and R. van Rooij. Relevance in cooperation and conflict. *Journal of Logic and Computation*, 22(1):23–54, 2012. 118, 166, 188

L. Frazier and K. Rayner. Making and correcting errors during sentence comprehension: Eye movements in the analysis of structurally ambiguous sentences. *Cognitive Psychology*, 14(2):178–210, 1982. 24

L. Frermann and M. Lapata. A Bayesian model of diachronic meaning change. *Transactions of the Association for Computational Linguistics*, 4:31–45, 2016. 46

L.T.F. Gamut. *Logic and Meaning Volume 1: Introduction to Logic*. University of Chicago Press, 1991a. Gamut is a pseudonym for J.F.A.K. van Benthem, J.A.G. Groenendijk, D.H.J. de Jongh, M.J.B. Stokhof, and H.J. Verkuyl. 6, 74, 81, 86, 129, 185

L.T.F. Gamut. *Logic and Meaning Volume 2: Intensional Logic and Logical Grammar*. University of Chicago Press, 1991b. Gamut is a pseudonym for J.F.A.K. van Benthem, J.A.G. Groenendijk, D.H.J. de Jongh, M.J.B. Stokhof, and H.J. Verkuyl. 118, 185

M. Gardner, J. Grus, M. Neumann, O. Tafjord, P. Dasigi, N.F. Liu, M. Peters, M. Schmitz, and L.S. Zettlemoyer. AllenNLP: A deep semantic natural language processing platform. *ArXiv:1803.07640*, 2017. 181

S. Garrod and A. Anderson. Saying what you mean in dialogue: A study in conceptual and semantic coordination. *Cognition*, 27:181–218, 1987. 37

J.M. Gawron, J. King, J. Lamping, E. Loebner, E.A. Paulson, G.K. Pullum, I.A. Sag, and T. Wasow. Processing English with a generalized phrase structure grammar. In *Proc. of the 20th Annual Meeting of the Association for Computational Linguistics*, Association for Computational Linguistics, pages 74–81, Toronto, Ontario, Canada, June 1982. http://www.aclweb.org/anthology/P82--1014 182

G. Gazdar. *Pragmatics, Implicature, Presupposition and Logical Form*. Academic Press, 1979. 138, 139

P. Geach. *Reference and Generality*. Cornell University Press, 1962. 87, 131

K. Georgila, J. Henderson, and O. Lemon. User simulation for spoken dialogue systems: Learning and evaluation. In *Proc. of the 9th International Conference on Spoken Language Processing (Interspeech)*, Pittsburgh, PA, 2006. 119, 168

M. Gerber and J. Chai. Beyond NomBank: A study of implicit arguments for nominal predicates. In *Proc. of the 48th Annual Meeting of the Association for Computational Linguistics*, Association for Computational Linguistics, pages 1583–1592, Uppsala, Sweden, 2010. https://www.aclweb.org/anthology/P10--1160 62

B. Geurts. Local satisfaction guaranteed. *Linguistics and Philosophy*, 19:259–294, 1996. 139, 171

J. Ginzburg. Resolving questions part I. *Linguistics and Philosophy*, 18(5):459–527, 1995a. 140, 155

J. Ginzburg. Resolving questions part II. *Linguistics and Philosophy*, 18(6):567–609, 1995b. 140, 155

J. Ginzburg. *The Interactive Stance: Meaning for Conversation*. Oxford University Press, 2012. 12, 162, 187

J. Ginzburg and R. Cooper. Clarification, ellipsis, and the nature of contextual updates. *Linguistics and Philosophy*, 27(3):297–366, 2004. 18

J. Godfrey, E. Holliman, and Jane J. McDaniel. Switchboard: Telephone speech corpus for research and development. In *Proc. of the IEEE International Conference on Acoustics, Speech, and Signal Processing (ICAPS)*, vol. 1, pages 517–520, 1992. 16

A. Göksel and C. Kerslake. *Turkish: A Comprehensive Grammar*. Routledge, 2004. 102

L.J. Green. Topics in African American English: The verb system analysis. Ph.D. thesis, University of Massachusetts Amherst, 1993. 100

E. Grefenstette. Towards a formal distributional semantics: Simulating logical calculi with tensors. In *Proc. of the 2nd Joint Conference on Lexical and Computational Semantics*, 2013. 93

H.P. Grice. Logic and conversation. In P. Cole and J.L. Morgan, Eds., *Syntax and Semantics Volume 3: Speech Acts*, pages 41–58, Academic Press, 1975. 15, 29, 118, 155, 163, 164, 165, 174

H.P. Grice. Utterer's meaning, sentence-meaning, and word-meaning. *Foundations of Language*, 4(3):225–242, 1968. 11

J. Groenendijk and M. Stokhof. Dynamic predicate logic. *Linguistics and Philosophy*, 14:39–100, 1991. 23, 77, 117, 118, 130, 131, 133

B. Grosz and C. Sidner. Attention, intentions and the structure of discourse. *Computational Linguistics*, 12:175–204, 1986. 108, 110, 187

B. Grosz, A. Joshi, and S. Weinstein. Centering: A framework for modelling the local coherence of discourse. *Computational Linguistics*, 21(2):203–226, 1995. 128, 129, 134

S. Gryllia. On the nature of preverbal focus in Greek: A theoretical and experimental approach. Ph.D. thesis, Leiden University, 2009. 157, 158

J.K. Gundel, N. Hedberg, and R. Zacharski. Cognitive status and the from of referring expressions in discourse. *Language*, 69:274–307, 1993. 151, 152, 153, 154

N. Haddock. Incremental semantics and interactive syntactic processing. Ph.D. thesis, Centre for Cognitive Science and Department of Artificial Intelligence, University of Edinburgh, 1988. 25

J. Hajič, E. Hajičová, M. Mikulová, and J. Mírovský. Prague dependency treebank. In N. Ide and J. Pustejovsky, Eds., *Handbook of Linguistic Annotation*, pages 555–594, Springer, 2017. 179

M. Halliday. Notes on transitivity and theme in English: Part 2. *Journal of Linguistics*, 3(02):199–244, 1967. 156, 157

M.A.K. Halliday. *A Course in Spoken English: Intonation.* Oxford University Press, 1970. 162

J. Halpern and L. Rêgo. Interactive unawareness revisited. In *Proc. of Theoretical Aspects of Rationality and Knowledge (TARK)*, pages 78–91, 2005. 121

C. Hamblin. *Fallacies.* Metheun, 1970. 11, 12, 107, 167

W.L. Hamilton, J. Leskovec, and D. Jurafsky. Diachronic word embeddings reveal statistical laws of semantic change. In *Proc. of the 54th Annual Meeting of the Association for Computational Linguistics (Volume 1: Long Papers)*, Association for Computational Linguistics, pages 1489–1501, Berlin, Germany, August 2016. http://www.aclweb.org/anthology/P16--1141 45, 46

S.O. Hansson. Changes in preference. *Theory and Decision*, 38(1):1–28, 1995. 121

Z.S. Harris. Distributional structure. *Word*, 10(2–3):146–162, 1954. 47

K. Haverinen, J. Kanerva, S. Kohonen, A. Missilä, S. Ojala, T. Viljanen, V. Laippala, and F. Ginter. The finnish proposition bank. *Language Resources and Evaluation*, 49(4):907–926, 2015. 178

D. Hebdige. *Subculture: The Meaning of Style.* Methuen, New York, 1984. 21

N. Hedberg, E. Görgülü, and M. Mameni. On definiteness and specificity in Turkish and Persian. In *Proc. of the Annual Meeting of the Canadian Linguistic Association*, 2009. 154

I. Heim. The semantics of definite and indefinite noun phrases. Ph.D. thesis, University of Massachussetts, 1982. 115, 117, 129, 130

J. Helmbrecht. Politeness distinctions in pronouns. In M.S. Dryer and M. Haspelmath, Eds., *The World Atlas of Language Structures Online*. Max Planck Institute for Evolutionary Anthropology, Leipzig, 2013. https://wals.info/chapter/45 103, 104

M. Hickmann and H. Hendriks. Cohesion and anaphora in children's narratives: A comparison of English, French, German, and Mandarin Chinese. *Journal of Child Language*, 26(2):419–452, 1999. 127

L. Hirschman and N. Chinchor. Coreference task definition (v3.0, July 13, 97). In *Proc. of the 7th Message Understanding Conference*, 1997. 123

J. Hobbs. An improper treatment of quantification in ordinary English. In *Proc. of the 21st Annual Meeting on Association for Computational Linguistics*, pages 57–63, 1983. 89

J.R. Hobbs. On the coherence and structure of discourse. *Technical Report CSLI-85–37*, Center for the Study of Language and Information, Stanford University, 1985. 109, 110

J. R. Hobbs, M. Stickel, D. Appelt, and P. Martin. Interpretation as abduction. *Artificial Intelligence*, 63(1–2): 69–142, 1993. 10, 108, 169, 187, 188

J.R. Hobbs. Coherence and coreference. *Cognitive Science*, 3(1):67–90, 1979. 9, 17, 30, 107, 132, 170

J.R. Hobbs and A. Kehler. A theory of parallelism and a case of VP ellipsis. In *Proc., of the 35th Annual Meeting of the Association for Computational Linguistics (ACL)*, pages 394–401, 1997. 124

J. Hockenmaier and M. Steedman. CCGbank: A corpus of CCG derivations and dependency structures cextracted from the Penn Treebank. *Computational Linguistics*, 33(3):355–396, 2007. 179

C.F. Hockett. A course in modern linguistics. *Language Learning*, 8(3–4):73–75, 1958. 157

J. Hoffmann. *Mundari Grammar and Exercises*. Gyan Publishing House, New Delhi, 1903. 78

P. Hofmeister and I.A. Sag. Cognitive constraints and island effects. *Language*, 86(2):366–415, 2010. 85

R. Huddleston and G. Pullum. *The Cambridge Grammar of English*. Cambridge University Press, 2002. 19

J. Hunter, N. Asher, and A. Lascarides. Integrating non-linguistic events into discourse structure. In *Proc. of the 11th International Conference on Computational Semantics (IWCS)*, pages 184–194, London, 2015. 27

J. Hunter, N. Asher, and A. Lascarides. A formal semantics for situated conversation. *Semantics and Pragmatics*, 2018. 28, 183

C. Innes and A. Lascarides. Learning structured decision problems with unawareness. In *Proc. of the 36th International Conference on Machine Learning (ICML)*, Long Beach, CA, 2019a. 121

C. Innes and A. Lascarides. Learning factored Markov decision processes with unawareness. In *Proc. of Uncertainty in Artificial Intelligence (UAI)*, Tel Aviv, Israel, 2019b. 121

H. Isahara, F. Bond, K. Uchimoto, M. Utiyama, and K. Kanzaki. Development of the Japanese WordNet. In *Proc. of LREC*, pages 2420–2423, Marrakech, 2008. 36, 66

Y. Ishizaki. A usage-based analysis of phrasal verbs in early and late modern English. *English Language and Linguistics*, 16(2):241–260, 2012. 68

A. Ivanova, S. Oepen, L. Øvrelid, and D. Flickinger. Who did what to whom?: A contrastive study of syntacto-semantic dependencies. In *Proc. of the 6th Linguistic Annotation Workshop*, Association for Computational Linguistics, pages 2–11, Jeju, Korea, 2012. 179

A. Ivanova, S. Oepen, R. Dridan, D. Flickinger, L. Øvrelid, and E. Lapponi. On different approaches to syntactic analysis into bi-lexical dependencies: An empirical comparison of direct, PCFG-based, and HPSG-based parsers. *Journal of Language Modelling*, 4(1):113–144, 2016. 182

R. Jackendoff. Morphological and semantic regularities in the lexicon. *Language*, pages 639–671, 1975. 44

R. Jackendoff. *The Architecture of the Language Faculty*. MIT Press, 1997. 44, 63

R. Jackendoff. English particle constructions, the lexicon, and the autonomy of syntax. In N. Dehé, R. Jackendoff, A. McIntyre, and S. Urban, Eds., *Verb-Particle Explorations*, pages 67–94, Walter de Gruyter, 2002. 67

A. Janin, D. Baron, J. Edwards, D. Ellis, D. Gelbart, N. Morgan, B. Peskin, T. Pfau, E. Shriberg, A. Stolcke, et al. The ICSI meeting corpus. In *Acoustics, Speech, and Signal Processing, Proceedings.(ICASSP). IEEE International Conference on*, vol. 1, pages I, 2003. 183

R.J. Jeffers and I. Lehiste. *Principles and Methods for Historical Linguistics*. MIT press, 1979. 46

M.R. Johnson. A semantic analysis of Kikuyu tense and aspect. Ph.D. thesis, The Ohio State University, 1977. 124

D. Jurafsky and J. Martin. *Speech and Language Processing*. Pearson Education India, 2000. 185

N. Kadman. *Formal Pragmatics*. Blackwell, 2001. 185

A. Kalouli and R. Crouch. GKR: The graphical knowledge representation for semantic parsing. In *Proc. of the Workshop on Computational Semantics beyond Events and Roles Pages*, pages 27–37, 2018. 143

H. Kamp. A theory of truth and semantic representation. In J. Groenendijk, T. Janssen, and M. Stokhof, Eds., *Formal Methods in the Study of Language*, pages 277–322, Mathematisch Centrum, Amsterdam, 1981. 23, 129

H. Kamp and U. Reyle. *From Discourse to Logic: Introduction to Modeltheoretic Semantics of Natural Language, Formal Logic and Discourse Representation Theory*. Kluwer Academic Publishers, 1993. 23, 31, 32, 86, 90, 107, 108, 117, 118, 129, 130, 131, 133, 179, 180, 182, 185, 187

D. Kaplan. Demonstratives. In J. Almog, J. Perry, and H. Wettstein, Eds., *Themes from Kaplan*. Oxford, 1989. 26, 27

L. Karttunen. Presupposition and linguistic context. *Theoretical Linguistics*, 1:181–194, 1974. 139

L. Karttunen. Presuppositions of compound sentences. *Linguistic Inquiry*, 4(2):169–193, 1973. http://www.jstor.org/stable/4177763 142, 143

D. Kastovsky. *Wortbildung und Semantik*. Bagel/Francke, Dusseldorf, 1982. 63

F. Katamba et al. Bantu nominal morphology. In D. Nurse and G. Philippson, Eds., *The Bantu Languages*, pages 103–120, Routledge, 2003. 127

M. Kay. Syntactic processing and functional sentence perspective. In *Theoretical Issues in Natural Language Processing: Supplement*, 1975. 3

E. Keenan and D. Westerståhl. Generalized quantifiers in linguistics and logic. In J. van Benthem and A. ter Meulen, Eds., *Handbook of Logic and Language*, pages 837–893, Elsevier, 1997. 83

A. Kehler. *Coherence, Reference and the Theory of Grammar*. CSLI Publications, Cambridge University Press, 2002. 17, 40, 107, 109, 128, 185

A. Kehler and H. Rohde. Evaluating an expectation-driven QUD model of discourse interpretation. *Discourse Processes*, 54(3):219–238, 2017. 132

A. Kehler, D. Appelt, L. Taylor, and A. Simma. The (non) utility of predicate-argument frequencies for pronoun interpretation. In *HLT-NAACL*, vol. 4, pages 289–296, 2004. 129

A. van Kemenade and B. Los. Particles and prefixes in Dutch and English. In G. Booij and J. van Marle, Eds., *Yearbook of Morphology*, pages 79–117, 2003. 67

R. Kempson, W. Meyer-Viol, and D. Gabbay. *Dynamic Syntax: The Flow of Language Understanding*. Wiley-Blackwell, 2000. 76, 114, 187

C. Kennedy. Comparatives, semantics of. In K. Brown, Ed., *Concise Encyclopedia of Philosophy of Language and Linguistics*, 2nd ed., pages 68–71, Elsevier Limited, Oxford, 2005. 77

J.S. Kessler, M. Eckert, L. Clark, and N. Nicolov. The 2010 ICWSM JDPA sentiment corpus for the automotive domain. In *4th International AAAI Conference on Weblogs and Social Media Data Workshop Challenge (ICWSM-DWC)*, 2010. http://www.cs.indiana.edu/~{}jaskessl/icwsm10.pdf 180

J.-D. Kim, T. Ohta, S. Pyysalo, Y. Kano, and J. Tsujii. Overview of BioNLP'09 shared task on event extraction. In *Proc. of the BioNLP 2009 Workshop Companion Volume for Shared Task*, pages 1–9, Association for Computational Linguistics, 2009. http://www.aclweb.org/anthology/W09--1401 89

J.-B. Kim and I.A. Sag. Negation without head-movement. *Natural Language and Linguistic Theory*, 20(2):339–412, May 2002. https://doi.org/10.1023/A:1015045225019 88

P. Kiparsky. Partitive case and aspect. In M. Butt and W. Geuder, Eds., *The Projection of Arguments*, CSLI, Stanford, 1998. 100

K. Knight and et al. Abstract meaning representation (AMR) annotation release 2.0, 2017. LDC2017T10. Web Download. 180

A. Knott. A data-driven methodology for motivating a set of coherence relations. Ph.D. thesis, University of Edinburgh, 1995. 111

A. Koller, K. Mehlhorn, and J. Niehren. A polynomial-time fragment of dominance constraints. In *Proc. of the 28th Annual Meeting of the Association for Computational Linguistics (ACL)*, Hong Kong, 2000. 76

A. Kratzer. An investigation of the lumps of thought. *Linguistics and Philosophy*, 12(5):607–653, 1989. 160

T. Krennmayer and G. Steen. VU Amsterdam metaphor corpus. In N. Ide and J. Pustejovsky, Eds., *Handbook of Linguistic Annotation*, pages 1053–1071, Springer, 2017. 180

S.A. Kripke. Presupposition and anaphora: Remarks on the formulation of the projection problem. *Linguistic Inquiry*, 40(3):367–386, 2009. 142

R. Krishna, Y. Zhu, O. Groth, J. Johnson, K. Hata, J. Kravitz, S. Chen, Y. Kalantidis, L. Li, D. Shamma, M. Bernstein, and L. Fei-Fei. Visual genome: Connecting language and vision using crowdsourced dense image annotations, 2016. https://arxiv.org/abs/1602.07332 181

G. Kumaran and J. Allan. Text classification and named entities for new event detection. In *Proc. of the 27th Annual International ACM SIGIR Conference on Research and Development in Information Retrieval*, pages 297–304, ACM, 2004. 126

S. Kuno. *The Structure of the Japanese Language*. The MIT Press, Cambridge, MA, 1973. 59, 60

T. Kwiatkowski, L. Zettlemoyer, S. Goldwater, and M. Steedman. Inducing probabilistic CCG grammars from logical form with higher-order unification. In *Proc. of the Conference on Empirical Methods in Natural Language Processing*, pages 1223–1233, Association for Computational Linguistics, 2010. 76

C. Kwok, O. Etzioni, and D. Weld. Scaling question answering to the Web. *ACM Transactions on Information Systems (TOIS)*, 19(3):242–262, 2001. 8

D.R. Ladd. *The Structure of Intonational Meaning: Evidence from English*. Indiana Press, Bloomington, 1980. 173, 175

D.R. Ladd. *Intonational Phonology*, 2nd ed., Cambridge University Press, 2008. 161

W. Ladusaw. *Polarity Sensitivity as Inherent Scope Relations*. Garland, New York, 1980. 83, 184

G. Lakoff. Cognitive semantics. *Meaning and Mental Representations*, 119:154, 1988. 2

G. Lakoff and M. Johnson. *Metaphors We Live By*. University of Chicago Press, 1980. 37, 49, 50, 51

K. Lambrecht. *Information Structure and Sentence Form: Topic, Focus, and the Mental Representations of Discourse Referents*. Cambridge University Press, Cambridge, UK, 1996. 157

T. Landauer and S. Dumais. A solution to Plato's problem: The latent semantic analysis theory of acquisition, induction and representation of knowledge. *Psychological Review*, 104(2):211–240, 1997. 92

S. Landes, C. Leacock, and R.I. Tengi. Building semantic concordances. In C. Fellbaum, Ed., *WordNet: An Electronic Lexical Database*, pages 199–216, MIT Press, Cambridge, MA, 1998. 177

R. Langacker. *Foundations of Cognitive Grammar: Theoretical Prerequisites*. Stanford University Press, 1987. 2

E. Laparra and G. Rigau. ImpAr: A deterministic algorithm for implicit semantic role labelling. In *Proc. of the 51st Annual Meeting of the Association for Computational Linguistics (Volume 1: Long Papers)*, Association for Computational Linguistics, pages 1180–1189, Sofia, Bulgaria, 2013. https://www.aclweb.org/anthology/P13--1116 62

M. Lapata, S. McDonald, and F. Keller. Determinants of adjective-noun plausibility. In *Proc. of the 9th Conference of the European Chapter of the Association for Computational Linguistics (EACL)*, pages 30–36, Bergen, 1999. 59

S. Lappin and H. Leass. An algorithm for pronominal anaphora resolution. *Computational Linguistics*, 20(4):535–561, 1994. 129

A. Lascarides and N. Asher. Agreement, disputes and commitment in dialogue. *Journal of Semantics*, 26(2):109–158, 2009. 11, 12, 29, 108, 173

A. Lascarides and A. Copestake. Default representation in constraint-based frameworks. *Computational Linguistics*, 25(1):55–105, 1999. 53

A. Lascarides and M. Stone. Discourse coherence and gesture interpretation. *Gesture*, 9(2):147–180, 2009. 27

A. Lascarides, E.J. Briscoe, N. Asher, and A. Copestake. Order independent and persistent typed default unification. *Linguistics and Philosophy*, 19(1):1–89, 1996a. 53

A. Lascarides, A. Copestake, and E.J. Briscoe. Ambiguity and coherence. *Journal of Semantics*, 13(1):41–65, 1996b. 40

P. Lasersohn. *Plurality, Conjunction and Events*. Kluwer, Dordrecht, 1995. 79

B.R. Lavandera. Where does the sociolinguistic variable stop? *Language in Society*, 7:171–182, 1978. 21

J. Lecarme. Focus in Somali. In G. Rebuschi and L. Tuller, Eds., *The Grammar of Focus*, pages 1–22, John Benjamins Publishing Company, Amsterdam/Philadelphia, 1999. 159

H. Lee, Y. Peirsman, A. Chang, N. Chambers, M. Surdeanu, and D. Jurafsky. Stanford's multi-pass sieve coreference resolution system at the CONLL-2011 shared task. In *Proc. of the 15th Conference on Computational Natural Language Learning: Shared Task*, pages 28–34, Association for Computational Linguistics, 2011. 127

H. Lee, A. Chang, Y. Peirsman, N. Chambers, M. Surdeanu, and D. Jurafsky. Deterministic coreference resolution based on entity-centric, precision-ranked rules. *Computational Linguistics*, 39(4), 2013. http://aclweb.org/anthology/J13--4004 181

K. Lee, L. He, M. Lewis, and L. Zettlemoyer. End-to-end neural coreference resolution. In *Proc. of the Conference on Empirical Methods in Natural Language Processing (EMNLP)*, 2017. 129

E. Lepore and M. Stone. *Imagination and Convention*. Oxford University Press, 2015. 2

B. Levin. *English Verb Classes and Alternations*. Chicago University Press, 1995. 58, 113

S. Levinson. *Pragmatics*. Cambridge University Press, 1993. 139

D. Lewis. Scorekeeping in a language game. *Journal of Philosophical Logic*, 8:339–359, 1979. 15, 131

M. Lewis and M. Steedman. Combined distributional and logical semantics. *Transactions of the Association of Computational Linguistics*, 1:179–192, 2013. 93

B. Li, Y. Wen, W. QU, L. Bu, and N. Xue. Annotating the little prince with Chinese AMRs. In *Proc. of the 10th Linguistic Annotation Workshop Held in Conjunction with ACL (LAW-X)*, pages 7–15, Association for Computational Linguistics, 2016. http://aclweb.org/antho logy/W16--1702 180

M. Liberman and I. Sag. Prosodic form and discourse function. *Chicago Linguistic Society*, 10:416–427, 1974. 173

D. Lin. Extracting collocations from text corpora. In *1st Workshop on Computational Terminology*, Montreal, 1988. 64

D. Lin, S. Zhao, L. Qin, and M. Zhou. Identifying synonyms among distributionally similar words. In *Proc. of the International Joint Conference in Artificial Intelligence (IJCAI)*, vol. 3, pages 1492–1493, 2003. 49

T.-Y. Lin, M. Maire, S. Belongie, J. Hays, P. Perona, D. Ramanan, P. Dollár, and C.L. Zitnick. Microsoft COCO: Common objects in context. In *European Conference on Computer Vision*, pages 740–755, Springer, 2014. 181

D. Litman and J. Allen. Discourse processing and commonsense plans. In J. Morgan P.R. Cohen and M. Pollack, Eds., *Intentions in Communication*, pages 365–388, MIT Press, 1990. 169

J. Liu, S. Cohen, and M. Lapata. Discourse representation structure parsing. In *Proc. of the 56th Annual Meeting of the Association for Computational Linguistics (Volume 1: Long Papers)*, Association for Computational Linguistics, pages 429–439, Melbourne, Australia, 2018. 188

N. Ljubešić, Z. Agić, F. Klubicka, V. Batanović, and T. Erjavec. hr500k–A reference training corpus of Croatian. In *Proc. of the Conference on Language Technologies and Digital Humanities*, Ljubljana, 2018. 179

K.E. Lochbaum. A collaborative planning model of intentional structure. *Computational Linguistics*, 24(4):525–572, 1998. 168, 169, 187, 188

D. Loehr. Gesture and intonation. Ph.D. thesis, Georgetown University, 2004. 27

R. Long, P. Pasupat, and P. Liang. Simpler context-dependent logical forms via model projections. In *Proc. of the 54th Annual Meeting of the Association for Computational Linguistics (ACL)*, pages 1456–1465, 2016. 181

J. Lu and V. Ng. Joint learning for event coreference resolution. In *Proc. of the 55th Annual Meeting of the Association for Computational Linguistics (Volume 1: Long Papers)*, pages 90–101. Association for Computational Linguistics, 2017. 126

J. Lyons. *Linguistic Semantics: An Introduction*. Cambridge University Press, 1995. 42

F. Mairesse, J. Polifroni, and G. Di Fabbrizio. Can prosody inform sentiment analysis? Experiments on short spoken reviews. In *IEEE International Conference on Acoustics, Speech and Signal Processing (ICASSP)*, pages 5093–5096, 2012. 20

S. Makino and M. Tsutsui. *A Dictionary of Basic Japanese Grammar*. The Japan Times, Tokyo, 1986. 105

F.S. Man. TOPIC and FOCUS in Cantonese: An OT-LFG account. Master's thesis, University of Hong Kong, 2007. 159

W.C. Mann and S.A. Thompson. Rhetorical structure theory: Description and construction of text structures. In G. Kempen, Ed., *Natural Language Generation: New Results in Artificial Intelligence*, pages 279–300, 1986. 17, 111, 182, 183

D. Marcu. The rhetorical parsing of unrestricted natural language texts. In P.R. Cohen and W. Wahlster, Eds., *Proc. of the 35th Annual Meeting of the Association for Computational Linguistics and Eighth Conference of the European Chapter of the Association for Computational Linguistics*, Association for Computational Linguistics, pages 96–103, Somerset, NJ, 1997. 188

D. Marcu. *The Theory and Practice of Discourse Parsing and Summarization*. MIT Press, 2000. 42

M.P. Marcus, B. Santorini, and M.A. Marcinkiewicz. Building a large annotated corpus of English: The Penn Treebank. *Computational Linguistics*, 19:313–330, 1993. 178

M. Marimon. Tibidabo: A syntactically and semantically annotated corpus of Spanish. *Corpora*, 10(3):259–276, 2015. 179

V. Mathesius. O passivu v moderní angličtině. *Sborní Filologický*, 5:198–220, 1915. 157

J. McCarthy. Circumscription—a form of non-monotonic reasoning. *Artificial Intelligence*, 13(1–2): 27–39, 1980. 11

S. McConnell-Ginet. The origins of sexist language in discourse. *Annals of the New York Academy of Sciences*, 433(1):123–135, 1984. 46

E. McCready. *The Semantics and Pragmatics of Honorification: Register and Social Meaning*. Oxford University Press, Oxford, 2019. 20, 104

D. McNeill. *Hand and Mind: What Gestures Reveal about Thought*. University of Chicago Press, 1992. 185

G. Miller, R. Beckwith, C. Fellbaum, D. Gross, and K. Miller. Introduction to WordNet: An on-line lexical database. *International Journal of Lexicography*, 3(4):235–244, 1990. 64, 66

G.A. Miller. Wordnet: A lexical database for English. *Communications of the ACM*, 38(11):39–41, November 1995. http://doi.acm.org.offcampus.lib.washington.edu/10.1145/219717.219748 35, 42, 177

E. Miltsakaki, R. Prasad, A. Joshi, and B. Webber. The Penn discourse treebank. In *Proc. of Linguistic Resources (LREC)*, 2004. 182

A.-L. Minard, M. Speranza, R. Urizar, B. Altuna, M.G.J. van Erp, A.M. Schoen, C.M. van Son, et al. MEANTIME, the NewsReader multilingual event and time corpus. In *Proc. of the 10th Language Resources and Evaluation Conference (LREC)*, Portorož, European Language Resources Association (ELRA), Slovenia, 2016. 180

T. Mitamura, Z. Liu, and E.H. Hovy. Overview of TAC KBP 2016 event nugget track. In *Text Analysis Conference*, 2016. 125

J. Mitchell and M. Lapata. Vector-based models of semantic composition. In *Proc. of ACL-08: HLT*, Association for Computational Linguistics, pages 236–244, Columbus, OH, June 2008. http://www.aclweb.org/anthology/P/P08/P08--1028 92

D. Moeljadi, F. Bond, and S. Song. Building an HPSG-based Indonesian resource grammar (INDRA). In *Proc. of the Grammar Engineering Across Frameworks (GEAF) Workshop*, pages 9–16, Association for Computational Linguistics, 2015. http://aclweb.org/anthology/W15--3302 182

M. Moens and M.J. Steedman. Temporal ontology and temporal reference. *Computational Linguistics*, 14(2):15–28, 1988. 98, 99

D. Monk. *Mathematical Logic*. Springer-Verlag, Berlin, 1976. 169

R. Montague. *Formal Philosophy*. Yale University Press, New Haven, CT. 1974. 7, 32, 84, 92, 97, 129, 169

T. Moor, M. Roth, and A. Frank. Predicate-specific annotations for implicit role binding: Corpus annotation, data analysis and evaluation experiments. In *Proc. of the 10th International Conference on Computational Semantics (IWCS), Short Papers*, Association for Computational Linguistics, pages 369–375, Potsdam, Germany, 2013. https://www.aclweb.org/anthology/W13--0211 62

R. Moot. A type-logical treebank for French. *Journal of Language Modelling*, 3(1):229–264, 2015. 180

R. Morante and E. Blanco. *SEM 2012 shared task: Resolving the scope and focus of negation. In *Proc. of the 1st Joint Conference on Lexical and Computational Semantics*, page 265–274, Montréal, Canada, June 2012. 89

M. Moravcsik. Aitia as generative factor in Aristotle's philosophy. *Dialogue: Canadian Philosophical Review*, 14(4):622–638, 1975. 41

A. Mostowski. On a generalization of quantifiers. *Fundamenta Mathematicae*, 44:12–36, 1957. 80

S. Müller and W. Kasper. HPSG analysis of German. In W. Wahlster, Ed., *Verbmobil: Foundations of Speech-to-Speech Translation*, pages 238–253, Springer, Berlin, 2000. 3, 182

P. Narayana, N. Krishnaswamy, I. Wang, R. Bangar, D. Patil, G. Mulay, K. Rim, R. Beveridge, J. Ruiz, J. Pustejovsky, and B. Draper. Cooperating with avatars through gesture, language and action. In K. Arai, S. Kapoor, and R. Bhatia, Eds., *Intelligent Systems and Applications*, Springer International Publishing, pages 272–293, Cham, 2019. 27

R. Navigli. Word sense disambiguation: A survey. *ACM Computing Surveys (CSUR)*, 41(2):10, 2009. 113

J. Nerbonne. Reference time and time in narration. *Linguistics and Philosophy*, 9(1):83–95, 1986. 124

V. Ng. Supervised noun phrase coreference research: The first fifteen years. In *Proc. of the 48th Annual Meeting of the Association For Computational Linguistics*, pages 1396–1411, 2010. 129

V. Ng and C. Cardie. Improving machine learning approaches to coreference resolution. In *Proc. of the 40th Annual Meeting of the Association for Computational Linguistics (ACL)*, pages 104–111, 2002. 129, 134

H.T.B. Nguyen. Contrastive topic in Vietnamese: With reference to Korean. Ph.D. thesis, Seoul National University, 2006. 159

J. Nichols. Head-marking and dependent-marking grammar. *Language*, 62(1):56–119, 1986. http://www.jstor.org/stable/415601 96

J. Nichols and B. Bickel. Locus of marking in the clause. In M.S. Dryer and M. Haspelmath, Eds., *The World Atlas of Language Structures Online*. Max Planck Institute for Evolutionary Anthropology, Leipzig, 2013. https://wals.info/chapter/23 96

R. Nordlinger. *A Grammar of Wambaya, Northern Australia*. Research School of Pacific and Asian Studies, The Australian National University, Canberra, 1998. 101

G. Nunberg. Transfers of meaning. *Journal of Semantics*, 12:109–132, 1995. 52

G. Nunberg, I.A. Sag, and T. Wasow. Idioms. *Language*, 70:491–538, 1994. 69, 70, 71

G. Nunberg. The pragmatics of deferred interpretation. *The Handbook of Pragmatics*, pages 344–364, 2004. 52

R.T. Oehrle. Boolean properties in the analysis of gapping in discontinuous constituency. In G.J. Huck and A.E. Ojeda, Eds., *Syntax and Semantics 20: Discontinuous Constituency*, vol. 20, pages 201–240, Academic Press, Orlando, 1987. 79

S. Oepen and J.T. Lønning. Discriminant-based MRS banking. In *Proc. of the 5th International Conference on Language Resources and Evaluation (LREC)*, pages 1250–1255, 2006. 179

S. Oepen, E. Callahan, C. Manning, and K. Toutanova. LinGO redwoods—A rich and dynamic treebank for HPSG. In *Proc. of the LREC Parsing Workshop: Beyond PARSEVAL, towards Improved Evaluation Measures for Parsing Systems*, pages 17–22, Las Palmas, 2002. 179

S. Oepen, M. Kuhlmann, Y. Miyao, D. Zeman, S. Cinková, D. Flickinger, J. Hajic, A. Ivanova, and Z. Uresova. Towards comparability of linguistic graph banks for semantic parsing. In *LREC*, vol. 16, pages 3991–3995, 2016. 179

Y. Okushi. Patterns of honorific use in the everyday speech of four Japanese women. Ph.D. thesis, University of Pennsylvania, 1997. 20

A. Oomen. Focus in the Rendille clause. *Studies in Afroasiatic Linguistics*, 9(1):35–65, 1978. 159

I. de Ottaviano. *Textos Tacana*. Instituto Linguistico de Verano, Riberalta, 1980. 20

M. Palmer, D. Gildea, and P. Kingsbury. The proposition bank: An annotated corpus of semantic roles. *Computational Linguistics*, 31(1):71–106, 2005. 57, 178

M. Palmer, C. Bonial, and J. Hwang. VerbNet: Capturing English verb behavior, meaning, and usage. In S.E.F. Chipman, Ed., *The Oxford Handbook of Cognitive Science*. Oxford University Press, Oxford, 2017. http://www.oxfordhandbooks.com/view/10.1093/oxford hb/9780199842193.001.0001/oxfordhb-9780199842193-e-15 56, 58, 178

B. Partee. Nominal and temporal anaphora. *Linguistics and Philosophy*, 7:243–286, 1984. 129

B. Partee. Topic, focus and quantification. In *Semantics and Linguistic Theory*, vol. 1, pages 159–188, 1991. 162

B. Partee and M. Rooth. Generalized conjunction and type ambiguity. In R. Bauerle, C. Schwarze, and A. von Stechow, Eds., *Meaning, Interpretation of Language*, pages 361–383, Walter de Gruyter, Berlin, 1983. 79

M. Pasca and S. Harabagiu. The informative role of WordNet in open-domain question answering. In *Proc. of NAACL-01 Workshop on WordNet and Other Lexical Resources*, pages 138–143, 2001. 42

P. Pauwels. *Put, Set, Lay, and Place: A Cognitive Linguistic Approach to Verbal Meaning*. Lincom Europa, Munich, Germany, 2000. 63

J. Pearl. *Probabilistic Reasoning in Intelligent Systems: Networks of Plausible Inference*. Morgan Kauffmann, 1988. 11

M. Peters, M. Neumann, M. Iyyer, M. Gardner, C. Clark, K. Lee, and L. Zettlemoyer. Deep contextualized word representations. In *Proc. of the Conference of the North American Chapter of the Association for Computational Linguistics: Human Language Technologies (NAACL)*, pages 2227–2237, New Orleans, LA, 2018. 49

M.J. Pickering and S. Garrod. Toward a mechanistic psychology of dialogue. *Behavioral and Brain Sciences*, 27:169–225, 2004. 187

S. Pinker, M. Nowak, and J. Lee. The logic of indirect speech. *Proc. of the National Academy of Science*, 105(3), 2008. 171

M. Poesio and D. Traum. Conversational actions and discourse situations. *Computational Intelligence*, 13(3):309–347, 1997. 187

M. Poesio and D. Traum. Towards an axiomatisation of dialogue acts. In J. Hulstijn and A. Nijholt, Eds., *Proc. of the 20th Workshop on the Formal Semantics and Pragmatics of Dialogue*, 1998. 12, 187, 188

C. Pollard and I.A. Sag. *Head-Driven Phrase Structure Grammar*. Chicago University Press, 1994. 93

M. Ponsonnet. A preliminary typology of emotional connotations in morphological diminutives and augmentatives. *Studies in Language*, 42(1):17–52, 2018. 19

C. Potts. Conventional implicature and expressive content. In C. Maienborn, K. von Heusinger, and P. Portner, Eds., *Semantics: An International Handbook of Natural Language Meaning*, vol. 3, pages 2516–2536, Mouton de Gruyter, Berlin, 2012. 164, 165

C. Potts. The expressive dimension. *Theoretical Linguistics*, 33(2):165–197, 2007. 19, 20, 142

L. Poulson. Meta-modeling of tense and aspect in a cross-linguistic grammar engineering platform. *UW Working Papers in Linguistics*, 28, 2011. 99

S. Pradhan and L. Ramshaw. OntoNotes: Large scale multi-layer, multi-lingual, distributed annotation. In N. Ide and J. Pustejovsky, Eds., *Handbook of Linguistic Annotation*, pages 521–554, Springer, 2017. 179

S. Pradhan, L. Ramshaw, M. Marcus, M. Palmer, R. Weischedel, and N. Xue. CoNLL-2011 shared task: Modeling unrestricted coreference in ontonotes. In *Proc. of the 15th Conference on Computational Natural Language Learning: Shared Task*, pages 1–27, Association for Computational Linguistics, 2011. http://www.aclweb.org/anthology/W11--1901 123

S. Pradhan, A. Moschitti, N. Xue, O. Uryupina, and Y. Zhang. CoNLL-2012 shared task: Modeling multilingual unrestricted coreference in ontonotes. In *Joint Conference on EMNLP and CoNLL—Shared Task*, pages 1–40, Association for Computational Linguistics, 2012. http://www.aclweb.org/anthology/W12--4501 123

R. Prasad, N. Dinesh, L. Alan, E. Miltsakaki, L. Robaldo, A. Joshi, and B. Webber. The penn discourse treebank 2.0. In *Proc. of the 6th International Conference on Language Resources and Evaluation (LREC)*, Marrakech, Morocco, 2008. 182

E.F. Prince. Toward a taxonomy of given-new information. *Radical Pragmatics*, pages 223–256, 1981a. 151

E.F. Prince. Topicalization, focus-movement, and Yiddish-movement: A pragmatic differentiation. In *Annual Meeting of the Berkeley Linguistics Society*, vol. 7, pages 249–264, 1981b. 160

A. Prior. *Time and Modality*. Oxford University Press, 1957. 97, 98

A. Przepiórkowski and A. Patejuk. Arguments and adjuncts in universal dependencies. In *Proc. of the 27th International Conference on Computational Linguistics*, pages 3837–3852, Association for Computational Linguistics, 2018. `http://aclweb.org/anthology/C18--1324` 58

M. Purver, A. Eshghi, and J. Hough. Incremental semantic construction in a dialogue system. In *Proc. of the 9th International Conference on Computational Semantics*, pages 365–369, Association for Computational Linguistics, 2011. 76

J. Pustejovsky. The generative lexicon. *Computational Linguistics*, 17(4):409–441, 1991. 40, 44, 48, 49, 54, 64, 90

J. Pustejovsky. *The Generative Lexicon*. MIT Press, 1995. 31, 37, 38, 49, 54, 90, 99

J. Pustejovsky, I. Mani, L. Belanger, B. Boguraev, B. Knippen, J. Litman, A. Rumshisky, A. See, S. Symonen, J. van Guilder, L. van Guilder, and M. Verhagen. Arda summer workshop on graphical annotation toolkit for timeML. *Technical Report*, MITRE, 2003. 126, 180, 184

J. Pustejovsky. Iso-timeML and the annotation of temporal information. In N. Ide and J. Pustejovsky, Eds., *Handbook of Linguistic Annotation*, pages 941–968, Springer, 2017. 180

W.V.O. Quine. *Word and Object*. MIT Press, 1960. 11

D. Radev, W. Fan, H. Qi, H. Wu, and A. Grewal. Probabilistic question answering on the Web. *Journal of the American Society for Information Science and Technology*, 56(6):571–583, 2005. 10

F. Rainer. Constraints on productivity. In *Handbook of Word-Formation*, pages 335–352, Springer, 2005. 44

C. Ramisch, S. Cordeiro, A. Savary, V. Vincze, V. Mititelu, A. Bhatia, M. Buljan, M. Candito, P. Gantar, V. Giouli, et al. ed. 1.1 of the parseme shared task on automatic identification of verbal multiword expressions. In *The Joint Workshop on Linguistic Annotation, Multiword Expressions and Constructions (LAW-MWE-CxG)*, pages 222–240, 2018. 178

C. Rashtchian, P. Young, M. Hodosh, and J. Hockenmaier. Collecting image annotations using amazon's mechanical turk. In *Proc. of the NAACL HLT Workshop on Creating Speech and Language Data with Amazon's Mechanical Turk*, pages 139–147, Association for Computational Linguistics, 2010. `http://aclweb.org/anthology/W10--0721` 181

S. Reddy, M. Lapata, and M. Steedman. Large-scale semantic parsing without question-answer pairs. *Transactions of the Association for Computational Linguistics*, 2:377–392, 2014. `http://aclweb.org/anthology/Q14--1030` 182

H. Reichenbach. *Elements of Symbolic Logic*. Macmillan, 1947. 26, 97, 98, 123

R. Reiter. A logic for default reasoning. *Artificial Intelligence*, 13:91–132, 1980. 11

P. Resnik. Selectional constraints: An information-theoretic model and its computational realization. *Cognition*, 61(1):127–159, 1996. `http://www.sciencedirect.com/science/article/pii/S0010027796007226` Compositional Language Acquisition. 59

U. Reyle. Dealing with ambiguities by underspecification: Construction, interpretation and deduction. *Journal of Semantics*, 10:123–179, 1993. 84, 90

F. Ribas. On learning more appropriate selectional restrictions. In *Proc. of the 7th Conference on European Chapter of the Association for Computational Linguistics*, pages 112–118, Morgan Kaufmann Publishers Inc., 1995. 59

S. Riehemann. A constructional approach to idioms and word formation. Ph.D. thesis, Stanford University, 2001. 72

V. Rieser and O. Lemon. *Reinforcement Learning for Adapting Dialogue Systems*. Springer, 2011. 118, 119, 168

C. Roberts. Modal subordination and pronominal anaphora in discourse. *Linguistics and Philosophy*, 12(6):683–721, 1989. 130, 131

C. Roberts. Information structure in discourse: Towards an integrated theory of pragmatics. *Semantics and Pragmatics*, 5(6):1–69, 2012. 161, 162, 164

H. Rohde. Coherence-driven effects in sentence and discourse processing. Ph.D. thesis, University of California, San Diego, 2008. 128

H. Rohde and A. Kehler. Grammatical and information-structural influences on pronoun production. *Language, Cognition, and Neuroscience, Special Issue on Production of Referring Expressions: Models and Empirical Data*, 29:912–927, 2014. 112

N. Rong. Learning in the presence of unawareness. Ph.D. thesis, Computer Science, Cornell University, 2016. 121

M. Rooth. A theory of focus interpretation. *Natural Language Semantics*, 1(1):75–116, 1992. 171

A. Rosenfeld and K. Erk. Deep neural models of semantic shift. In *Proc. of the Conference of the North American Chapter of the Association for Computational Linguistics: Human Language Technologies (NAACL-HLT)*, vol. 1, pages 474–484, 2018. 46

W.M. Rule. *A Comparative Study of the Foe, Huli, and Pole Languages of Papua New Guinea.* Number 20, University of Sydney, 1977. 101

J. Ruppenhofer, C. Sporleder, R. Morante, C. Baker, and M. Palmer. SemEval-2010 task 10: Linking events and their participants in discourse. In *Proc. of the 5th International Workshop on Semantic Evaluation*, Association for Computational Linguistics, pages 45–50, Uppsala, Sweden, 2010. https://www.aclweb.org/anthology/S10--1008 62

J. Ruppenhofer, M. Ellsworth, M.R.L. Petruck, C.R. Johnson, C.F. Baker, and J. Scheffczyk. *FrameNet II: Extended Theory and Practice*, 2016. 57

H. Sacks, E.A. Schegloff, and G. Jefferson. A simplest systematics for the organization of turn-taking in conversation. *Language*, 50(4):696–735, 1974. 174, 184

I. Sag, T. Baldwin, , F. Bond, A. Copestake, and D. Flickinger. Multiword expressions: A pain in the neck for NLP. In *International Conference on Intelligent Text Processing and Computational Linguistics*, pages 1–15, Springer, 2002. 63, 64

G. Şahin and E. Adalı. Annotation of semantic roles for the Turkish Proposition Bank. *Language Resources and Evaluation*, 52(3):673–706, 2018. 178

M. Sailer and S. Markantonatou, Eds. *Mutliword Expressions: Insights from a Multi-lingual Perspective, in Phraseology and Multiword Expressions*. Language Science Press, Berlin, 2018. 63

T. Sanders. Semantic and pragmatic sources of coherence: On the categorization of coherence relations in context. *Discourse Processes*, 24:119–148, 1997. 111

A. Sanford and A. Graesser. Shallow processing and underspecification. *Discourse Processes*, 42:99–108, 2006. 89

A. Sanford and P. Sturt. Depth of processing in language comprehension: Not noticing the evidence. *Trends in Cognitive Sciences*, 6:382–386, 2002. 89

R. Saurí and J. Pustejovsky. Factbank: A corpus annotated with event factuality. *Proc. on the Conference on Language Resources and Evaluation (LREC)*, 43(3): 227, 2009. 184

L. Savage. *The Foundations of Statistics*. John Wiley, 1954. 118, 168

N. Schenk and C. Chiarcos. Unsupervised learning of prototypical fillers for implicit semantic role labeling. In *Proc. of the Conference of the North American Chapter of the Association for Computational Linguistics: Human Language Technologies*, Association for Computational Linguistics, pages 1473–1479, San Diego, CA, 2016. `https://www.aclweb.org/anthology/N16--1173 62`

D. Schlangen. A coherence-based approach to the interpretation of non-sentential utterances in dialogue. Ph.D. thesis, University of Edinburgh, 2003. 187

J. Schlöder and R. Fernandez. Pragmatic rejection. In *Proc. of the 11th International Conference on Computational Semantics (IWCS)*, Oxford, 2015. 173

N. Schneider and N.A. Smith. A corpus and model integrating multiword expressions and supersenses. In *Proc. of the Conference of the North American Chapter of the Association for Computational Linguistics: Human Language Technologies (NAACL-HLT)*, pages 1537–1547, 2015. 178

N. Schneider, D. Hovy, A. Johannsen, and M. Carpuat. Semeval-2016 task 10: Detecting minimal semantic units and their meanings (dimsum). In *Proc. of the 10th International Workshop on Semantic Evaluation (SemEval)*, pages 546–559, 2016. 178

G. Scontras, M. Polinsky, C.-Y.E. Tsai, and K. Mai. Cross-linguistic scope ambiguity: When two systems meet. *Glossa: A Journal of General Linguistics*, 2, 2017. `http://doi.org/10.5334/gjgl.198 89`

J. Searle. *Speech Acts*. Cambridge University Press, 1969. 14

E. Selkirk. Sentence prosody: Intonation, stress, and phrasing. In J.A. Goldsmith, Ed., *The Handbook of Phonological Theory*, 1st ed., pages 550–569, Blackwell, Cambridge, MA, 1995. 158

P. Sgall, E. Hajicová, J. Panevová, and J. Panevova. *The Meaning of the Sentence in its Semantic and Pragmatic Aspects*. Springer Science & Business Media, 1986. 179

E. Shriberg, R. Dhillon, S. Bhagat, J. Ang, and H. Carvey. The ICSI meeting recorder dialog act (MRDA) corpus. In *Proc. of the 5th SIGdial Workshop on Discourse and Dialogue at HLT-NAACL*, 2004. `http://aclweb.org/anthology/W04--2319 183`

M. Siegel, E.M. Bender, and F. Bond. *Jacy: An Implemented Grammar of Japanese*. CSLI Studies in Computational Linguistics. CSLI Publications, Stanford CA, November 2016. 103, 182

J. Sikos, Y. Versley, and A. Frank. Implicit semantic roles in a multilingual setting. In *Proc. of the 5th Joint Conference on Lexical and Computational Semantics*, Association for Computational Linguistics, pages 45–54, Berlin, Germany, August 2016. `https://www.aclweb.org/anthology/S16--2005 62`

C.S. Smith. *The Parameter of Aspect*. Kluwer Academic Publishers, Dordrecht, 1991. 99

L.M. Solan and P.M. Tiersma. *Speaking of Crime: The Language of Criminal Justice*. University of Chicago Press, Chicago, IL, 2005. 171

S. Song. *Modeling Information Structure in a Cross-Linguistic Perspective*. Language Science Press, 2017. http://langsci-press.org/catalog/book/111 157, 158, 160

W. Soon, H. Ng, and D. Lim. A machine learning approach to coreference resolution of noun phrases. *Computational Linguistics*, 27(4):521–544, 2001. 125

R. Soricut and D. Marcu. Sentence level discourse parsing using syntactic and lexical information. In *Proc. of Human Language Technology and North American Association for Computational Linguistics*, Edmonton, Canada, 2003. 135

R. Speer. Conceptnet numberbatch 17.04: Better, less-stereotyped word vectors. Blog post, https://blog.conceptnet.io/2017/04/24/conceptnet-numberbatch-17--04-better-less-stereotyped-word-vectors/, accessed July 6, 2017. 48

D. Sperber and D. Wilson. *Relevance*. Blackwells, 1986. 187

D. Sperber and D. Wilson. *Relevance: Communication and Cognition*. Blackwells, 1995. 168

R. Stalnaker. Pragmatic presuppositions. In K. Munitz and P. Unger, Eds., *Semantics and Philosophy*, pages 197–213, New York University Press, New York, 1974. 139

R.C. Stalnaker. Assertion. In P. Cole, Ed., *Syntax and Semantics*, pages 315–322, Academic Press, 1978. 15

R. Stalnaker. On the representation of context. In *Semantics and Linguistic Theory*, vol. 6, pages 279–294, 1996. 115

L. Stassen. *Comparison and Universal Grammar*. Blackwell, Oxford, 1985. 77, 78

M. Steedman. *The Syntactic Process*. MIT Press, 2000. 76, 84, 93, 175

M. Steedman. *Taking Scope*. MIT Press, 2012. 85

M. Steedman. The surface-compositional semantics of English intonation. *Language*, pages 2–57, 2014. 156

M.J. Steedman. *Surface Structure and Interpretation*. MIT Press, 1996. 25

R. Stevenson, A. Nelson, and K. Stenning. The role of parallelism in strategies of pronoun comprehension. *Language and Speech*, 38(4):393–418, 1995. 128

A. Stolcke, K. Ries, N. Coccaro, E. Shriberg, D. Jurafsky, R. Bates, P. Taylor, R. Martin, C. van Ess-Dykema, and M. Meteer. Dialogue act modeling for automatic tagging and recognition of conversational speech. *Computational Linguistics*, 26(3):339–374, 2000. 15

M. Stone. Modality in dialogue: Planning, pragmatics and computation. Ph.D. thesis, University of Pennsylvania, 1998. 25

T. Strzalkowski. *Reversible Grammar in Natural Language Processing*, vol. 255, Springer Science and Business Media, 2012. 3

A. Suhr, M. Lewis, J. Yeh, and Y. Artzi. A corpus of natural language for visual reasoning. In *Proc. of the 55th Annual Meeting of the Association for Computational Linguistics (Volume 2: Short Papers)*, pages 217–223, Association for Computational Linguistics, 2017. `http://aclweb.org/anthology/P17--2034` 181

A. Suhr, S. Zhou, I. Zhang, H. Bai, and Y. Artzi. A corpus for reasoning about natural language grounded in photographs. *ArXiv Preprint ArXiv:1811.00491*, 2018. 181

R. Sutton and A. Barto. *Reinforcement Learning: An Introduction*. MIT Press, 1998. 119

L. Talmy. *Toward a Cognitive Semantics*. MIT press, 2000. 2

M. Tanenhaus, M. Spivey-Knowlton, and J. Hanna. Modeling thematic and discourse context effects within a multiple constraints framework: Implications for the architecture of the language comprehension system. In M. Pickering, M. Crocker, and C. Clifton, Eds., *Architectures and Mechanisms for Language Processing*. Cambridge University Press, 2000. 25

A. Tarski. The concept of truth in formalized languages. *Logic, Semantics, Metamathematics*, 2:152–278, 1956. 7

S. Tellex, T. Kollar, S. Dickerson, M. Walter, A. Banerjee, S. Teller, and N. Roy. Understanding natural language commands for robotic navigation and mobile manipulation. In *Proc. of the 25th AAAI Conference*, pages 1507–1514, 2011. 27, 28

N. Tersis. *Forme et Sens des Mots du Tunumiisiut*. Peeters, Paris, 2008. 20

N. Tersis. Lexical polysynthesis. In *Variations on Polysynthesis, the Eskaleut Languages*, vol. 86, pages 51–64, Benjamins, 2009. 19

D. Tompkins. *How to Wreck a Nice Beach: The Vocoder from World War II to Hip Hop, the Machine Speaks*. Melville House Publishing, 2010. 21

J. Tonhauser, D. Beaver, C. Roberts, and M. Simons. Toward a taxonomy of projective content. *Language*, 89(1):66–109, 2013. 141, 142

E.C. Traugott and R.B. Dasher. *Regularity in Semantic Change*, vol. 97, Cambridge University Press, 2001. 45

D. Traum. A computational theory of grounding in natural language conversation. Ph.D. thesis, Computer Science Department, University of Rochester, 1994. 187

D. Traum and S. Larsson. The information state approach to dialogue management. In R. Smith and J. van Kuppevelt, Eds., *Current and New Directions in Discourse and Dialogue*, pages 325–353, Kluwer Academic Publishers, 2003. 187

C. Tschichold. Multi-word units in natural language processing. Ph.D. thesis, University of Basel, 1998. 63

P. Turney. Similarity of semantic relations. *Computational Linguistics*, 32(3):379–416, 2006. 47

P. Turney and P. Pantel. From frequency to meaning: Vector space models in semantics. *Journal of Artificial Intelligence Research*, 37:141–188, 2010. 49

I. Txurruka. Particion of informacional en el discourso. Ph.D. thesis, University of the Basque Country, Donostia, Spain, 1997. 149

I. Txurruka. Natural language disjunction in discourse. In *Proc. of the 5th International Workshop on Formal Semantics and Pragmatics of Dialogue (Bi-Dialog)*, Bielefeld, 2001. Also to appear in P. Kühnlein, H. Rieser, and H. Zeevat Eds., *The Semantics and Pragmatics of Dialogue*, John Benjamins. 149

A. Vaidya, J.D. Choi, M. Palmer, and B. Narasimhan. Analysis of the Hindi proposition bank using dependency structure. In *Proc. of the 5th Linguistic Annotation Workshop*, pages 21–29, Association for Computational Linguistics, 2011. 178

E. Vallduví. *The Informational Component*. Outstanding Dissertations in Linguistics. Garland Publishing, New York, 1992. 157

R. van der Sandt. Presupposition projection as anaphora resolution. *Journal of Semantics*, 9(4):333–377, 1992. 139, 140, 145, 148, 171

G. van Noord. Reversible unification based machine translation. In *Proc. of the 13th Conference on Computational Linguistics (COLING)*, pages 299–304, Association for Computational Linguistics, 1990. 3

G. van Noord, G. Bouma, R. Koeling, and M.-J. Nederhof. Robust grammatical analysis for spoken dialogue systems. *Natural Language Engineering*, 5(1):45–93, 1999. 3

R. van Noord, L. Abzianidze, A. Toral, and J. Bos. Exploring neural methods for parsing discourse representation structures. *Transactions of the Association for Computational Linguistics*, 6:619–633, 2018. 182

R. van Rooij. Signalling games select horn strategies. *Linguistics and Philosophy*, 27:493–527, 2004. 166, 188

Z. Vendler. Verbs and times. *Philosophical Review*, 46:143–160, 1957. 99

M. Verhagen, R. Saurí, T. Caselli, and J. Pustejovsky. SemEval-2010 task 13: TempEval-2. In *Proc. of the 5th International Workshop on Semantic Evaluation*, Association for Computational Linguistics, pages 57–62, Uppsala, Sweden, July 2010. https://www.aclweb.org/antho logy/S10--1010 180

V. Vincze, I. Nagy, and G. Berend. Multiword expressions and named entities in the wiki50 corpus. In *Proc. of the International Conference Recent Advances in Natural Language Processing*, pages 289–295, 2011. 178

V. Vincze, G. Szarvas, R. Farkas, G. Móra, and J. Csirik. The BioScope corpus: Biomedical texts annotated for uncertainty, negation and their scopes. *BMC Bioinformatics*, 9(11):S9, 2008. 89

K. von Fintel. What is presupposition accommodation, again? *Philosophical Perspectives*, 22(1):137–170, 2008. 139

W. Wahlster, Ed. *Verbmobil: Foundations of Speech-to-Speech Translation*. Springer, 2000. 89

M. Walker. Inferring acceptance and rejection in dialogue by default rules of inference. *Language and Speech*, 39(2), 1996. 173

I.S. Wang, P. Liang, and C. Manning. Learning language games through interaction. In *Proc. of the 54th Annual Meeting of the Association for Computational Linguistics (Volume 1: Long Papers)*, pages 2368–2378, Association for Computational Linguistics, 2016. http://aclweb.org/a nthology/P16--1224 118, 121, 188

S.I. Wang, S. Ginn, P. Liang, and C.D. Manning. Naturalizing a programming language via interactive learning. In *Association for Computational Linguistics (ACL)*, 2017. 188

A. Warner. English auxiliaries without lexical rules. In R. Borsley, Ed., *Syntax and Semantics Volume 32: The Nature and Function of Syntactic Categories*, pages 167–220, Academic Press, San Diego and London, 2000. 88

B.L. Webber. Structure and ostension in the interpretation of discourse deixis. *Natural Language and Cognitive Processes*, 6(2):107–135, 1991. 109, 110

B.L. Webber, A. Knott, M. Stone, and A. Joshi. Anaphora and discourse structure. *Computational Linguistics*, 29(4):545–588, 2003. 17, 111, 114

D. Westerståhl. Quantifiers in formal and natural languages. In *Handbook of Philosophical Logic*, pages 1–131, Springer, 1989. 81, 83

D. Wetzel and F. Bond. Enriching parallel corpora for statistical machine translation with semantic negation rephrasing. In *Proc. of the 6th Workshop on Syntax, Semantics and Structure in Statistical Translation*, pages 20–29, Association for Computational Linguistics, 2012. http://www.aclweb.org/anthology/W12--4203 89

P.J. Wetzel. Japanese social deixis and discourse phenomena. *The Journal of the Association of Teachers of Japanese*, 22(1):7–27, 1988. http://www.jstor.org/stable/489333 105

A.S. White, D. Reisinger, K. Sakaguchi, T. Vieira, S. Zhang, R. Rudinger, K. Rawlins, and B. Van Durme. Universal decompositional semantics on universal dependencies. In *Proc. of the Conference on Empirical Methods in Natural Language Processing*, pages 1713–1723, Association for Computational Linguistics, 2016. http://aclweb.org/anthology/D16--1177 181

M. White and J. Baldridge. Adapting chart realization to CCG. In *Proc. of the 9th European Workshop on Natural Language Generation (ENLG) at EACL*, 2003. 3

J.D. Williams and S.J. Young. Partially observable Markov decision processes for spoken dialog systems. *Computer Speech and Language*, 21(2):231–422, 2007. 118, 119, 168, 169

T. Wilson, J. Wiebe, and P. Hoffmann. Recognizing contextual polarity in phrase-level sentiment analysis. In *Proc. of Human Language Technology Conference and Conference on Empirical Methods in Natural Language Processing*, Association for Computational Linguistics, pages 347–354, Vancouver, British Columbia, Canada, October 2005. http://www.aclweb.org/anthology/H/H05/H05--1044 20

T. Wilson, J. Wiebe, and C. Cardie. MPQA opinion corpus. In N. Ide and J. Pustejovsky, Eds., *Handbook of Linguistic Annotation*, pages 813–832, Springer, 2017. 180

T. Winograd. *Understanding Natural Language*. Academic Press, New York, 1972. 9

N. Xue and M. Palmer. Adding semantic roles to the Chinese Treebank. *Natural Language Engineering*, 15(1):143–172, 2009. 178

Y. Yang and J. Eisenstein. Unsupervised multi-domain adaptation with feature embeddings. In *Proc. of the Conference of the North American Chapter of the Association for Computational Linguistics: Human Language Technologies*, pages 672–682, 2015. 37

L. You and K. Liu. Building Chinese FrameNet database. In *Natural Language Processing and Knowledge Engineering, IEEE NLP-KE. Proc. of IEEE International Conference on*, pages 301–306, 2005. 178

Y. Yu, A. Eshghi, and O. Lemon. Training an adaptive dialogue policy for interactive learning of visually grounded word meanings. In *Proc. of SIGDIAL*, pages 339–349, Los Angeles, 2016. 27, 76

W. Zaghouani, M. Diab, A. Mansouri, S. Pradhan, and M. Palmer. The revised Arabic Prop-Bank. In *Proc. of the 4th Linguistic Annotation Workshop*, pages 222–226, Association for Computational Linguistics, 2010. 178

B. Zeller and S. Padó. A search task dataset for German textual entailment. In *Proc. of the 10th International Conference on Computational Semantics (IWCS)*, pages 288–299, 2013. 8

L. Zettlemoyer and M. Collins. Online learning of relaxed CCG grammars for parsing to logical form. In *Proc. of the Joint Conference on Empirical Methods in Natural Language Processing and Computational Natural Language Learning (EMNLP-CoNLL)*, pages 678–687, 2007. `http://www.aclweb.org/anthology/D/D07/D07--1071` 76

Y. Zhang and R. Wang. Cross-domain dependency parsing using a deep linguistic grammar. In *Proc. of the Joint Conference of the 47th Annual Meeting of the ACL and the 4th International Joint Conference on Natural Language Processing of the AFNLP*, pages 378–386, Association for Computational Linguistics, 2009. `http://aclweb.org/anthology/P09--1043` 182

Y. Zhou and N. Xue. The Chinese discourse treebank: A Chinese corpus annotated with discourse relations. *Proc. of Language Resources and Evaluation (LREC)*, 49(2):397–431, 2015. 182

Authors' Biographies

Emily M. Bender

Emily M. Bender is a Professor in the Department of Linguistics and Adjunct Professor in the School of Computer Science & Engineering at the University of Washington. Her primary research interests lie in multilingual grammar engineering, the incorporation of linguistic knowledge in NLP, computational semantics, and ethics in NLP. She is the PI of the Grammar Matrix project, which is developed in the context of the DELPH-IN Consortium (Deep Linguistic Processing with HPSG Initiative). More generally, she is interested in the intersection of linguistics and computational linguistics, from both directions: bringing computational methodologies to linguistic science and linguistic science to natural language processing.

Her Ph.D. (in linguistics) is from Stanford University. She has authored or co-authored papers in *Transactions of the ACL*, *Linguistic Issues in Language Technology*, the *Journal of Research on Language and Computation*, *English Language and Linguistics*, the *Encyclopedia of Language and Linguistics*, and *Linguistic Typology*, and the proceedings of conferences such as ACL, COLING, EMNLP, IJCNLP, and IWCS, and associated workshops. She is the author of a previous volume of this series, *Linguistic Fundamentals for Natural Language Processing: 100 Essentials from Morphology and Syntax*, Synthesis Lectures on Human Language Technologies #20.

Alex Lascarides

Alex Lascarides is Personal Chair in Semantics at the School of Informatics, University of Edinburgh. Her research is in formal and computational semantics and pragmatics, focusing mainly on the interaction between discourse coherence and discourse interpretation. Together with her colleague Nicholas Asher, she developed the semantic framework Segemented Discourse Representation Theory (SDRT). She has published work on many semantic phenomena, including tense and aspect, presuppositions, lexical semantics, indirect speech acts, the semantics of questions and requests, strategic conversation, agreement and denial, negotiation and persuasion, human-robot interaction, symbol grounding, intonation, and embodied conversation, including the meaning spontaneous hand gestures. More recently, her research has focused on non-linguistic phenomena in Artificial Intelligence, particularly on learning optimal strategies in complex games, and algorithms for adapting graphical representations of sequential decision problems when during the learning process the learner discovers unforeseen factors that are critical to success.

Her Ph.D. in Cognitive Science is from the University of Edinburgh. She has co-authored a book on SDRT (published by Cambridge University Press), a textbook on Cognition and Communication (published by MIT Press), journal papers in Formal Semantics (*Linguistics and Philosophy*, *Journal of Semantics*, *Semantics and Pragmatics*), Philosophy (*Synthese*, *Review of Philosophy and Psychology*, *Journal of Logic, Language and Information*), Computational Linguistics (*Computational Linguistics*, *Natural Language Engineering*) and Artificial Intelligence (*Journal of Artificial Intelligence Research*), and papers in conferences such as ACL, COLING, EMNLP, IWCS, SEMDIAL, AAMAS, CoRL, UAI, ICML, and Intellysis.

General Index

Index of Languages

Printed in the United States
by Baker & Taylor Publisher Services